The Retirement Survival Guidebook

Secrets to Tax-Free Savings, Worry-Free Spending, Fool-Proof Planning, and Low-Cost Living

Publisher's Note

This book is intended for general information only. It does not constitute medical, legal, or financial advice or practice. The editors of FC&A have taken careful measures to ensure the accuracy and usefulness of the information in this book. While every attempt has been made to assure accuracy, errors may occur. Some websites, addresses, and telephone numbers may have changed since printing. We cannot guarantee the safety or effectiveness of any advice or treatments mentioned. Readers are urged to consult with their professional financial advisors, lawyers, and health care professionals before making any changes.

Any health information in this book is for information only and is not intended to be a medical guide for self-treatment. It does not constitute medical advice and should not be construed as such or used in place of your doctor's medical advice. Readers are urged to consult with their health care professionals before undertaking therapies suggested by the information in this book, keeping in mind that errors in the text may occur as in all publications and that new findings may supersede older information.

The publisher and editors disclaim all liability (including any injuries, damages, or losses) resulting from the use of the information in this book.

Therefore, since we are surrounded by such a great cloud of witnesses, let us throw off everything that hinders and the sin that so easily entangles. And let us run with perseverance the race marked out for us.

Hebrews 12:1 NIV

The Retirement Survival Guidebook: Secrets to Tax-Free Savings, Worry-Free Spending, Fool-Proof Planning, and Low-Cost Living and all material contained therein copyright © 2018 by FC&A Medical Publishing. All rights reserved. Printed in the United States of America.

This book or any portion thereof may not be reproduced or distributed in any form or by any means without written permission of the publisher. For information, or to order copies, contact:

FC&A Medical Publishing®
103 Clover Green
Peachtree City, GA 30269
www.fca.com

Produced by the staff of FC&A
ISBN 978-1935574699

Table of Contents

Money management: Brilliant ideas to keep more of what you earn 1

Increase wealth — and lower stress — with these
simple tips 1

'Un-fix' retirement income with your dream job 4

Boost your bottom line with these fun and easy
moneymakers 6

Fraud alert: Protect yourself from 4 sly scams 8

Second hand is grand: 13 things to always buy used . . .10

End the paper chase: What to keep, what to shred,
and where to put it all 13

Missing in action: How to replace your
lost documents 14

Keep cash in your pocket with a shipshape
clutter-free smartphone 16

12 ways to keep your motor running 17

Snag killer deals on wheels with these
secret strategies 19

Smooth selling: Drive a hard bargain when you
post online 22

5 tips drive down the cost of filling up 23

Repair rip-offs: 5 ways your mechanic takes you for
a ride 26

Brains over brawn — fresh tech keeps you safe on
the road 27

6 tips power down pricey electric bills 29

Don't let this bill drain your wallet 31

Never pay this monthly bill again 33

Dial up $720 in yearly savings by switching your
    cell strategy 34

Block bothersome robocalls for good 37

7 ways to slash your grocery bill by 50 percent 38

Like free groceries? Insider tips help you stock up
    on savings 41

Dynamite dining deals: Simple ways to take a bite
    out of your restaurant bill .43

Sizzlin' senior deals: More exciting perks for folks
    over 50 45

End credit card chaos: Safe and smart ways to manage your plastic 47

3 ways to erase credit card debt fast 47

Should you pad your savings while paying off debt? 49

Don't let debt collectors dredge up the past 50

Clue into credit ratings to score big savings 51

5 steps move your credit score toward a perfect 850 52

Credit checkup: Free ways to give your report a
    once-over 54

Stay sharp — spot errors on your credit report and
    save hundreds 56

New rules protect you from old fines 58

Spend smarter — the right credit card can help you
    save big 59

The best card for poor credit .61

How to spot a bad card from a mile away 62

4 common ways credit cards waste your money 64

Transferring a balance? 3 tests your card needs to pass 66

No. 1 way to put the freeze on ID sharks 67

Scammed? Take back your identity with these
    simple steps 68

5 smart ways to buff up your online security 70

Check fraud — don't give thieves carte blanche to
    drain your savings 73

Protect privacy by destroying docs and digital files
    the right way 74

Sniff out phishy emails and phony calls 76

Dispute charges to wipe away billing boo-boos 77

Small print surprise — don't sign away your right
    to sue 79

All rights reserved: 4 rules repel credit card swindles . . .80

Safeguard your own credit to save hundreds 83

Better banking: Boost your savings and sidestep sneaky fees 85

Outfox the foxes with a better way to save 85

How to shop for the best senior-friendly checking 87

4 surefire steps to swapping banks without a hitch 88

Put the freeze on fees: Virtual banking saves you
    real dollars 91

Are you making this simple banking blunder? 93

Load up on savings with online banks 94

Get smart — use your phone to scan and sign
    important docs 98

Thwart hackers by bulking up your virtual
    protection 99

Block ATM scammers by going cardless 102

Prepaid cards — pay ahead to save later 103

4 common loan mistakes that will cost you
a bundle 106

Don't get trapped by zero-interest offers 108

Home and auto loans: Pain-free steps to paying less 111

Discover the hidden perks of managing a mortgage
in your golden years 111

An ARM might save you thousands if you're
between homes 114

3 routes to finding a lender you can write
home about 115

Credit crunches curtailing your dream move?
Not anymore 118

4 costly mortgage mistakes you don't want to make . . .119

Trading equity for income — is a reverse mortgage
right for you? 122

3 ways to pocket your reverse mortgage money 124

2 surefire strategies to fight foreclosure 126

Stay a step ahead to stop mortgage scammers 127

3 common car-leasing myths you need to bust 129

Auto loan checklist: How to get the best deals 131

Refinance your auto loan to stuff your wallet 133

Home and auto insurance: Clever ways to safeguard your property. 135

10 ways to save a heap on home coverage 135

Coverage checkup: 3 questions you need to ask 138

Check your homeowners coverage: What you don't
know could cost you 139

An umbrella policy keeps your assets covered 141

Slam the door on scammers with these savvy tips 143

5 ways to put the brakes on rising car
    insurance costs 145

Time to review your auto coverage? Follow
    these signs 148

The spy in your dash can drive down
    your premiums 149

Accident not your fault? You may still pay more 150

Crash for cash: Dodge these common highway cons 151

Steer clear of costly tow-truck scams 153

If you dent a rental, are you sure you're insured? 154

Personal insurance: The best protection at rock-bottom prices. 157

5 smart reasons to use a health savings account 157

Qualify for an HSA: It's as easy as 1, 2, 3 159

Stretch your health care dollars with a flexible
    spending account 160

HSA and FSA: Your heath plan's one-two punch 161

Making sense of Medicare and Medicaid: Your
    benefits in a nutshell 163

Medicare savings programs keep money in
    your pocket 166

Make the most of annual Medicare freebies 169

Scammers use new card to swindle seniors 170

Take the quiz: How Medicare savvy are you? 172

Buying medical supplies: A little hassle, a lot
    of savings 173

Plugging the gaps: Pick a plan that's right for you 176

Sick of medical bills? 3 tips to make you feel
  all better 178

Take the pain out of prescriptions — get your
  meds for free 179

Rx for a secure ID: Take steps to keep your privacy
  in the pink 180

Turn that frown upside down with a great
  dental deal 182

Give yourself a little financial TLC with LTCi 184

5 clever ways to beat skyrocketing premiums 186

Solve your life insurance dilemma — love it or
  lose it? 187

Lost policy? Here's how to track it down 189

Real estate wisdom: How to buy, sell, remodel, or age in place 191

Get moving: How to sell your home in any market . . .191

Test drive your dream home before you buy 194

Make the right move: Should you buy or sell first? 195

Seal your lips to seal the deal 198

Senior experts make housing decisions a breeze 199

Get an appraisal that's right on the money 201

Step up curb appeal for less than $200 203

Choose these hues to score higher profits 204

4 easy ways to increase your home's value
  by thousands 206

Make your house safe — and stylish — for your
  golden years 208

Can't afford to renovate? Help is closer than
  you think 210

Live mortgage free: The money-saving secret smart
  homeowners should know 212

House or condo: Make the move that's right for you . .216

Upsize or downsize — how to right-size your life 217

HOAs: Check the 'dues' and don'ts to avoid
  pricey penalties 220

Intelligent investing: Smart moves to make your money grow 223

Pay taxes up front to save thousands later 223

Simplify your 401(k) swap in a few easy steps 224

Super savings plans for the self-employed 225

401(k) rollover: 3 deadly don'ts could cost
  you dearly 226

Get Wall Street advice for a Main Street price 228

Don't derail your investments with these blunders 230

4 can't-miss tips for getting your mutual funds on
  the right track 232

Kick-start your investing with these surefire steps 234

Want to hit the target? Consider this mutual fund 236

Unscrambling annuities — the pros and cons of
  buying in 237

QLACs — upgrade your retirement with
  guaranteed income 239

Taking stock: Avoid the perils of probate 240

Build your portfolio drip by drip 242

How to build a bulletproof bond portfolio 244

Climb the ladder to financial stability 246

Sold on holding your bonds? You may miss a
  big payday 248

Find the right balance for your investments 250

Investment nightmares: Avoid falling into
  these traps 252

4 savvy ways to outsmart scam artists 254

Tax secret: Perfectly legal ways to deduct more, file faster, and pay less 257

Terrific tax breaks just for seniors 257

Caring for a senior parent? Don't miss these
  tax breaks 259

4 changes to tax law you won't want to miss 261

Savvy tricks to save your inheritance from the IRS 264

Hit with high property taxes? Here's an
  'appealing' answer 266

Paying your parents' mortgage? How to make sure
  you get the deduction 269

Small business owner? Don't 'pass through'
  this deduction 271

Business deductions: There's no place like home 272

Don't fall into this vacation home tax trap 274

Mess up your tax return? Here's how to fix it 276

Get the most from giving when you donate
  to charity 277

IRS notice: It's no reason to panic 279

5 audit red flags you need to know about 281

Watch your excuses when it comes to the IRS 283

Simple and smart ways to file for free 284

Protect yourself from these 4 tax scams 285

Forewarned is forearmed: How to
  outsmart fraudsters 288

A richer retirement: Simple strategies to make your nest egg last **289**

7 secrets to a happy, comfortable retirement 289

Retire these myths for a shock-free financial future . . .291

3 mistakes that can ruin your retirement 292

Budget your way to retirement readiness 294

Retirement rundown: Secrets to a successful
    second act 296

Cherry-pick a spending plan to further your funds . . .298

Beneficiary blunders: Heir today, gone tomorrow 300

Loosen Uncle Sam's grip with these retirement
    fund tax tips 301

Retirement account Q&A — bring your questions
    to the table 304

Early retirement offers: Look before you leap 304

5 factors to consider when choosing a
    pension payout 306

When to take benefits: A question for the ages 309

Size up your projected payout to sidestep surprises . . .312

Social Security and Medicare: Where to go to stay
    in the know 313

5 Social Security windfalls you don't want to miss 314

Is your check missing money? 5 facts you need
    to know 316

Fraud alert: Steer clear of these 3 sneaky scams 318

3 keys to living well on a fixed income 321

Thinking of downsizing? Prime signs it's time
    to move 322

Leaving a legacy: Estate planning essentials for your family's future **325**

3 reasons you must think ahead 325

Secure your finances after the death of a loved one . . .328

'Til debt do us part: How to keep creditors from
   eating up your estate 330

Stay ahead of the curve with 1 important document 331

How to stop a 'no-way' on your POA 333

4 will-writing rules that may catch you by surprise . . .334

Do-it-yourself will — smart savings or
   major mistake? 336

5 must-do's for finding a missing will 338

Agreed to be an executor? Avoid these 5 missteps 339

When a will is not your best choice 340

Put your trust in the right hands 342

Don't let a catastrophic illness drain your savings 343

Think twice before setting up joint ownership 345

Living will: 3 things you must include 346

The end of the road: Have you mapped out a plan? 347

5 ways to dodge costly funeral flimflam 349

Spare yourself a grave injustice: Write your
   own obit 351

Say R.I.P. to grave-robbing identity thieves 353

Paying for a funeral the smart way 354

Going, going, gone: Cash in your estate with a
   profitable partnership 356

Index **359**

Money management

Brilliant ideas to keep more of what you earn

Increase wealth — and lower stress — with these simple tips

Do money problems have you stressed out? You're not alone. Nearly three out of four Americans say their finances cause them stress at least once a month. Two-thirds report losing sleep over money worries like health care costs and retirement planning. And to add insult to injury, research shows that people who worry about money often look older than those who don't fret over finances.

Stop the money madness. The following tips can help you set up an easy budget that simplifies your life and creates wealth you never knew you had. Imagine. You're just a few steps away from financial freedom — and a good night's sleep.

Be a goal setter. What are the top three things you want to do with your money? Retire well? Provide an education for your children or grandchildren? Travel the world? Write down your goals and post them in plain sight. Then review them regularly to be sure you're headed in the right direction.

Track and trim spending habits. Keep tabs on your wallet for at least one month to see where your money is actually going. Can you get a better deal on cable or internet? Spend less on groceries? A money manager like *mint.com* can help you set up a budget, pay your bills, and even monitor your credit score.

Ditch your credit card debt. Seems like a no-brainer, right? But listen up. If your credit card has an interest rate of 16 per- cent, paying off that balance is like giving yourself a 16 percent tax-free return. What's the best way to pay off multiple cards? Some experts say to pay off the card with the highest interest rate first, while others say start with the smallest balance. Pick a plan that works for you, and stick to it.

> If you're paid biweekly — that's every other week instead of twice a month — here's a tip that could add thousands to your savings. In two months of each year, you'll receive three paychecks instead of two. Don't fritter them away. Stash the extra cash in your savings account or 401(k).

Set it and forget it. Stash away part of your income — some experts recommend at least 10 percent of each paycheck — into a savings account. Think of it as your cash cushion. Simply set up your accounts so the money is transferred automatically.

Save your raise. Congratulations! Your boss upped your pay. Don't blow it all on the latest electronic gear. Instead, tuck it away in your savings account or 401(k). You won't miss it, but it'll be there when you need it.

Live long and prosper in retirement. And while you're at it, sock away some funds for when you retire. Researchers say you need to save about 15 percent of your paycheck to fund a comfy retirement. And make sure you put away enough to fully match your employer's contribution. You don't want to waste that free money.

Type your way to unclaimed gold

Nancy couldn't believe her eyes. But there it was, plain as day on her computer screen. The state of Pennsylvania was holding $4,000 from a 1983 life insurance policy naming her as beneficiary. All she had to do was fill out the forms to claim it.

You could be next.

According to the National Association of Unclaimed Property Administrators, about $42 billion is up for grabs. Insurance payments, abandoned checking and savings accounts, certificates of deposit — all waiting for you to claim them.

Nancy found her fortune at *creditkarma.com/unclaimed-money*, but you can also try your luck at *missingmoney.com* or *unclaimed.org*. Type in the details, and if you have missing money in your name, your information will pop up on the screen. Then follow the directions to stake your claim. Searching is free.

An easy way to prospect, wouldn't you say? No picks or shovels required.

DOLLARS & SENSE

'Un-fix' retirement income with your dream job

Discover hundreds of ways to make extra money after you retire. It's the perfect time to try out a job you've always dreamed about. So take a close look at the skills you've gained over your lifetime, and see if they match up with the daydreams of your youth. Channel your inner child — and consult with your inner adult — to find a "second half" career that works for you.

Think back to when you were a kid. What did you enjoy that sparked your imagination?

You wanted to be just like the Wright brothers. Still in love with the wild blue yonder? Learn to fly a UAV — an unmanned aerial vehicle or drone. Skilled UAV operators are in demand by real estate agents, photographers, law enforcement officials, and even farmers. The possibilities are endless. With the right skills, you could earn up to $50 an hour.

You gobbled up Nancy Drew books like candy. Release your inner author and earn an average of $25 per hour as a freelance writer. Find out about writing opportunities in your local paper or community magazine. Or search for jobs online at *freelancewritinggigs.com* or *nDash.co*.

You dreamed of a Super Bowl ring. It's too late for you to join Merlin Olsen and the Fearsome Foursome on the Rams' front line, but sports is still a big part of your life. Ever think about coaching? Average salaries for athletic coaches run around $40,000. A degree in physical education is a plus. Or pick up some extra bucks working as a personal trainer, and pocket up to $50 an hour.

Dr. Doolittle was your hero. Talking to the animals just comes naturally to you. Pet sitting, which can include feeding, walking, and basic grooming, is a great way to connect with your four-legged friends. And it can pay $12 to $17 per pet visit.

You never missed an episode of Davy Crockett. In fact, you still dream of being "King of the Wild Frontier." So go to work for the National Park Service, and enjoy the great outdoors — while earning a salary. To explore open-air opportunities, visit *usajobs.gov*, and use the keywords "national park service." Coon-skin cap optional.

You dreamed of guest-starring on The Ed Sullivan Show. You may be too old for American Idol auditions, but you can still carry a tune with the best of them. How about offering voice lessons? Or maybe piano lessons? Both will bring in $30 to $40 an hour — sure to have you humming a happy tune.

Stash away cash with a zero-spending day

Think of it as a one-day break from spending money. No $4 morning coffee, no $11 lunch. One day a week, chug a cup of joe at home. Brown-bag a sandwich to work. Skip the extra trip to the grocery store, and make a meal out of what's already in your pantry.

How much will you save? The creator of the Zero Day Challenge said he cut his spending by more than $1,500 each month — that's over $18,000 a year. He admits to being a big spender before starting the plan, so you may not save as much as he did. But if you pocket just $20 every week, you'll save more than $1,000 by year's end. That leaves you a nice stack of cash to stash away in the old 401(k).

DOLLARS & SENSE

Boost your bottom line with these fun and easy moneymakers

In kindergarten, you ran a lemonade stand to fatten up your piggy bank. During your teen years you earned mad money as the neighborhood yard boy or everybody's go-to baby sitter. A steady cash flow was your secret to living well as a youngster, and things haven't changed much now that you're a senior on a fixed income.

Imagine what you could do if you found an extra $200 in your budget every month. How about an extra $300, $500, or even $1,000 a month? It's not as hard as it sounds. Read on to find out about 17 moneymakers you can do in your spare time.

▶ Still enjoy babysitting? Go for it. The average sitter makes around $16 per hour.

▶ Yard work pays big. According to Angie's List, lawn maintenance workers charge between $35 and $50 to cut, trim, and edge a yard.

▶ Handy around the house? Bet your neighbors would be happy to pay you to shovel snow, paint, clean gutters, or wash windows.

▶ Are you a numbers person? Senior adults who struggle with their finances need your bookkeeping skills.

▶ Let your organizational skills pay off. Consider becoming a senior move manager — someone who helps older people downsize.

- Savvy with a saw and hammer? Market your skills to older folks who need home renovations to help them age in place.

- Are you crafty? Sell your creations on Etsy, a unique online store for handmade and vintage items. It's easy to get started. Just go to *etsy.com* and click "Sell on Etsy."

Don't waste your time or money on these three jobs when they require you to send in money to buy their materials or supplies — envelope stuffing, assembly or craft work, and mystery shopping. The Federal Trade Commission warns to steer clear of companies that promise big pay days for easy work.

- Rent yourself out as a grandma. Perform Nana duties like babysitting or cooking while earning $14 to $20 an hour. Sign up at *rentagrandma.com*, or ask around to see what opportunities are available near you.

- Are you a teacher at heart? Look into online tutoring. Streamline the process by signing up on sites like *chegg.com/tutors* and *tutorme.com*.

- Become a personal shopper for residents of a local retirement home. Lots of those folks would gladly pay you to pick up their essentials.

None of these jobs tickle your fancy? Check out the website *seniorjobbank.org* to find your perfect job — right in your own neighborhood. You'll see ads for receptionists, tech support staffers, call center reps, substitute teachers, and even deckhands for steamboats or cruise ships.

Or turn your passion for volunteering into a paid gig. Retired teachers Bob and Judy were passionate about their volunteer work at a homeless shelter. Their dedication paid off when the shelter director rewarded their efforts with a monthly salary. The couple now enjoy a satisfying part-time job that helps pay the bills.

But even if it doesn't turn into a moneymaker, volunteering has its own rewards. Find an opportunity to serve your community at *volunteermatch.org*.

Fraud alert: Protect yourself from 4 sly scams

You've trimmed your budget to the bone, making every penny count and squirreling away cash like acorns for the winter. And it's working. Your 401(k) and savings accounts are blossoming. But beware. Smooth-talking con artists lurk in the shadows, trying to get their mitts on your hard-earned cash.

Be on the lookout — that's BOLO to you crime show fans — for these four scams.

"Grandma, I need your help." You answer the phone and hear, "Granny, do you know who this is? I know I sound weird. I have a cold." Your heart does a little leap when you realize your grandson is calling. And when he asks for money to buy his college textbooks, you're happy to help out. But he has lost his identification card and asks you to wire the cash via a money-transfer service so he can collect your gift without an ID.

Except it's not really your grandson on the line. It's one of those bad guys. And you've just been scammed, using the most powerful secret scammers have — appealing to your emotions.

It doesn't matter how smart you are. Studies show older adults are more likely to fall prey to con artists arousing fear, excitement, anger, or frustration. Protect yourself by refusing to rush into any decisions until you can check out the situation.

Brace yourself for this Medicare scam. A colorful, professional-looking postcard arrives in the mail, offering to send you a back or knee brace — for free. Well, isn't that nice? All you have to do is send them your Medicare information, and they'll ship it right to you.

You may actually receive a cheap, Velcro band for your knee or back. But then the scammer bills Medicare for hundreds of dollars for the device — much more than your brace is worth. And now the crooks have your info so they can continue to bill Medicare in your name for services you will never receive.

> What do you do if you're the victim of a scam? Don't be afraid to let someone know what happened. Contact the police and your bank. You should also reach out to the Adult Protective Services. To find an agency near you, go to *napsa-now.org/get-help/ help-in-your-area* and select your state.

"Hello, it's me?" Your cellphone rings, and to your surprise, your number comes up on the caller ID. What's going on here? Scammers try to make you believe they're calling from your phone provider, which is why your number shows up on the screen.

Once they get you on the line, the bad guys threaten to disconnect your service — claiming they've noticed suspicious activity — unless you verify your account by giving them info like your Social Security number.

The lesson here? Never give out your private information over the phone, no matter what the caller says. Just hang up.

Alexa, I've been scammed. Amazon customers, watch out. You're the prime target for this scam. The bad guys send you an email, stamped with an authentic-looking Amazon logo, requesting that you verify your account.

Don't do it. Once you enter your username and password into their fake form, the scammers head to your account and change the information. You're locked out, and their shopping spree begins — financed by your credit card.

Second hand is grand: 13 things to always buy used

Recycled. Hand-me-down. Pre-owned. Just nice ways of saying used. Does the thought of buying someone else's nearly new stuff turn you off? It shouldn't, especially if you're fond of saving money. Here are 13 items you should never buy new. Get them used every time. They'll be just as good, and you'll save a bundle of cash.

- ▶ **Cars.** New cars start to lose their value the minute you drive them off the lot. Quality used cars are a better value.

- ▶ **Furniture.** You can find bargains at estate sales, consignment sales, and even yard sales. But never, ever buy used mattresses.

- ▶ **Boats, motorcycles, and RVs.** Anything with a motor eventually goes down in value. Buy used and save.

▶ **Books, CDs, and DVDs.** You'll find them on the cheap at most yard sales and secondhand shops. Check out *amazon.com*, too.

▶ **Sports gear.** From hand weights to treadmills, you can find exercise equipment for rock-bottom prices at garage sales and online sites like *craigslist.org*.

▶ **Jewelry.** Quality jewelry doesn't always hold its value well, so it's a good idea to buy used. But before you buy, get a professional appraisal.

▶ **Tools.** Find just-like-new hammers, saws, and more in newspaper classified ads or on Craigslist.

▶ **Musical instruments.** Buy online, or purchase them used at local music stores. You may even find a store with a rent-to-buy plan, in case your want-to-be musician changes his mind.

▶ **Toys and games.** Stock up for the grandkids at yard sales and thrift shops.

▶ **Formal wear.** From wedding gowns to special occasion dresses, save up to 50 percent when you shop online for preloved dresses.

▶ **Tech items.** Save big when you buy used or refurbished electronics and technology at sites like *bestbuy.com*.

▶ **Pre-owned gift cards.** Sites like *cardpool.com* and *giftcardgranny.com* sell gift cards at up to 30 percent off their face value.

▶ **Gently used clothing.** Find great deals on clothing for the whole family at online thrift stores like *swap.com* and *thredup.com*. You could score discounts of up to 90 percent off retail value.

Grab and go — documents you need in case of crisis

Suppose disaster strikes. Think fire, flood, or earthquake. What documents should you always have on hand in case of an emergency? The Federal Emergency Management Agency (FEMA) says you need to have these papers ready to go at the drop of a hat.

- vital records like driver's licenses and birth certificates

- insurance documents for your home and property

- dental and medical records, including immunization documents for your pets

- financial records, including bank account and credit card numbers

- property records such as real estate deeds and mortgage documents

- photos, a video, or a printed list of your household possessions

- personal records like your address book, a list of your online passwords, and a key to your safe-deposit box

Store your items in a fireproof box or protect them in a three-ring binder with plastic sleeves.

End the paper chase: What to keep, what to shred, and where to put it all

Does your filing cabinet look like a pack rat has turned it into his home sweet home? It's difficult to decide what you need to keep — and what you can put through the shredder. Unravel the rat's nest and make sense out of all the confusion by following these tips to organize your important records the easy way. Send that rat packing, once and for all.

Never destroy these nine documents. The Federal Trade Commission recommends safeguarding these important official papers.

▶ Social Security cards

▶ Birth certificates, death certificates, and adoption papers

▶ Passports and citizenship papers

▶ Marriage and divorce decrees

▶ Tax returns

Stick to this shredder schedule. Hang on to tax-related receipts and canceled checks for seven years before you send them off to the shredder. Why? The IRS has up to seven years to audit you.

Other papers, like your bank statements and medical bills, can be destroyed after one year. Scrap your pay stubs, too, as long as they match up with your W-2. But shred your credit card and utility bills every month, as soon as you pay them.

And don't worry about keeping track of most sales receipts. Go ahead and shred them — unless they're related to your taxes, insurance, or warranties. You may want to keep receipts from home improvement projects as well. Certain expenses may help lower capital gains taxes if you make a large profit when you sell your home.

Keep them safe and secure. Now that you have your papers in order, how should you store them? Documents like bank records, pay stubs, medical bills, and tax documents are best kept in a fireproof safe.

For records that are difficult to replace, like birth certificates and Social Security cards, invest in a safe-deposit box at your local bank. You'll rest easier knowing your paperwork is organized and protected.

> Use your phone to scan receipts, medical records, or other documents for safekeeping. Buy an app like TurboScan, Scanner Pro, or Prizmo, or give freebie Genius Scan a try. You can store documents as PDFs or JPEGs on your phone, in the cloud, or on your computer.

Missing in action: How to replace your lost documents

After a late-night visit to the emergency room, Gloria discovered that her wallet was missing from her purse. Social Security, Medicare, and insurance cards — all gone. Now what? How do you replace your important papers?

Social Security card. The good news? You can replace your Social Security card for free. The bad news? Not every state allows you to replace it online.

Go to *ssa.gov/ssnumber* to see the requirements for your state. If you're not eligible to order a new card online, print out the application and mail it to your local Social Security office, which will be listed on the website.

You'll need to include your driver's license, state-issued identity card, or passport. The Social Security Administration won't accept photocopies. They only take originals or copies certified by the issuing agency, so you may feel safer applying in person.

Medicare card. To request a new Medicare card, log in to your Social Security account, or create a new account if you don't already have one. Click on the Replacement Documents tab, and find "Mail my replacement Medicare card." Your new card will arrive in about 30 days. If you don't want to use the online service, you can call 800-772-1213 to request a replacement.

Birth certificate. Born in the United States? Contact the Vital Records Office in the state where you were born. Go to *cdc.gov/nchs/w2w/index.htm* to find the address you need, along with the price tag for the service. Unfortunately, a new birth certificate is not free.

Passport. Head on over to *travel.state.gov* to report it as lost or stolen. That's also where you'll find the replacement application, Form DS-11, and a list of local offices.

Need a replacement in two weeks or less? You can make an appointment at a passport agency or center. No plans to travel that soon? Apply at an authorized passport acceptance facility, which may be a post office or library. If your passport goes missing while you're traveling out of the country, contact the nearest U.S. embassy or consulate. Fees for a replacement passport? $135. Ouch.

Keep cash in your pocket with a shipshape clutter-free smartphone

Do you have dozens of unanswered emails gumming up your inbox? Is your phone packed full of family photos that gobble up your storage space? And how about your passwords? Using one like "ABC123" certainly won't protect your bank account and credit cards from internet hackers.

Need some help getting it all under control? Organize your digital life — and safeguard your online accounts — with these simple tips.

Clean out your inbox. Before you spend your hard-earned cash on a new memory card for extra storage on your phone, try cleaning out your email inbox. Here's how.

First, sort your messages by date. Then create a dedicated folder — you can call it something like "Clean Sweep" so you remember what it's for. Drag the oldest emails into the folder. You're not deleting anything yet, just sweeping the clutter away until you have time to deal with it.

The result? A nice, clean, organized inbox and — once you go through and delete the old stuff — more storage space, too.

Store your pictures in a digital shoebox. Are your pics and videos hogging more than their fair share of space? Get them under control with a free app like Shoebox. It will automatically store your photos and videos on your computer or tablet — even in the cloud. You can still use your phone to view your pictures and videos, but they won't use up your memory. Genius, huh?

Want more ways to free up space? Comb through your phone for old audiobooks, podcasts, or music you're tired of. And don't forget to delete all those space-stealing texts, especially the ones that include videos or pictures.

Protect your accounts with a password manager. Tired of creating new passwords and then promptly forgetting them? A password manager, like Dashlane or LastPass, generates unique passwords for all your online accounts and keeps track of them. Go to *dashlane.com* or *lastpass.com* for more information. The best part? They're free.

12 ways to keep your motor running

"The ultimate driving machine," brags BMW. "The best built cars in the world," touts Toyota. And don't forget this favorite from Ford — "Designed for living. Engineered to last."

Auto manufacturers make all kinds of promises to sell you a car. But after you drive it off their lot, it's up to you to keep your new wheels rolling smoothly. Here are 12 keys that could make your car last practically a lifetime. And not one of them is difficult or expensive.

▸ Your car may require a little extra TLC if you rack up more than your share of city miles or if you make lots of short trips. Climate impacts your engine life, too. Do you live near the ocean or in the mountains? Is your car exposed to very hot or very cold weather? Check your owner's manual for the severe-use or extreme-use maintenance schedule. It may advise you to change your oil and other fluids more often in order to keep your motor purring along.

▶ Change your car's oil and oil filter according to the schedule in your owner's manual.

▶ Be sure to check the air filter. Your engine needs a breath of fresh air every now and then.

▶ Buy a vehicle service manual — a more detailed version of the owner's manual. It will explain what engine problems to look out for, and may even guide you through minor repairs.

▶ Cheap parts and fluids could void your warranty — or even damage your car. Purchase brands recommended by your car's manufacturer.

▶ Check your tire pressure once a month, when the tires are rested.

▶ Get your tires rotated every six months or 6,000 to 8,000 miles.

▶ Avoid jackrabbit stops as well as starts that swallow up gas and hinder your engine's performance.

▶ Protect your car's exterior with a regular wash and wax.

▶ You'll enjoy owning your car for a lifetime if its interior is clean as a whistle. Vacuum thoroughly as needed.

▶ Park in a garage or carport to avoid sun damage and tree sap.

▶ Find a mechanic you can trust. Regular maintenance performed by a skilled technician will keep your car up and running, smooth as a little Deuce Coupe.

Grand slam! Score super savings at warehouse clubs

You shop at membership clubs to find bargains on bulk items or pick up a few groceries on the cheap. But a car? You bet. In just one year, members bought almost 500,000 cars through Costco. And the savings are grand. Literally. Experts say you can save up to $1,000 on a new car if you buy it through the warehouse club.

Cruise by *costcoauto.com* to connect with a local dealership that has been hand-selected to offer you the best deal available. You'll need to enter your membership number and answer a few questions about your ideal car's make and model. What you won't have to do is haggle over the price. And you'll even get discounts on service and parts.

Warehousers like BJ's and Sam's Club offer similar programs. Paper towels, chips, and a brand new car — it's a grand deal for members only.

DOLLARS & SENSE

Snag killer deals on wheels with these secret strategies

"Come away with me, Lucille, in my merry Oldsmobile." When Billy Murray crooned these lyrics in 1905, Lucille's state-of-the-art, Curved-Dash ride sold for $650. The last Olds to come off the assembly line, on the other hand, recently auctioned for a whopping $42,000. Car prices certainly have changed, and so have car-buying styles. Want to save hundreds — even thousands — on your new wheels? Read on to uncover the secrets car salesmen don't want you to know.

Buying a car doesn't have to be a hassle if you shop online.
Search for your new ride from the comfort of your own home.
Need some easy-to-navigate sites to get you started? Try
truecar.com, edmunds.com, or *cars.usnews.com.*

These web resources will ask you to enter information about
the car model you want to buy. They'll also need your email
address, phone number, and ZIP code. Then, hang on. Offers
by the dozens will start rolling in from internet salesmen at all
the local dealerships.

Test-drive your email to work out the details. Communicating
with salesmen through email allows you to shop and compare
with several dealerships at the same time. Once you've snagged
a great deal, take that quote to the dealer of your choice, and see
if the salesmen will match it. If not, walk away — straight to
another dealership.

Buy your next car at the price you want to pay. You can
eliminate the middleman and avoid that unpleasant haggling
in the dealer's finance room. Just arrange your own loan online
through a national lender, or visit a local bank or credit union.
The interest rate you get will be the best rate you qualify for —
without the pricey dealer markup of up to 2 percent.

That markup adds up. Take on a seven-year loan of $30,000
with a 5 percent interest rate from the dealership, and you'll pay
about $2,300 more over the course of the loan than if you had
scored a 3 percent rate.

And you might get caught in this roadblock — "So what monthly
payment are you looking for today?" asks the grinning salesman.

Don't answer. This is a sneaky strategy some finance departments use to add on extra fees and charges that can bump up the overall price of your car. But with your financing in place, you're free to give a thumbs down to add-ons and extended-warranty offers you don't want.

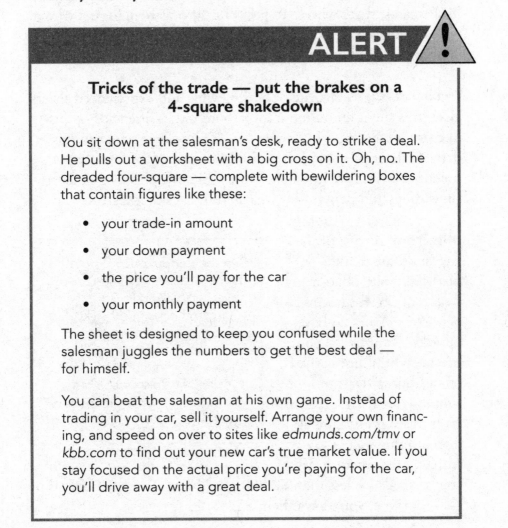

ALERT

Tricks of the trade — put the brakes on a 4-square shakedown

You sit down at the salesman's desk, ready to strike a deal. He pulls out a worksheet with a big cross on it. Oh, no. The dreaded four-square — complete with bewildering boxes that contain figures like these:

- your trade-in amount
- your down payment
- the price you'll pay for the car
- your monthly payment

The sheet is designed to keep you confused while the salesman juggles the numbers to get the best deal — for himself.

You can beat the salesman at his own game. Instead of trading in your car, sell it yourself. Arrange your own financing, and speed on over to sites like *edmunds.com/tmv* or *kbb.com* to find out your new car's true market value. If you stay focused on the actual price you're paying for the car, you'll drive away with a great deal.

Smooth selling: Drive a hard bargain when you post online

You may strike the best deal for your car if you sell it yourself. But where are all the buyers? Surfing the internet and looking for bargains, that's where. To get your car out there for the whole world wide web to see, start by choosing the right strategy for your sale. Drive by these popular sites to see if one works for you.

Craigslist.org. A favorite of both newbie and experienced sellers alike, this site is an online smorgasbord of classified ads — just like you used to find in newspapers. Except here, you can post a detailed description with a handful of pictures for free. And potential buyers are just a click away. Include photos that clearly show dings and dents — as well as your car's best features.

eBay.com. As one of the largest online market-places, this site offers a wealth of tips for beginner sellers. And you have options. Want to sell your car outright? Choose the "Buy It Now" feature. Would you rather auction it off to see if buyers will drive up the price? Go with an eBay auction. If your car sells for less than $2,000, you'll pay eBay a $60 fee. If it goes for more, you'll owe them $125.

> Pick the perfect price. To get the inside scoop on what local buyers are willing to pay for your car, check out sites like cars.usnews.com/cars-trucks/used-cars. The prices you'll find are based on national transactions. Experts also recommend you leave a little wiggle room in your asking price for negotiation.

Autotrader.com. This popular site offers several selling plans, including a basic package for $25. Your ad will run for one month, and you can upload three photos to draw in customers.

If you choose the pricier "Run 'till It Sells" option, you'll pay $100. But it comes with additional perks like a featured listing and an ad tracker that helps you gauge viewer interest.

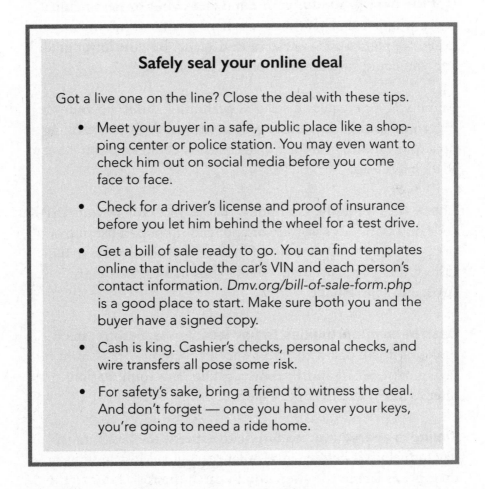

Safely seal your online deal

Got a live one on the line? Close the deal with these tips.

- Meet your buyer in a safe, public place like a shopping center or police station. You may even want to check him out on social media before you come face to face.

- Check for a driver's license and proof of insurance before you let him behind the wheel for a test drive.

- Get a bill of sale ready to go. You can find templates online that include the car's VIN and each person's contact information. *Dmv.org/bill-of-sale-form.php* is a good place to start. Make sure both you and the buyer have a signed copy.

- Cash is king. Cashier's checks, personal checks, and wire transfers all pose some risk.

- For safety's sake, bring a friend to witness the deal. And don't forget — once you hand over your keys, you're going to need a ride home.

5 tips drive down the cost of filling up

The all-time highest average price for a gallon of gas, according to the American Automobile Association (AAA)? $4.11. Yikes. Hopefully, the days of $4 gas are long gone, but you still want to give your pennies a good pinch at the pump. Good news — you can save 20 cents on every gallon of gas with these cost-saving secrets.

Get the best grade for your car. Check your owner's manual to see what kind of gas you need. If your car can run on less-expensive regular gas instead of mid-grade, buy the lower grade and you could save up to 27 cents a gallon.

And if you buy regular instead of premium? Bump up your savings to more than 50 cents a gallon. Just think. If you're filling up a minivan, for example, that one trick could save you close to $10 on a fill-up.

Check with a buddy. GasBuddy, that is. Just type in your ZIP code on GasBuddy's website or app, and up pops a list of gas prices at stations in your area. Find the cheapest, and save the cash. Other popular money-saving apps include Gas Guru, AAA, and Fuel Finder.

Cash in on opportunities to pay less. Some stations offer a discount if you pay with cash rather than credit card. Count on saving between 10 and 15 cents a gallon. But some stations may offer as much as $1 off per gallon.

Timing is everything. According to experts, the best time of day to fuel up is before dawn or late at night. Most stations raise their prices late in the afternoon to catch the rush-hour traffic.

The best day to buy? Studies show you'll save more by pumping earlier in the week, especially Monday. But this can vary from state to state. Check with GasBuddy before heading out to the station for a fill-up.

Reap the rewards of smart shopping. For every dollar you spend at some supermarkets, you'll earn points that lower your price at the pump. It's easy. Earn 100 fuel points at Kroger grocery stores, for example, and you'll save 10 cents per gallon on your next gas purchase. Check with your local store to see how you can save.

Top-tier fuel keeps your engine in tiptop shape

A spic-and-span sedan may turn heads, but it's what's under the hood that counts. For pennies more a gallon, keep your engine clean as a whistle with TOP TIER certified gasoline.

Fuels that meet TOP TIER performance standards contain higher amounts of detergents. These additives keep harmful deposits from forming in your engine.

But you thought all fuel was the same? Not quite. Experts crash-tested the theory and found that lower-quality additives can slash fuel economy by 4 percent.

"AAA was surprised to learn the extent to which detergent additives impact gasoline quality," says John Nielsen, AAA's managing director of Automotive Engineering and Repair. "As advertised, tested TOP TIER gasolines kept engines remarkably cleaner than other fuels we tested."

Popular certified brands include BP, Chevron, and Texaco. Typically, service stations will display the TOP TIER logo, but for a full list, check *toptiergas.com/licensedbrands*.

Repair rip-offs: 5 ways your mechanic takes you for a ride

Julie's aging Fiat sedan stopped dead in the middle of a busy road. Again. Once she got it started, she headed straight to the auto repair shop where — just two weeks earlier — the mechanic had promised her car troubles were over for good. Although he had charged her, he obviously hadn't fixed the problem. He would now.

"You drive," she ordered, tossing him the keys. Before they got out of the lot, the car broke down again. And this time, the mechanic took her complaint seriously. He ordered the correct parts and repaired her car.

Take a page from Julie's book, and don't let your mechanic off the hook. Make sure he completes the repairs that show up on your bill. And be on the lookout for four more car repair scams.

Dodge the big flush. You take your car in for an oil change, and once that's done, the mechanic recommends extra work like flushing radiator coolants or replacing power steering, transmission, and brake fluids. Your car may not need all that. Newer cars, for example, often use an extended-life coolant that lasts up to 100,000 miles. When in doubt, let your owner's manual be your guide for scheduled maintenance.

Don't buy new when a patch will do. For your tire, that is. If the tread on your tire is still in good condition, consider a $20 patch instead of a $100 replacement tire.

Head off the front-end flimflam. Did the mechanic recommend front-end work like new ball joints or an alignment?

If your car is driving fine, don't let his warning about steering loss scare you into spending more money. Instead, get a second opinion before you make any repairs.

Beat the boot bamboozle.
A broken axle boot can be pricey, but be prepared to bite the bullet and have it fixed — if the damage comes from normal wear and tear. But beware. Some mechanics will cut the rubber boots just to make a little extra money for themselves.

Ask to see the damaged part before you OK the repair. A torn boot should be jagged and dirty from use. If it's not, you're being hoodwinked. The auto shop should fix it at no cost to you.

> Can your neighborhood mechanic wreck your car's warranty? Not according to the Federal Trade Commission. A dealer can't deny your warranty just because you had routine maintenance — like oil changes and fluid checks — performed somewhere else. Protect yourself by keeping thorough records of the service date, your mileage at the time, and the work completed.

Once you're certain car repairs are needed, how do you know if you're getting a good deal? Call around to check prices at local auto shops, or try Consumer Reports' Car Repair Estimator at *consumerreports.org/cars/repair* for prices in your neighborhood.

Brains over brawn — fresh tech keeps you safe on the road

Oh, Eleanor, sweet Eleanor. The '73 Mustang Mach 1 made famous in the flick "Gone in 60 Seconds" — how you dreamed of taking her for a spin on the open road. Or maybe the Duke boys' General Lee, that Dixie-blaring Dodge Charger, was more your style.

Does it seem like your life has taken a detour from muscle cars — straight to the Metamucil aisle? Don't despair. Here are some tips to help you choose tech-savvy safety tools that will put you right back in the driver's seat.

When it comes to safety, technology tops muscle. Three out of four drivers age 50 and older who plan to buy a new car in the near future say technology is key to keeping them safe on the streets.

Tools that top their wish list? Blind spot and lane departure warning systems are the most sought after. Both can help if you have difficulty turning your head to scan the traffic around you.

A forward collision warning system is another popular choice. Get too close to the car in front of you, and an alert sounds. Some models even hit the brakes for you.

Update your car with do-it-yourself add-ons. Not in the market for a new car? No problem. You can add safety features to your present car. But get out your wallet. A system that includes lane departure and forward collision warning can cost you around $1,000 including installation. And a blind spot detection system will run you about $240.

Looking for cheaper options? Install your own dash cam. You can find popular models that act as a collision warning system for around $130 online.

A backup camera is a great tool for parallel parking or maneuvering down that long, winding driveway. A system you put in yourself will cost less than $140 at auto parts stores or online. But you may just want to save your money for a new ride instead. All those shiny new cars at your local dealership now come with backup cameras as standard equipment.

So maybe Bandit's '77 Trans Am did have plenty of muscle to spare. But it wasn't nearly as smart — or as safe — as today's models. And where driver safety is concerned, brains beat muscle every time.

6 tips power down pricey electric bills

Every month your electric bill sends shock waves straight to the heart of your budget. But you can save more money on your power bills than you think.

One way? Pack up and head off to New Mexico, the Land of Enchantment. With bills averaging about $76 a month, these folks have the lowest power tabs in the country. Maybe you're not ready to make the move to Santa Fe, but still want in on the cheaper bills. These tried-and-true tips can get you started.

▶ Electric companies may charge more for daytime power. For example, your provider might have summer rates that spike from 2 p.m. to 8 p.m. Monday through Friday, but drop at night and on weekends. So put off that extra load of laundry until Saturday, or power up your computer after the evening news. And consider a laptop for your next home computer. They use less power than desktop models, and you can easily unplug during peak hours.

▶ Many electronic devices and appliances continue to soak up electricity after you've turned them off. Plug them into a power strip, and turn it off when not in use. Pull the plug on all those phone and tablet chargers, too. They gobble up energy even when your gadgets aren't hooked up.

▶ Who knew wall color could save you money? If you want a warmer room, paint the walls with warm colors like reds and oranges. Your room may seem six to 10 degrees warmer. Want to cool off? Select cooling blues and greens instead. And next time you paint, ask about the color's Light Reflectance Value (LRV), the amount of light it will reflect back into the room. Spaces painted with a higher LRV color require less artificial light, saving electricity and money.

▶ Give wet clothes one more spin in the washer. Why? Your washing machine uses less energy than your dryer. And to save time and cold, hard cash, use the dryer's moisture sensor mode instead of the timed option.

▶ Plant deciduous trees — the kind that lose their leaves in autumn — on the south and west sides of your home. The trees will help cool your house in the summer, but allow the sun to shine through your windows to warm you up in the winter.

▶ Put a lid on those ice tea pitchers. Refrigerators use energy to lower the humidity inside the icebox, which helps your food stay cool 24/7. That's why your fridge has to work overtime to bring down the temp when you store open containers of liquids. Cover them up and save money.

A finely tuned home keeps you wealthy — and healthy

"Energy efficiency leads not only to lower energy bills, but also to greater comfort, and in some cases improved health," says David Lee, a program manager with the U.S. Department of Energy. So how can your house protect your health?

Experts say energy-efficient homes are especially beneficial for people with allergies and asthma. "You're sealing the house up from outside allergens," says Lee. That includes health-harming dust mites and pollen.

And then there's mold. If your house isn't insulated or sealed properly, humid air can leak in, he says. This causes moisture to form on your walls and windows — or on other surfaces you can't see. And then your home can become a giant petri dish.

For tips on transforming your house into a healthy, energy-efficient home, go to *energy.gov* and click "Save Energy, Save Money."

Don't let this bill drain your wallet

Too much of your hard-earned cash is going straight down the drain with those pricey water bills. Looking for some practical tips to stem the costly flow from your faucet and put cash back in your pocket? Here are six simple strategies, ready and waiting to buoy your bank account.

▶ Avoid washing your dishes by hand. You'll save up to
4 gallons of water if you use an Energy Star dishwasher, or
2 gallons if you have a regular one. Make sure you wash
when you have a full load, or you'll send your savings down
the pipes. And don't pre-rinse your dishes. Scrape them by
hand instead.

Fighting the urge to rinse? Try this. Mix water and a little
dish detergent in a spray bottle, and keep it by the sink.
Spray your dishes before you load them into the dishwasher.

▶ Don't defrost frozen cuisine in running water. Instead, thaw
food in the fridge overnight or use the microwave, and
you'll save 2 gallons of water every minute.

▶ Don't leave the water running when you shave or brush
your teeth. You've heard this one many times before, so why
are you still doing it? Kick the habit, and it will save you 3
gallons of water every day.

▶ Take a Navy shower. Turn off the tap while you soap up.
You'll conserve 2 1/2 gallons every minute you leave the
water off.

▶ Install low-flow toilets or convert those you already have.
Save 2 to 5 gallons per flush.

▶ Take your ride to a car wash that recycles water instead of
lathering on the suds at home. You'll knock at least 100
gallons off your water bill, and you'll be helping the envi-
ronment. Saving money while you save the planet — now
that's a bargain.

Pocket $900 every year by scaling down your water routine

Helen's family of four uses 600 gallons of water every day. That's 150 gallons per person. Her monthly water bill? A hefty $109. But what if she could get her family to cut down their usage to 50 gallons each by practicing water-saving strategies?

Helen's bill would drop to just $34. She would save $75 a month for a grand total of $900 each year. And that makes quite a splash in her bank account.

DOLLARS & SENSE

Never pay this monthly bill again

You're tired of paying sky-high cable bills — just to watch TV every now and then. Well, you can forget about those monthly satellite or cable bills. Just pay for this once and watch TV forever, including shows you'd never see otherwise.

Join the cord-cutters and disable your cable. More than 22 million customers have already cut ties with their cable or satellite company. Ready to join them? Buy an antenna. Find them online or in stores like Best Buy and Walmart. They sell for as little as $7 to more than $300. But cheaper models often do as well as — or even better than — the more expensive ones.

Location, location, location. The channels you receive with your antenna will depend on where you live. For example, if you're close to a city, you will probably be able to get standard stations like ABC, CBS, FOX, NBC, plus many more.

Many stations also offer subchannels that let you tune into your old TV favorites or pick up public channels that aren't offered by your expensive cable provider. An extra bonus? You may be pleasantly surprised to see your picture quality is head and shoulders above what you're used to with cable.

Rabbit ears are for bunnies, not your TV. Today's antennas don't look anything like the rabbit ears of your childhood. They're sleek and modern, and many indoor models can attach to your wall or window. Some can even be painted to match your decor.

You can choose an indoor antenna to pick up signals 30 miles away, an attic-mounted style for signals within a 60-mile range, or a roof-mounted antenna — just right for signals more than 100 miles away.

Ready to jump on the "kill the cable" bandwagon? Hold on. Don't cut your cable until you check out *tvfool.com* or *antennaweb.org* to see what stations are available in your area. Just type in your address or ZIP code to get started.

Dial up $720 in yearly savings by switching your cell strategy

It's a fact. More than 95 percent of Americans now own some kind of cellphone. And 77 percent of those folks have "smart-phones" — the ones that allow you to access your email, update your Facebook status, and make video calls. Very handy. But let's face the music — most cellphone plans are no bargain. In fact, the average American household pays $1,074 each year for cell-phone service. Yikes. Want to know the secrets to cutting your cellphone bill in half? Read on.

Strike a better deal with your carrier. Before you call customer service to negotiate your bill, get your facts and figures ready. Find the least expensive rate available for the plan or package you want. See if you can find the "new customer" rate, too. It could be the cheapest. If your provider offers a lower rate in your area, jump on it. If another company has a better offer, use it as leverage.

Jump ship to save a mint. If haggling the price doesn't work, just switch to the provider that offers the best deal. In one *Consumer Reports* survey, nearly half of participants who changed phone companies saw their monthly bill drop $20 or more. A crisp Andrew Jackson a month back in your pocket — just by switching phone providers? That's a cool $240 a year.

Ties that bind may cost big bucks. Ah, the dreaded cell-phone contract. It's supposed to guarantee perks like free phone upgrades every few years and better coverage. But it could be ballooning your bill to new heights.

Almost 51 percent of American homes don't have a landline, says the National Center for Health Statistics. Consider cutting yours, especially if you have good cellphone service at home and at work. You could shave up to $30 off your bill every month — that's $360 to plump up your piggy bank every year.

The average family pays almost $90 every month for their phone service. But you just want a simple, easy-to-use phone. No frills needed. Sound about right? Then it's time to ditch the pricey contract and take a look at budget providers like Boost Mobile or Cricket. You can find unlimited monthly plans with great coverage starting around $30. That's a savings of up to $60 each month — a whopping $720 every year.

Add 'em up: 13 ways to save $100 a month on utilities

Want to shave 10, 30, or even 50 percent off your monthly power and water tabs? You know from experience that hot summer days or icy winter temps usually mean higher utility bills. Not this year. Find out what you can do to save up to $100 a month on energy bills.

	Monthly Savings*
Seal up airleaks around windows and doors.	$14
Use a power strip for electronics, and turn it off when not in use.	$8
Install low-e exterior storm windows.	$24
Turn back your thermostat 7 to 10 degrees for 8 hours a day.	$7
Weatherstrip double-hung windows.	$7
Replace five frequently used light fixtures or bulbs with Energy Star models.	$6
Fix leaky faucets.	$3
Use sleep mode and power-management features on your computer.	$3
Install a WaterSense toilet.	$8
Insulate your hot water pipes.	$1
Insulate water heater tank.	$4
Plant shade trees.	$10
Lower water heater temperature.	$5

*Based on Department of Energy statistics. Actual savings may vary.

TOTAL SAVINGS $100

Block bothersome robocalls for good

Another dinnertime, another pesky robocall. Ring a bell? If so, you're not alone. According to the Federal Communications Commission (FCC), Americans put up with more than 2 billion robocalls every month.

And the calls aren't just irritating. Sometimes scammers are on the other end of the line, hoping to get enough personal information to steal your identity. But you can protect yourself. Here are some tips to stop telemarketers from calling — for good. You won't learn these from a salesman.

Your first line of defense. The National Do Not Call Registry was created by the FCC to put an end to unwanted sales calls. You can register your landline or wireless phone numbers on *donotcall.gov*. Or call toll-free at 888-382-1222 with the phone you want to register.

It's simple — and free — to add your number to the list, and the registration never expires. In fact, the registry already contains nearly 230 million phone numbers. Humorist Dave Barry jokingly calls this list "the most popular federal concept since the Elvis stamp."

But remember, the Do Not Call Registry is designed to stop sales calls only. You may still get a ring from political parties, charities, or debt collection agencies.

Block that robocall. Need more help? Ask your phone provider about robocall-blocking technology. Verizon, AT&T, Sprint, and other carriers offer their own call-blocking features — which may tack on additional fees to your monthly bill. Or you can click on over to *ctia.org/consumer-tips/robocalls* and do your own search for apps that will work with your phone.

You can also purchase a call-blocking device that works with your landline phone. These blockers allow you to program certain numbers to come through — like those belonging to friends and family. That's your "whitelist." Many of the devices also come complete with a factory-installed "blacklist" that's ready and waiting to block thousands of spam numbers.

Phone still ringing off the hook? You may still get a buzz from companies you've recently done business with or from agencies you've given written permission to contact you. If you don't want to hear from them, let them know you don't consent to the call. They have to honor your request. Just be sure to record the phone number and date you asked to be removed from their call list.

You can report unwanted sales calls after your number has been on the Do Not Call Registry for 31 days. File a complaint online at *complaints.donotcall.gov.*

7 ways to slash your grocery bill by 50 percent

Fans of the hard rock band Guns N' Roses remember Saul Hudson — aka Slash — as the group's lead guitarist. But do you know how he got his nickname? One wacky rumor says he worked at a grocery store where his job was to slash prices for really big sales.

It sure would be handy to shop with your own guitar-shredding price slasher. Luckily, you can follow these tips to slice up to 50 percent off your grocery bill. That's a savings even Slash would be proud of.

No-frills grocers save you a bundle. Save 40, 50, even a whopping 70 percent when you buy the store brands — and even some name-brand products — at discount grocers like Aldi, Save-A-Lot, and Grocery Outlet.

Cheaper by the bag. Experienced shoppers know that prebagged produce usually costs less. Just be sure you weigh a few bags before plopping one in your cart to make sure you're getting the most bang for your buck. A *Consumer Reports* staffer weighed bags of apples, each labeled 3 pounds. The heaviest bag tipped the scales at 3.36 pounds. That's a tasty 12 percent bonus.

Only buy food when it's on sale. Really on sale. Like 30 to 50 percent off — at least. But don't buy something just because it's discounted. Make sure you pick out food your family won't grumble about when they see it on the dinner table.

Some stores charge 10 cents for each plastic bag used to pack your groceries. Try reusable bags instead. But beware. Bacteria left behind from meat and produce could contaminate other food. So keep your bags in the cleanest area of your car, and wash them with soapy water once a month.

Stockpile the cereal. Most shelf items — like cereal, for example — go on sale every six to eight weeks. Watch store circulars to see when your family favs are discounted, and be sure to stash away enough to last. If you run out before the sales cycle starts again, you might have to pay full price.

Keep more cash in your pocket — no coupons needed

An average married couple over the age of 51 spends about $500 every month on groceries. Quite a chunk of change. But by making one simple switch, you can save up to 60 percent at your local grocery store every time you shop.

The secret to these super savings is simple — buy store brands. Shopping experts stacked name-brand foods against store brands, and found that you save an average of 25 percent when you buy store varieties — that's $125 a month for the happy couple. And some store labels help you save even more — up to 60 percent.

Worried about the taste of store brands? In a fair food fight, researchers discovered that supermarket varieties were often just as tasty as foods with famous logos. Compare the ingredients list and nutritional information on the products. They might be exactly the same — except for the price.

DOLLARS & SENSE

The time of day matters. You've felt it in your gut, but now researchers at Cornell University have scientific proof. Don't shop hungry. You're less likely to buy the healthy stuff and more likely to buy high-calorie foods between 4 p.m. and 7 p.m., those hungry hours right after work.

Buy off the bargain rack. Those bananas with the brown spots. The bruised and battered tomatoes. You can tell by looking at them — their clock is ticking. And that means extra savings for you. But only buy what you know you can use quickly.

Eggs at the drugstore? When you're heading to the local CVS or Walgreens to pick up a prescription, check the store's sales ads and website for great deals on food items like cereal, dairy products, and eggs — yes, eggs. You may also find super-slashed prices on personal care items like toothbrushes, toothpaste, and makeup.

Like free groceries? Insider tips help you stock up on savings

Want to get grocery items for pennies — or even free? Here are some clever coupon tricks to help you outsmart your supermarket every time you shop. Fill your cart with bargains by using these simple secrets the grocery stores hope you never learn.

> The pennies and nickels you save using coupons may not seem like much. But if you deposit those savings in the bank, the change will really add up. Do the same with a supermarket loyalty program. Check your receipt to see how much you saved, and deposit that amount into your account.

Double your savings with this BOGO tip. The sign by the soup grabbed your attention with ginormous red letters that spelled out "buy one, get one free." Now heap up extra savings by pairing this deal with a coupon. Cha-ching.

Stack 'em high with a triple play. Combine your coupons just right, and you could get items for free. Start with a good store sale, and dig up a manufacturer's coupon. Then throw a store coupon on top, and watch your savings pile up.

Store brands aren't always the best deal. Surprise! Do the math before you buy. You may save more if you use a coupon to purchase a brand-name item that's already on sale.

Savings don't go out of date. Coupon expired? Your store may still accept them. Ask at the courtesy counter.

Rack up a real bargain. You can often use coupons on products off the bargain rack, too. You may find you get the items for free — or nearly free.

Coupons plus rebates equals more savings. Combine your coupons with a rebate you find online, and watch your savings come rolling in. Click on over to popular sites like *ibotta.com* and *checkout51.com* for details.

Use a coupon for each item you buy. It's a simple but often overlooked couponing tip. For example, if you buy two boxes of cereal, use two coupons. You'll get an even better deal if you wait until the item is on sale. Check store circulars and supermarket websites before you head to the store.

Delicious discounts are just a click away

Find a buffet of bargains at *Restaurant.com*. Type in your ZIP code to locate participating restaurants in your area. Then purchase a discounted certificate for your favorite eatery. For example, you can pay $10 for a $25 certificate to Partners Pizza, or $4 for a $10 deal at Dickey's Barbecue.

Print out your certificate or just show it to your server on your phone, and enjoy a great meal at a rock-bottom price. The certificates usually range in value from $5 to $100, and they never expire. And with over 62,000 restaurants to choose from, you'll never go hungry.

DOLLARS & SENSE

Dynamite dining deals: Simple ways to take a bite out of your restaurant bill

You'd like to skip a night of kitchen duty — but you're worried the added expense of a fancy restaurant meal will bust your budget. Did you know you can dine out for less than the price of a home-cooked meal — and even free in some restaurants? Here's how.

Tuck into savings by mapping out your menu. Before you head out for your special dinner, mosey over to the restaurant's website and take a gander at the menu. You'll know just how much your meal will cost, so you can set a budget and skip the surprises when the check comes. And take a peek at the restaurant's Facebook page for special offers.

Here's a giveaway just for you chocolate lovers. Join the Godiva Loyalty Program to receive perks like a special birthday offer every year, a free chocolate once a month, and free shipping on one online order. It's quick and easy to register online or at a Godiva boutique. Yum. Free chocolate — now that's a sweet deal.

Savvy searching pays off. This trick is a favorite among coupon hunters. Open up your internet browser, and type in the restaurant's name along with the word "coupon" to see what pops up. And look for special meal-deal perks on sites like *retailmenot.com* and *seniordiscounts.com*.

Mystery solved — eat for free. Always dreamed of being a person of mystery? Here's your chance. Sign up to be a mystery shopper. You'll dine at local restaurants, shop at certain stores — even visit banks. Then simply complete a survey about your experience. You'll be reimbursed for whatever you spend, and you may even get paid a little something extra.

Just look out for companies that promise to send a check in advance or ask you to pay to become a shopper. And always reach out to the agency directly. Big names in the business like Market Force Information and BARE International say scammers often contact folks out of the blue and pretend to be from legit companies.

Jaw-dropping deals at a glance. Isn't it fun to score special offers and discounts — just because you're over 50? Check out these secret benefits and hard-earned dining-out perks no one told you about.

Age 50+	Age 55+	Age 60+
Krispy Kreme	Arby's	Applebee's
White Castle	Fuddruckers	Burger King
Pollo Tropical	TCBY	Culver's
	Chili's	Einstein Bros. Bagels
	Popeyes	Sonic
	Wendy's	Subway
	El Pollo Loco	Sweet Tomatoes
		Golden Corral
		Ben & Jerry's
		Village Inn

Check locations near you for details. Discounts vary and may change without notice.

Senior discounts at restaurant chains can range from a free beverage with a meal to 20 percent off any menu item. The table on the previous page lists how old you have to be to get a 10 percent discount at some of the most popular restaurants in town. See if your favorite spot made the cut.

Sizzlin' senior deals: More exciting perks for folks over 50

When Walter turned 50, he decided to grow a beard, thinking his salt-and-pepper facial hair would say "Distinguished gentleman." Uh, nope. Turns out it said "Senior discount, please!" At first, Walter was a little blue about going gray — until he discovered all the incredible discounts he could get as part of the 50-plus crowd. Find out how seniors like you can save money on just about everything.

Sock away extra dollars with these super discounts. Know when to shop at your favorite stores, and you could pack your piggy bank with extra cash.

Store	Discount day	Age	Savings
Belk	First Tuesday of month	62+	15%
Bealls	Every Tuesday	50+	15%
Kohl's	Every Wednesday	60+	15%
Ross	Every Tuesday	55+	10%
Michaels	Every day	55+	10%

Discounts vary and may change without notice.

Pinch your pennies till they squeak with frugal pharmacy deals. Some drugstores host a senior day once a year. But why wait? You can score sweet discounts at these pharmacies every day.

  ▶ **Costco.** The Costco Member Prescription Program allows members to save up to 80 percent. For details, check with your local store.

  ▶ **Rite Aid.** Sign up for the free Rite Aid Rx Savings Program, and you'll save 20 percent on many brand-name and generic medications.

  ▶ **CVS.** For the best deals at this pharmacy, sign up for their free ExtraCare program. Earn coupons and 2 percent back on select purchases.

  ▶ **Local pharmacies.** The pharmacists at locally owned drugstores may offer you a great deal on your prescriptions.

Buy just about everything — on the cheap. Looking for a discount on your favorite flick? How about a haircut? Need new tires? You can find savings everywhere — from Ace Hardware all the way to Verizon Wireless. Check out discount sites like *theseniorlist.com* or apps like Sciddy for senior deals. And show off those silver strands with pride.

End credit card chaos

Safe and smart ways to manage your plastic

3 ways to erase credit card debt fast

The average credit card user racks up $5,600 in debt — and if you carry a balance from month to month, you probably have a bit more. Put those dollars back in your pocket with these simple tips.

Go above and beyond the bare minimum. You want to clear your balance ASAP. But if you only shell out the minimum payment every month, you drag out your timeline and even increase debt by adding on all that interest.

For example, a $2,500 balance with a 15 percent interest rate could cost you more than $1,400 in interest over 6 1/2 years if you only make minimum payments of $50. Yikes. But if you double up and pay $100, you could save more than $930 — and get out of the red four years sooner.

Make a plan and stick to it. Do you carry a balance on multiple cards? Pick one of these strategies to cut down debt at warp speed.

▶ Tackle the balance with the highest interest rate first. Focus on cards that charge the most interest, and you might save more money in the long run.

▶ Knock out the lowest balance first. You'll pay it off sooner, and then you can put the extra money toward the bigger ones.

Remember to make minimum payments on all your cards regardless of which method you choose. Both are savvy options, but you need to have a plan in place.

"My advice is to focus on the one you think will keep you motivated to reach the goal of being debt-free. It's more important that you get to the finish line and don't get caught up in what saves you the most money over time," says Bruce McClary, vice president of communications at the National Foundation for Credit Counseling (NFCC).

Phone a financial friend. If your money matters seem out of control, you can always turn to credit counseling services. They'll help you understand your situation, create a budget, and form a plan to pay off debt. Look for reputable nonprofit programs, and do your research to see if they charge fees or have any unresolved complaints.

McClary says you can reach out to an advisor anytime you want to learn more about managing your money. And he certainly recommends getting help if you know you're about to fall behind on bills.

"If somebody is facing a financial crisis and they're having diffi-culty managing their debt, it's important they reach out to a credit counselor as soon as possible," he says. You can find approved counselors at *NFCC.org* or by calling 800-388-2227.

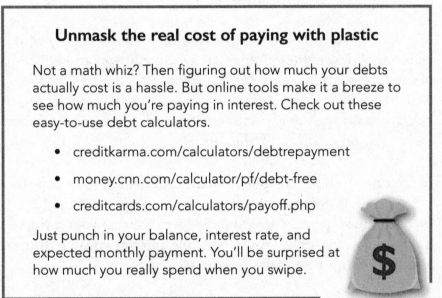

Unmask the real cost of paying with plastic

Not a math whiz? Then figuring out how much your debts actually cost is a hassle. But online tools make it a breeze to see how much you're paying in interest. Check out these easy-to-use debt calculators.

- creditkarma.com/calculators/debtrepayment

- money.cnn.com/calculator/pf/debt-free

- creditcards.com/calculators/payoff.php

Just punch in your balance, interest rate, and expected monthly payment. You'll be surprised at how much you really spend when you swipe.

DOLLARS & SENSE

Should you pad your savings while paying off debt?

Erasing debt is important, but if you leave yourself with no backup plans, you might wind up right back where you started. Take Mark — he wanted to be debt-free by the end of the year, so he made a new budget and began funneling all his extra cash into paying off his credit card bills. He was almost there, but when his water heater sprung a leak he didn't have any money set aside. His credit card covered the cost, but he was dealing with debt all over again.

You can't plan for a trip to the doctor or a flat tire, but you can be certain you'll face some kind of financial emergency eventually. And dipping back into your credit line can be costly. "Credit card debt is one of the most expensive forms of debt there is," says Bruce McClary, spokesperson for the National Foundation of Credit Counseling.

McClary, who worked as a credit counselor for 16 years, knows all too well how common this Catch-22 credit scenario is. "A lot of the people reaching out for help are in situations where they were living on the edge financially and did not have savings to help them through unexpected emergencies," he says. "And they had to rely on credit to fill the gap."

He recommends getting out of credit card debt as soon as possible, but not at the expense of your savings account. "You don't ever want to stop your forward progress in growing your savings," he says. "You may just have to limit the amount you're putting aside as you prioritize debt repayment."

Financial guru Dave Ramsey advises setting aside at least $1,000 for your emergency fund before you begin seriously paying down debt. When you're out of the hole, bump up your savings to six months of net income, says McClary. It'll pay on a rainy day.

Don't let debt collectors dredge up the past

Your old debts might not cost as much as you think. Debt collectors only have a limited amount of time to legally collect on those bills. Otherwise, the balances might become time-barred — meaning the collection agency can't sue you for them.

If a debt collector calls to dig up dues on a credit card bill you forgot about 10 years ago, ask if it has passed its statute of limitations. He is legally required to tell the truth, though he may opt to not answer.

Just because a debt is time-barred doesn't mean you won't face consequences. Choosing not to pay up could hurt your credit score, making it hard to get loans, insurance, or credit cards. But making a partial payment reactivates outstanding charges, which means debt collectors can sue you for the full amount.

If you choose to settle these old debts, get a signed letter detailing your payment plan. You might be able to pay it off in a series of small installments or one lump sum. But you'll need to come to an agreement with the debt collector before you start clearing the balance. Make sure to have a plan in writing so you have a record of restarting the payments.

Clue into credit ratings to score big savings

How do banks, insurance companies, and creditors decide to lend you money? About 90 percent of top lenders use your FICO score, which tells them what kind of risk you might be.

An excellent credit score, like 800, can save you hundreds on everything from your mortgage to your insurance payments. But if you're sitting below 600, you might be in trouble.

Use the chart on the following page to understand how companies calculate your score — and what factors you can focus on to boost that number.

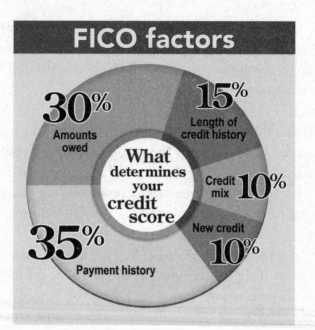

FICO factors

30% Amounts owed

15% Length of credit history

What determines your credit score

Credit mix 10%

New credit 10%

35% Payment history

5 steps move your credit score toward a perfect 850

Bob and Paul both have $1,500 on their credit cards. But Bob's credit limit is $2,000 and Paul's is $20,000. Even though they owe the same amount of money, Bob's credit score will take a hit. Knowing why will help you hook that magic number.

Keep your credit card bills low. Overspending can drive down your credit score if you're not careful. When your balance gets too close to your credit limit, like Bob's, banks and other lenders think you're a risky customer. Keep your spending under 30 percent of your limit. For Bob, that means he should never charge more than $600.

He could also lower his percentage by asking the lender to raise his credit limit. But if you go this route, don't let the increase tempt you into spending more. You should still pay off your balance in full each month.

Lump loan applications together. When you apply for a loan, credit card, or even a new apartment, companies pull your credit report to see if you'll be a good customer. But each checkup costs you a few points.

The good news is reports filed within 30 days of each other only count as one inquiry. So you can keep the damage to a minimum if you apply for your loans all at once.

Mix up your credit categories. Lenders like to team up with people who can juggle balances on different types of accounts. So if you make regular payments on your credit cards, mortgage, and car loan, your credit score will reap the benefits. Just be careful not to get into debt you can't pay off.

Pay your bills on time. Want to build up your credit score? Show lenders you're a responsible spender. Create a solid payment history by opening up a credit card if you don't have one. And if you already have a card, make sure to pay your bills in full and on time.

> Don't sweat the small drops. When you get a new car loan or mortgage, your credit score might take a plunge. That's because fresh debt affects two FICO factors — amounts owed and new credit. But it also boosts your credit mix. So make regular payments, and your score will be on the rise in no time.

Keep an eye on your credit score. One out of 20 credit reports has a serious error that could slash your score and cost you big.

Check yours on a regular basis to catch mistakes before they sky-rocket the interest rate on your next credit card or mortgage.

Taking these steps will save you hundreds of dollars in the long run. A better score means you'll pay less for your house and car. And in certain states, you can save hundreds of dollars on auto insurance. *(See table.)*

	Estimated monthly payment		Monthly savings with good credit
	With a low credit score	With a high credit score	
$250,000 30-year fixed rate mortgage	$1,424	$1,185	$239
$30,000 5-year new car loan	$724	$550	$174
Average auto insurance rates	$153	$73	$80
Total	$2,301	$1,808	$493

Credit checkup: Free ways to give your report a once-over

You're the victim of identity theft. You've been denied a loan based on your credit score. You believe there's an error on your report. All these situations get you a free pass to view your credit report. But why wait until problems develop?

Keeping an eye on your credit score can be a great way to know just how healthy your wallet is. And checking your report at least once a year can keep you safe from mistakes and identity theft.

Your first report is on the government. You're entitled to one free credit report every year from each of the three major credit bureaus — Equifax, Experian, and TransUnion. All you need to do is log on to *AnnualCreditReport.com* to get yours. If you would rather not get your report on the internet, you can mail a request form to the Annual Credit Report Request Service or call them toll-free at 877-322-8228.

Check your state laws — you might get a discount. You can always purchase another credit report if you've already received your free annual one, but don't shell out the cash just yet. Depending on where you live, you could be eligible for free reports or a discount. For example, Georgia residents get two credit reports on the house every year on top of

> Heads up! Rental companies may run a credit report if you rent your wheels using a debit card. Don't want to pay the full bill with your credit card? Just use it to make the reservation and skip the credit review. The final payment can always be made with a check or your debit card.

their free federal one. Minnesota residents get a discount rate for their reports, with the first ringing up at just $3. Check your local laws to see what is available to you.

Watch out for websites that promise free credit reports. Free credit checks might not actually be free. Some online ads are scams that try to trick you into giving out your credit information or bill you for their so-called free reports. Stick with websites you trust, and don't take any chances.

ALERT

Shopping for a money mentor?
Watch out for online traps

Avoid internet ads or websites that promise to get you out of debt fast. They might be for-profit firms with no intention of helping you get out of the red. Instead, these companies are after your cash.

So what do you do? Susan Grant, the director of consumer protection and privacy at the Consumer Federation of America, says to stay away from organizations that only exist online.

"There are rules that prohibit asking for fees upfront for debt consolidation services. If you put a number where consumers can call you, you fall under those rules," she says. "But the Federal Trade Commission (FTC) does not have the authority to enforce promises made solely on the internet."

So if you come across a debt relief company online, look for a phone number. And never go with an agency that asks for payment right off the bat. According to the FTC, they can't charge you a fee without first providing the service.

Stay sharp — spot errors on your credit report and save hundreds

Lisa always pays her bills on time, has a reasonable mortgage, and keeps her monthly spending low. So when she was turned down for a car loan because of a bad credit score, she couldn't understand what went wrong. It turns out, the credit company accidentally put a different Lisa's debts on her report. Here's what to look for so slips don't sink your score.

Dodge a case of mistaken identity. A simple name mix-up could wreck your credit score. Reports for people with common names are especially prone to error, so make sure your address, phone number, and full name all check out.

Identity theft is another cause of errors. Loans or accounts you don't remember opening could be the work of thieves, so take care of them as quickly as possible.

Communication breakdowns could cost you big. Occasionally companies make a mistake when they update your account status for credit bureaus, so stay on top of them to make sure nothing goes wrong. Your bank could report closed accounts as open or put in the wrong payment dates. If they say you've missed payments for months when you're only a few days late, your credit score could wind up dropping like a stone. Keep good records to help you spot these slip-ups early.

Defend yourself from duplicates. Do your debts show up twice on your report? It's a simple mistake, but it could tank your credit score. Get this taken care of, otherwise potential lenders might think you're drowning in debt.

Watch out for balance blunders. Check your report to make sure your credit limits and bank accounts are correct. If companies accidentally mark you down with a low credit limit, your score could suffer.

Finance fixer-upper: Easy actions repair your report

Uh-oh — your credit report listed your mortgage twice, so now lenders think you're in over your head. Fortunately, it's a fast and easy fix.

When you catch an error, the first thing you need to do is get in touch with the credit bureau that provided the report. Start by sending them a written complaint, either by mail or email, and point out the error.

Include all the information the company needs to sort it out, like your full name, address, and report confirmation number, if available. Don't forget a copy of the report and supporting documents, so you can point out exactly where the mistake is and make your case.

If the error came from somebody else — like your bank or a collection agency — contact them to let them know what went wrong. They can help the credit company get the mistake off your record.

New rules protect you from old fines

Tut-tut, your neighbor says. You shouldn't have let those library fines go by the wayside. Rumor has it, the fees on all the books you neglected to return on time will end up in a collection agency. And that could damage your credit score.

It was true once. But now you can tell your nosy neighbor about new rules set in motion by the three major credit bureaus — companies can only report debts that come from contracts or other prearranged agreements. This excludes traffic and parking tickets as well as those pesky library fees.

That doesn't mean you should willy-nilly blow off your fines. But it does mean credit bureaus are taking steps to make sure your credit report is more accurate. So what else is new? The National Consumer Assistance Plan calls for these changes.

▸ Companies can't report medical debts until a 180-day period has passed, allowing time for insurance payments to kick in. And reporting agencies must remove previously listed medical collections that have been or are being paid by your insurance.

▸ Debt collectors must regularly update the status of your outstanding debts and remove old ones no longer being pursued for collection.

▸ If you're the victim of identity theft, fraud, or other ID mix-ups, you get special attention. And when you successfully dispute an error on your free annual credit report, you can request another free report without waiting a whole year.

Spend smarter — the right credit card can help you save big

The *Guinness World Records* book claims Walter Cavanagh has a whopping 1,497 credit cards. If you stack them end-to-end, they are taller than a four-story building. While you may cringe at having that many cards, chances are you have two or three. And if you're like most other Americans, you haven't changed them in over a decade.

These days, you have more options than ever, and picking the right card could save you hundreds in interest and even put money back in your pocket. So, as a popular commercial says, "What's in your wallet?"

Frequent fliers: look for a card with airline miles. These cards are great for people who love to travel. Using your credit card can help you earn points for flights, hotel stays, and other great travel benefits.

But not all these cards are the same. Some offer better rewards, like allowing you to use your miles on any airline. Some limit the time you have to use them. Use websites like *MileCards.com* to help you find a card that works best for you.

Cash-back cards help you cash in. If your free time isn't spent on the road, air miles aren't much good to you. You may want a card that gives you cash or rewards on things you use every day, like gasoline and groceries.

Look for cards that offer points for every dollar spent, and avoid ones with unrealistic expiration dates and limits. Choose carefully and spend wisely, and you'll get a nice bonus from buying the essentials.

Low-interest cards are a great back-up plan. A card that offers a low interest rate isn't only for people with debt. It's also great for people who might need cash in an emergency.

You always want to pay off your credit card bills in full, but sometimes life hands you an unexpected expense. A smashed window, a flat tire, or a leaky roof can come out of nowhere, and if you don't have cash on hand you'll be out of luck.

Fortunately, low-interest cards can let you pay off these damages and keep your debt from spiraling out of control.

A CLOSER LOOK

Abigail signed up for a few department store credit cards, thinking those 15 to 20 percent discounts would save her big on Christmas shopping. But she wasn't expecting to see her credit score drop by the new year.

While opening an account can be a great way to take advantage of discounts or rewards, it can hurt you in the long run. Every time you apply for a credit card, companies pull your report. And each inquiry knocks a couple points off your credit score. If you're not careful, this can add up quickly.

When you open a new card, it's a good idea to wait at least six months before applying for another. Better yet, think twice about whether the rewards are even worth it.

The best card for poor credit

If you've dug yourself into a credit hole, don't panic. You can dig yourself out with help from a secured credit card.

Companies offer these cards to customers with low credit scores who have trouble qualifying for other credit. The cards usually have low credit limits and require a deposit that's equal to or over that limit.

A good company will let you know about these fees upfront, and they'll even give you a timeline of how long it should take to get your credit score up. If you keep your bills low and make your payments on time, you'll raise your credit score and qualify for a better card before you know it.

Just be careful of cards that seem too good to be true. They may be trying to take advantage of you.

ALERT ⚠️

Don't let old cards come back to haunt you

When you get a new credit card, the last thing you should do is toss your old one in the trash. Even if your card is deactivated or expired, it is still loaded with sensitive personal information.

Make sure to cut up your old cards into tiny pieces, and throw them away in separate trash bags. If you want to go even further, run a strong magnet along the strip on the back before you cut it up. This wipes off all the info. And if you have a chip on your card, make sure to cut it in half, too.

How to spot a bad card from a mile away

Vivian had less than stellar credit, so when a card offer came in the mail offering zero APR, it seemed perfect. She signed up, but before she knew it she was drowning in fees. Unfortunately, Vivian's experiences aren't uncommon. Some credit card companies try to take advantage of you, but with a little know-how you can learn to avoid their traps.

Ditch too-good-to-be-true offers that come in the mail.
Many direct-mail offers target people who don't know much
about their credit score. If your FICO number is in the low
range, and you get an offer with a fabulous interest rate and
high credit limit, it probably has a catch.

Do a bit of research and find out what a fair interest rate looks
like for your credit score. For example, a recent government
report showed the average rate for scores below 550 hovered
around 17 percent. If you fall into that group and get an offer
for much less than that, toss it in the trash.

Don't buy into cards you can't understand. Does your credit
card contract look like Greek? Predatory companies write confusing contracts on purpose. They hope you'll gloss over the fine
print and wind up trapped.

Credit agreements are actually getting easier to understand, says
the Consumer Financial Protection Bureau. So if you get one
that even your Ph.D. brother-in-law can't figure out, a warning
bell should go off. Read the fine print, and pass on offers that
don't make sense.

Watch out for fees that blow up your balance. Fees are small
potatoes for big credit card issuers, but that's not the case for
predatory lenders. These sly companies haul in more than half
their money from customer fees.

These cards try to nickel-and-dime you for every little thing,
and it could wind up costing you big. One company even
charges a 25 percent fee each time you increase your credit limit.
If you were to bump your limit by just $200, you'd have to pay
a whopping $50.

Scan the card's agreement and research its policy for late fees, add-ons, and other ways the company may try to get your money. If it seems like the little fees might add up to a big problem, pass on the credit card offer.

Wipe out late fees with a single phone call

Oh no! You forgot to pay the credit card bill and it was due two days ago. Now you'll get charged a hefty late fee. Don't panic. If you call the company's customer service hotline, they may be willing to help you out.

Just ask Rose. "I mistakenly paid the minimum instead of the full balance one month," she said. "Since I thought I'd paid my bill, I didn't pay attention to the next email reminder I got. But when the following one mentioned a collection agency, I immediately called to straighten things out."

That's when she learned she'd been slapped with a $27 late fee on her $35 bill. Ouch. "I told them about the mix-up and that I didn't think I should have to pay a late fee, and they agreed to take it off."

Some companies will waive fees, like late charges or over-limit fees, for loyal customers and first-time offenders. So never hesitate to give it a try.

DOLLARS & SENSE

---

4 common ways credit cards waste your money

That little piece of plastic in your wallet sure makes shopping easy, doesn't it? Almost too easy. If you're not careful your cards could end up costing you a bundle. Keep some extra dollars in your pocket by avoiding these common credit card mistakes.

Don't store all your cards in your wallet. Sometimes it's smarter to leave them at home. Research shows credit card users often don't think about how much things cost when they shop. Let's face it, if you had to pull $75 out of your wallet to pay for that cute blouse, you'd probably think twice.

So fight the urge to make impulse buys by making a shopping list. And don't be afraid to leave your credit cards behind once in a while. If you have a favorite online store you shop at, don't save a card number to your account. You'll splurge less often if you have to put a bit of extra thought into what you buy.

Making the minimum payment is making you poor. If you don't pay your credit card bill off in full, you're not alone. Only 1 out of 4 people pay off their entire bill each month. But all you're doing is throwing money down the drain.

Interest builds up, meaning everything you buy costs you a bit more. If you let the $40 you spent on gas stay on your bill, that 15 percent interest rate will add an extra $6 over time. That adds up — especially when you keep using your card — so try to pay your bills off in full every month. And only use your card for purchases you can afford.

Letting due dates slide by hits you where it hurts. Forgetting to pay your credit card bill on time is an easy way to spiral into debt. Not only does interest build up, but the company will slap you with a late fee of up to $27, more if you're repeatedly late.

Put reminders on your calendar to keep track of when you need to pay your bills. If you have online banking, you can set up automatic bill payment so you'll never miss a deadline.

These cards could be bleeding you dry. Rewards cards are great, but most come with a not-so-great companion — annual fees. If you're smart about your spending, you can earn back the fee and more in cash, points, or airline miles. But not everyone spends enough to cover this cost.

Suppose your card charges an annual fee of $99, and one rewards point is worth 1.9 cents. You'd have to spend a whopping $5,210 annually just to offset the fee and start benefiting from the rewards. If that's not happening, consider switching to a card without an annual fee.

Transferring a balance? 3 tests your card needs to pass

Jerry needed to get his credit card debt under control, so he jumped at a new promotion that let him transfer his balance and pay no interest for a year. But when he got his first statement, he was shocked to find out interest was piling up anyway.

It turns out the contract he signed let the company charge interest on any new purchases made with his balance-transfer card. And he had no grace period in which to pay them off. So when he charged a week's worth of groceries and a tank of gas, interest started building up right away.

The worst part is, the bank applied Jerry's payment to his transfer amount and not his new purchases. That means he'll be charged interest on them every month unless he pays the entire amount — including the transferred funds — in full.

According to the Consumer Financial Protection Bureau, this happens all too often. Companies sneak fine print into credit card contracts that can wind up costing you thousands.

If you want to transfer debt to a new card, make sure the offer passes these tests.

> ▶ **It's clear and easy to understand.** Sometimes companies hope to trap you with confusing statements so you don't know what you've agreed to. If you can't make sense of a contract, don't sign it.

> ▶ **It gives you zero percent interest on both balance transfers and new purchases.** A good card will let you pay down your balance and buy the essentials at the same time. If you think you might be charged interest, don't use the card for anything besides paying off debt.

> ▶ **It comes from a company you trust.** Be on the lookout for offers from reputable credit card issuers. Websites like *magnifymoney.com* can help you find the best deals. Do a little research, and you'll track down the right card to pay off your debt responsibly.

No. 1 way to put the freeze on ID sharks

A stolen identity can destroy your life. And since hackers swiped the personal data of millions of Americans — from Social Security numbers to birth dates — in the infamous Equifax breach, protecting your identity is more important than ever. So how do you put the kibosh on identity thieves? All you have to do is call up each of the major credit bureaus and tell them you want to freeze your credit.

You'll have to pay a small fee, but the price is more than worth the peace of mind. After freezing your credit, nobody can access your report without your permission, which makes it harder for crooks to open accounts in your name. Even banks, insurance companies, and credit card vendors can't get their hands on your report unless you've cleared it.

When you make the request, you'll receive a PIN or password. You'll need this to temporarily lift the freeze if you ever apply for a loan or credit card. Get started by calling each bureau toll-free.

- Equifax — 800-349-9960

- Experian — 888-397-3742

- TransUnion — 888-909-8872

Scammed? Take back your identity with these simple steps

Denied. The rejection stamped across Greg's latest loan application didn't make any sense. He never once missed a payment, and his credit card bills were never too high. So what happened? His identity was stolen. Like many people, he didn't discover the damage until it was too late.

If you notice unusual withdrawals from your bank account or start getting unexpected calls from debt collectors, you might be the victim of identity theft. Contact your bank or credit card provider to straighten things out. Then ring up one of the major credit bureaus and ask them to place a free fraud alert on your report. They should contact the other two for you.

A fraud alert makes it a lot harder for thieves to open up accounts in your name. That's because it forces companies to verify your identity before they supply credit. The alert stays on your report for 90 days, but you can renew it if you need to.

From there, the steps vary depending on what the thieves have stolen. The federal government has a one-stop resource to help guide you through the process. Go to *identitytheft.gov/steps* to find out exactly what your next move should be.

ALERT ⚠

Sound the alarm: Stop rip-offs in real-time with notifications

A house alarm gives you the heads-up thieves are trying to break in, and fraud alerts do the same for your wallet. Banks and credit card companies offer services that keep tabs on your accounts. Take advantage of them, and you could catch cons before they wreck your finances.

Call your bank and credit card company to see what options are available. Many let you set up text or email alerts that warn about suspicious activity like unusual purchases or account changes. You should also review your bank statements and credit reports to catch fraudulent charges.

5 smart ways to buff up your online security

Out-of-print books, old car parts, and imported cheeses are only a few clicks away when you shop online. But internet retailers don't tell you just how vulnerable your identity is, especially if you're not tech savvy. To protect yourself from online scammers and identity thieves, remember these five security strategies.

Vault the door to online accounts with strong passwords. A safe chock-full of money and jewels wouldn't be secure if it didn't have a lock, and the same is true for your online profiles. Thieves can use your email and other online data to learn all about you.

So you need to set up strong passwords on any website with a login — that includes Amazon, Facebook, and your email account. And it's best to use a different one for each site. Create passwords with a mix of symbols, letters, and numbers. Avoid using your hometown, birthday, or other bits of information people know about you.

Double up on online protection. A bank wouldn't let somebody withdraw money without an ID, so why should things be different for virtual banks? You can't show your driver's license and passport to a computer screen, but you can take advantage of two-factor identification on most bank, email, and social media accounts.

Set up this feature in your security settings, and a code will be sent to your cellphone or email whenever you try to log on. You'll need this code to get into your account. So even if your password gets stolen, thieves can't access your information without your phone or email. And as an added bonus, you'll know if anybody tries to break into your account.

Wipe out wireless worries by keeping your internet under lock and key. Your online accounts need a strong password, but so does your Wi-Fi connection. If your internet access isn't safe, anybody within range of your Wi-Fi signal can hook up to your network and retrieve information from your computers and tablets.

To put an uncrackable password in place, you'll need to access your router — the device that connects your home network to the internet. Contact your internet provider or dig out the user manual for instructions.

> Scammers can use social media websites to learn all about you. Your posts and profile pages give them hints about your login information, so only share content with close friends and family. You should also avoid posting your phone number, address, and full name online.

And if you use public Wi-Fi networks, avoid sending personal information through websites or apps. That means you should be extra careful if you do any online shopping at the local coffee shop.

Take a leaf from a secret agent's playbook to keep your identity safe. Every spy worth his salt uses secret codes to send letters and radio messages. Believe it or not, you can do the same on your computer with encrypted websites.

You won't have the glamorous ciphers and invisible inks, but you'll protect your identity all the same. These secure sites work by scrambling your data, so only the people sending and receiving the info can make sense of it.

To make sure you're on an encrypted website, look for "https" at the beginning of the web address. The "s" stands for secure.

Stick with what you know. It's best to do all your online shopping on trusted websites. Confirm the seller's contact information, like the address and phone number, before you hand over any cash.

If pop-up ads ask for credit card numbers or other personal information, don't click on them. They're definitely scams. And don't send credit card numbers or other financial information over email either. If an online retailer doesn't have a secure way to shop, avoid doing business with them.

ALERT ⚠️

Don't get duped by this 2-factor trick

Watch out — thieves have fashioned a new scam to target your two-factor security measures. Here's how it works.

They pretend to be from the company you have an account with and send you a message saying they've noticed suspicious activity. They tell you they're going to send you a verification code, which you must text back to them so you won't get locked out of your account. Then they try to log in to your account. This prompts the two-factor feature and sends the ID code to your phone.

But if you send them the info, you're handing over everything they need to steal your data. Don't ever text or email your login information to people. And if you do suspect a problem with your online accounts, contact the company directly.

Check fraud — don't give thieves carte blanche to drain your savings

Anybody with a computer and a printer can make a fake check — just ask Bill. Crooks swiped one of his checks, and before he knew it, his bank was cashing checks he never wrote. "They not only bought stuff with a check from our account, it had been duplicated right down to the scenery, colors, and markings. And it was written off a check we had not even used yet — one that was still in my checkbook," he says.

Modern technology makes it a piece of cake to copy checks. So be extra careful with your pocketbook or it could cost you your life savings.

Pay with plastic or cash — especially if you shop somewhere new. You may not think twice about whipping out your checkbook at the grocery store or gas station. But being quick on the draw might put your finances at risk.

Checks are loaded with personal information, and if the store mishandles or misplaces one, you could be in a lot of trouble. Don't pay with a check if you don't trust the person handling it 100 percent. And if you do use checks regularly, keep an eye on your bank statements to make sure fraudulent charges don't pop up.

You should never write checks with a ballpoint pen. Ink isn't as permanent as you might think, especially if it comes from a regular old pen. Scammers can wash the info right off your checks. And a $10 trip to the gas station could end up costing hundreds. But not all inks are easy to wash off. Gel-based pens are much safer, so pick up a box of them instead.

Clean out your mailbox every day. Think about all the important things that wind up in your mailbox — credit card offers, insurance statements, and even new checks. If somebody gets to them before you do, your bank account could be wiped clean.

Check your mail every day. If you're going away for a few days, call up your post office and get a vacation hold on your mail. And don't send or receive checks at your house unless you have a locking mailbox.

Protect privacy by destroying docs and digital files the right way

You wouldn't hand out your credit card number to a stranger on the street, would you? But if you're careless with your old letters and computers, you might as well write your Social Security number on a T-shirt and wear it around town. Follow these simple steps to ward off potential identity thieves.

Put private papers through the shredder. You need to hang on to receipts and bank statements for tax season, but you shouldn't keep them around too long. If they get lost or wind up in the wrong hands, your identity will be in jeopardy.

It's important to get rid of documents when you don't need them anymore. But don't just chuck them in the garbage — cut them into tiny pieces or run them through a crosscut shredder. Be sure to get one beefy enough to shave old credit cards. They'll be useless to anybody who wants to steal your identity.

Digitally destroy your old computers. If you throw away a piece of paper, it's not really gone. It ends up in a dump or — if you're really unlucky — the hands of somebody who's up to no good. The same is true for your computer, too.

Just dragging files into the trash can doesn't completely erase them. They get sent off to a virtual landfill, and if you ever sell your computer they might be unearthed. Before you get rid of old laptops or desktops, use a utility program to wipe out the lingering data.

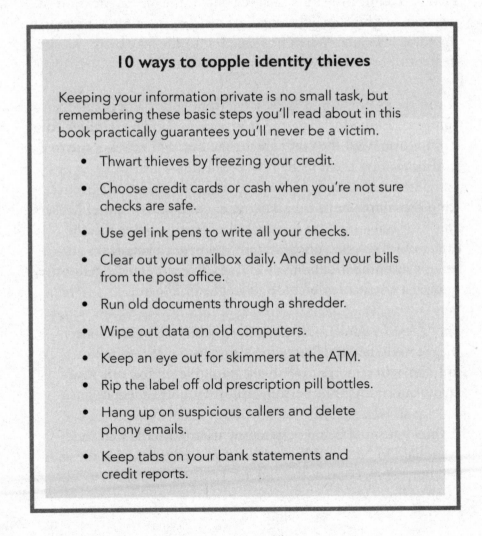

10 ways to topple identity thieves

Keeping your information private is no small task, but remembering these basic steps you'll read about in this book practically guarantees you'll never be a victim.

- Thwart thieves by freezing your credit.
- Choose credit cards or cash when you're not sure checks are safe.
- Use gel ink pens to write all your checks.
- Clear out your mailbox daily. And send your bills from the post office.
- Run old documents through a shredder.
- Wipe out data on old computers.
- Keep an eye out for skimmers at the ATM.
- Rip the label off old prescription pill bottles.
- Hang up on suspicious callers and delete phony emails.
- Keep tabs on your bank statements and credit reports.

Sniff out phishy emails and phony calls

Panic set in when Fred got an email saying his bank account had been compromised. He clicked the link, logged into his account, but didn't see anything out of the ordinary. Little did he know, he had just been swindled.

Don't get hooked by email scams. Nothing was wrong with Fred's account. Instead, he fell for one of the oldest tricks on the internet — phishing. The email came from a scammer pretending to be his bank. When he logged in to the fake bank website, he handed over his username and password.

If you get an email or text message from your bank or another company asking for account information, don't be so quick to hand it over. Call the company or go directly to its website to find out if a problem really exists.

Ring the alarm bells on suspicious callers. Computer hackers aren't the only ones out to steal your identity. Some thieves prefer old-fashioned phone fraud. If you get a ring from an unknown number telling you about a free trip, credit card offer, or even a charitable donation, it might be a scam.

Spot these fraudulent calls by asking who's calling and why they're so desperate to get your information. If they're not upfront with you, it's probably a scam. Never give out your credit card number or personal information to these callers.

If you can't stand being pestered by telemarketers, join the National Do Not Call Registry at *donotcall.gov*. And if the calls still don't stop, contact the Federal Trade Commission to file a complaint.

Dispute charges to wipe away billing boo-boos

One missed credit card bill can weigh heavily on your wallet. Make a simple slip-up, and debt collectors are all over you. But when your credit card company makes a mistake, it gets swept under the rug. Even worse, when you're overcharged by merchants, you're on the hook for money you shouldn't have to pay. But if you know your rights, you can safeguard your savings with confidence.

The law is on your side — credit companies can't charge you for their slip-ups. A billing blunder could be as simple as an incorrect charge on your statement. Or it could be as big as failure to deliver your bill to the right address, resulting in monstrous late fees. If you discover an error on your credit card statement, don't fret. The law protects you from paying for other people's mistakes.

First, contact your credit card company in writing. Let them know you're disputing the charges, and point out the errors. You need to send the notice within 60 days of receiving your bill. Otherwise, they don't have to investigate. It's a good idea to use certified mail so you know when it reaches your creditor.

After the company gets the letter, they have 90 days to look into your claims. You're not responsible for paying any money on the disputed charge during this period, and the outstanding fees can't affect your credit score. But don't forget to pay the rest of your bill.

In the event your card issuer doesn't get back to you within the allotted time, you're legally off the hook. Even if the charges were correct, you don't owe a dime.

Get your money back from sellers who over promise and under deliver. Suppose a landscaping company charged you, but never returned to finish the job. Or maybe you ordered fleece Snuggies, but received cotton blankets with holes cut in the front. Your credit card company can help you get money back if you run into problems with a seller.

In fact, anything you purchased in your home state for more than $50 is subject to something called a chargeback. You can kick-start the process after you've tried to resolve the dispute with the seller directly.

Your credit card company then becomes a valuable ally. Submit your complaint with them, and they'll review the dispute and take action for you. This process could take a while, and you may be responsible for footing the bill in the meantime. But if you win your case, you'll get your money back.

A CLOSER LOOK

Keith's brand new laptop broke down just days after the warranty expired. He thought he'd be out of luck, but fortunately, he paid for the computer with a credit card. Some cards, like Keith's, come with purchase protection. That means if you file a claim for lost, damaged, or stolen items on recent purchases, you might be able to get your money back.

Check to see if your card offers this perk. To reap the benefits, you'll need to send in the receipt and the credit card statement with the original charge. For stolen items, make sure to get a copy of the police report.

Some cards offer price protection, too. So if you buy something with a credit card but find it cheaper later, you can get the difference back straight from your credit card company.

Small print surprise — don't sign away your right to sue

You never want to take your credit card company to court, but if you're trying to settle a long-standing squabble, it might be your last option. Little do you know, you probably signed away your rights to sue them.

A number of credit card companies have mandatory arbitration clauses in their terms of service. These restrictions limit your ability to take legal action against them — like going to court or joining class-action lawsuits.

If you have a dispute, it must be settled by a third party chosen by the credit card company. And that often means less money for you. So what can you do?

▸ Shop around for a new card with a company that doesn't have these restrictions.

▸ When you sign up for a card that has an arbitration clause, see if you can opt out. Some companies will remove the terms from your contract if you send them a letter, as long as you do this within a certain timeframe.

▸ If you're already a loyal customer, go back and read the fine print. Most user agreements make certain exceptions. For example, some credit card providers allow you to go to small claims court.

ALERT ⚠️

Add-ons could whisk away hard-earned cash

Watch out. Credit card companies often pitch extra services, like credit monitoring or identity protection, when you sign up for a card. But these add-ons could add a pretty penny to your monthly or annual membership fees. Fortunately, you don't have to buy them.

In fact, many experts recommend you steer clear of these programs because they often cost a lot for little to no benefit. Just ask Alex. He paid $200 a month for debt protection services, but found that when he needed to tap into the benefits, he wasn't eligible due to a loophole in the terms and conditions.

If you are set on buying an add-on, make sure you get the terms in writing and weigh your options carefully. Even contracts for free trials can contain tricky language that allows the company to automatically charge you at the end of the test run.

All rights reserved: 4 rules repel credit card swindles

Astronomical late fees, soaring interest rates, and narrow bill-pay windows aren't just annoying — they are illegal, too. The good news is the Credit CARD Act protects your wallet from the tricks of the trade. Here's how.

Know what you owe. You have a right to know how much your bills will set you back, interest and all. That's why your monthly statement must include:

▸ how long it will take you to pay off your balance if you only make the minimum payments — plus the cost with all that added interest.

▸ how much you'd have to pay each month to clear the balance in three years or less.

Time is on your side. Credit card companies have to give you at least 21 days to pay your bill after the statement is mailed or delivered. And the due date must be the same every month. No surprises. Card issuers also can't legally charge you late fees if your payment doesn't arrive because of weekends or holidays.

Plus they can't set time requirements for payments. So gone are the days of extra charges for not making that 5 p.m. cutoff. What a relief.

Little mistakes can't cost you big. If you're a first-time late-payment offender, the fee is capped at $27. But after that, you're open to harsher penalties. The best solution is to make sure you always pay your tab on time. But if a due date does slip your mind every now and then, companies can't charge a fee of more than $38.

Rates can't change on a dime. Companies aren't allowed to drive up your annual percentage rate, or APR, on a whim. Legally, they have to give you 45-days' notice before they make any changes to your account.

This includes raising your APR based on your credit history. So even if you're having trouble keeping up with utility bills, your card company can't jack up your rates with no warning. Even better, any changes in interest rates won't apply to old charges.

But promotions and other variables in your contract might let companies bump up your interest rate. Read the fine print, and keep an eye on your APR.

What if your credit card company breaks the rules and doesn't respond to your concerns? It's time to file a complaint with the Consumer Financial Protection Bureau. Contact them at *consumerfinance.gov/complaint* or 855-411-2372.

ALERT

Are you tangled up in the dark web?

Hackers and scammers are common online boogeymen, but there's a whole underworld lurking beneath the surface of the internet. Hidden websites where thieves can buy and sell everything from drugs to stolen credit card numbers make up something known as the darknet or dark web.

It takes some serious technical know-how just to find these websites. You can't do it on your average web browser. But some ID protection services now devote efforts to sweeping these black markets for any mention of your info.

So far, experts say it's unclear whether these programs, known as dark web scans, are worth the cost. That's because they let you know your info is out there, but can't actually stop crooks from trading your data. Keep your info safe by freezing your credit, securing your accounts, and following the other advice in this book.

Safeguard your own credit to save hundreds

Credit monitoring services promise to take the hassle out of keeping your identity safe. Just pay a few dollars a month, and you'll never have to worry about identity theft or fraud again. But are these services really all they are cracked up to be?

Built-in protection already shields you from credit crooks. Cleaning up after identity theft is ugly. It can be a huge pain, but at the end of the day, you're not legally liable for accounts made by credit thieves. And fraudulent charges won't cost you a dime if:

▸ the swindler swiped your card number, but not your card.

▸ you reported your card as stolen before the shopping spree started.

Even if thieves run wild with your cards, you're not responsible for any charges past the first $50. In comparison, credit monitoring services can cost more than $300 a year.

Monitoring is a lot of bark without much bite. Credit monitoring services are like home burglar alarms that go off when the bad guys sell your stuff on eBay. Since they can only monitor transactions and account openings, they won't actually keep thieves from stealing your identity.

They do pick up on suspicious activity quickly so you can act fast. And many offer to help resolve your case if you do get in a bind. But don't fall for the marketing hype that these services can stop crooks from swiping your private details and having a field day with your ID.

Why pay for something you can get for free? Many credit monitoring services offer access to your credit reports and scores. But they'll factor this perk into the price of your membership. Don't forget — you can get free reports from various other services, including *AnnualCreditReport.com*.

Curb the urge to splurge

We may splurge a lot more than we think we do. According to a recent survey, the average consumer makes three unplanned purchases a week, adding up to $450 a month. That's a whopping $5,400 a year.

Food seems to be the biggest culprit, with 7 out of 10 people confessing to spur-of-the-moment grocery buys. To keep that money in your pocket, try this.

Grab a pen and several sheets of paper. At the top of each sheet, write the name of one of your credit cards. Every time you use a credit card, pull out its sheet. Write down the date, what you bought, and how much you charged. At the end of every week, total the numbers to find out how much you spent.

If you're an impulse buyer, you'll soon see how much money you lose to those purchases. And just knowing that number can help you resist temptation.

Better banking

Boost your savings and sidestep sneaky fees

Outfox the foxes with a better way to save

The average savings account earns a measly 0.06 percent annual interest. That means if you keep $10,000 locked away in your bank, you'll earn just $30 in interest over the next five years. What bankers don't want to tell you is that if you're saving your money the traditional way, you're losing out. Here's how to get more bang for your buck.

Spend a little now to save a lot tomorrow. When you know you won't need to touch your savings for a few years, certificates of deposit (CDs) might be your best bet. Think of these investments as loans from you to your bank. You give them a few thousand dollars, and in a few years you'll get your money back plus interest.

CDs do come with a downside — you can't get your money early unless you pay a hefty fee. But the interest you earn could make the wait worth it. If you take the same $10,000 and put it in a CD earning 1.5 percent interest, you'll make more than $750 in five years. Rates vary depending on a number of factors.

▸ the type of CD

▸ the length of time until it matures

▸ how much you invest

▸ which bank you go to

When you shop for CDs, check out credit unions, community banks, and even online-only banks. They tend to offer better rates.

Get the best of both worlds with money market accounts. These bank accounts are set up to earn more interest than your plain old savings account, while still giving you some access to your money. You usually need at least $5,000 to $10,000 just to set up a money market account.

You won't earn a fixed interest rate on your returns. Instead, your profits are based on the strength of your bank and their investments.

Most accounts let you write a few checks and make some withdrawals each month without any penalties. In general, the more you invest, the higher your interest rate

Banks and credit unions offer product bundles, claiming you'll save when you get everything from your credit cards to savings accounts at one place. Even without a bundle, you might get a higher-yield savings account at a credit union or a better deal on a credit card at an online-only bank.

will be. It won't be as high as the rate on a CD, but that's the price you pay for having easier access to your money.

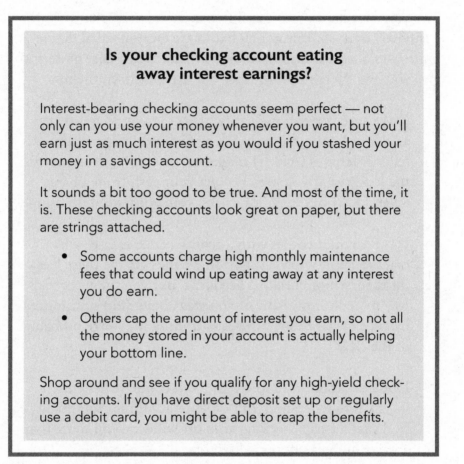

Is your checking account eating away interest earnings?

Interest-bearing checking accounts seem perfect — not only can you use your money whenever you want, but you'll earn just as much interest as you would if you stashed your money in a savings account.

It sounds a bit too good to be true. And most of the time, it is. These checking accounts look great on paper, but there are strings attached.

- Some accounts charge high monthly maintenance fees that could wind up eating away at any interest you do earn.

- Others cap the amount of interest you earn, so not all the money stored in your account is actually helping your bottom line.

Shop around and see if you qualify for any high-yield checking accounts. If you have direct deposit set up or regularly use a debit card, you might be able to reap the benefits.

How to shop for the best senior-friendly checking

Most people would jump at the chance to have a checking account with free checks and no fees. If you're a senior, you've hit the jackpot. Banks are targeting you with offers of discounts and free services that will make your head spin. But are they really worth it?

The very best banks waive maintenance fees and offer perks for customers over 65. But not all banks are created equal. Some businesses advertise senior accounts that actually cost more and give you less. Here's how to filter out the best from the rest.

▸ Make sure you can use the benefits. Senior accounts that advertise free cashier's checks or reduced fees at automatic teller machines (ATMs) might not save you any money in the long run if you prefer to get your cash from a bank teller. Don't pay extra for things you won't wind up using.

▸ If the account comes with a maintenance fee, see what it takes to get it wiped away. Some banks charge these fees for their senior checking accounts, but you might have a way to get out of them. If you stay above your minimum balance or have direct deposits coming in, you're probably in the clear.

▸ Don't be afraid to shop around and compare benefits. Check different banks and types of accounts. You might find that a basic checking account will save you more than an account geared toward seniors.

4 surefire steps to swapping banks without a hitch

Have you been loyal to your bank through poor customer service and rocketing fees? You're not alone — more than half of folks who want to change their bank give up because it's just too hard to figure out. It doesn't need to be difficult, though. Follow these simple steps to take back your financial freedom.

Don't jump ship until your new accounts are ready. The first thing you need to do is open an account with your new bank or credit union. You should do this at least a week or two before you plan on switching banks so you can make sure everything is properly set up and ready to go.

You can link your new account to your old one for an easy way to move your money over. Search "linking bank accounts" online for instructions. If you can't figure it out, talk to your new bank for help.

> When neither a big bank or credit union meets your needs, look for a community bank. Smaller, local banks have a lot of the same advantages as credit unions, like great customer service and competitive interest rates. But you don't have to become a member to open an account.

Don't leave behind direct deposits or automated bills. If you get any money from direct deposits, like paychecks or Social Security benefits, switch them to your new bank account.

And if you have automatic bill pay set up, change your information so you're not drawing from the old account. But make sure you have enough money in the new account to cover these costs. You wouldn't want to get hit with overdraft fees right after joining a new bank.

Keep slip-ups from sinking your savings. No matter how much you prepare, chances are somebody will make a mistake. A direct deposit check might end up in the wrong account, or you might forget to switch over an automated bill. But don't sweat it.

Keep some money stashed in the old account until you're 100 percent sure you won't need it anymore. That way you won't get smacked by a surprise overdraft fee as a bittersweet goodbye.

You should also keep good records of everything you're moving around. You'll be able to find mistakes faster and get them fixed easier when you can point them out to your bank.

Shutter your old accounts right to avoid losing money.
When you're finally ready to move on from your old bank, contact them to find out how to officially close the account. You'll probably need to send them a letter in writing.

And don't forget to withdraw leftover money. Take cash if a small amount remains, or get a cashier's check. Don't use a personal check because if you can't process it before the account is closed, you'll be out of luck.

A CLOSER LOOK

Imagine a bank that isn't in it for the money. And all the savings are passed on to you. The fees are low or nonexistent, and the savings accounts boast high interest rates. Sounds far-fetched, right? Turns out credit unions, nonprofit financial organizations, may provide just that.

Jane was blown away by the potential savings. A huge corporate bank in her city offers a 0.01 percent interest rate on savings accounts. So if she kept $20,000 tucked away, she'd have to wait 50 long years before she made $100 in interest.

On the other hand, her local credit union offers savings accounts that rake in 1.45 percent. So if Jane decided to take her money there instead, she'd earn almost $300 in interest after only one year.

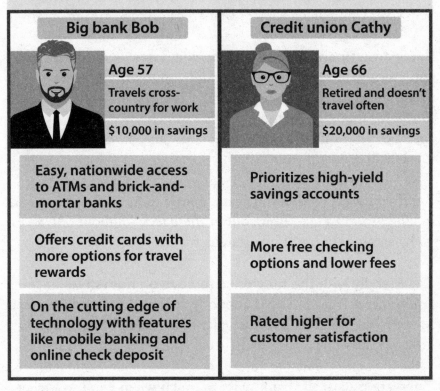

Banks vs. Credit Unions — what suits your savings?

Banks aren't one-size-fits-all, so how do you know which one is best for you? Take a look at Bob and Cathy. Even though they live in the same town, he uses a big bank and she's a member of a credit union. Check out the features that won them over.

Big bank Bob

Age 57

Travels cross-country for work

$10,000 in savings

Easy, nationwide access to ATMs and brick-and-mortar banks

Offers credit cards with more options for travel rewards

On the cutting edge of technology with features like mobile banking and online check deposit

Credit union Cathy

Age 66

Retired and doesn't travel often

$20,000 in savings

Prioritizes high-yield savings accounts

More free checking options and lower fees

Rated higher for customer satisfaction

Put the freeze on fees: Virtual banking saves you real dollars

If you're not ready for the digital age, it's going to cost you. Literally. Want your statement mailed to you? That'll be $3. Need to talk to a teller? Another $5. Bankers, brokers, and credit card companies are now tacking on extra charges to your monthly bills for not taking advantage of their online services. And those sneaky fees can cost you thousands.

You probably know how to avoid the common fees for over-drafts, withdrawals, and inactivity, but here are a few tricks to help you avoid paying for fees that aren't quite so run-of-the-mill.

Paper-free financing cuts the bank's costs — and it'll save you money, too. Banks hate sending you mail. The costs of paper, printer ink, and postage really add up, and somebody has to pay for them. Unfortunately, that somebody is you. Physical copies of your bills, account statements, and other paper documents will drive up your monthly fees.

But if you want to save your bank a little money, they'll respond in kind. You can take a bite out of these fees — about $36 a year — by signing up for online statements.

Get friendly with the machines to save on human teller fees. Louise never trusted ATMs after one ate her debit card, so every Monday she walked up to the teller at her bank to get cash. But little did she know, her weekly ritual added up to $20 a month.

Transactions cost the bank twice as much when you use a teller instead of an ATM. So they tack on a little fee to cover their expenses. Simple transactions like deposits or withdrawals won't cost you a dime if you handle them at the self-service kiosks. But if you need to tackle a task a machine can't handle, don't worry — banks won't charge you if you have no alternative.

Don't get duped into thinking your rewards are free. It's easy to think your credit card rewards won't cost you a penny. After all, you've earned them by purchasing with plastic.

Unfortunately, you might just have to spend money to access your points, especially if you have a travel rewards card. Some cards charge you $50 just to redeem your airline miles at the ticket counter or over the phone. You can usually get around these fees by taking care of everything online.

Don't let ATMs double dip into your savings

Getting slapped with ATM fees can add up — it costs an average of $4.35 just to use an out-of-network ATM. If you're far away from a fee-free money machine, use these tricks to get your money without having to pay for the privilege.

- Next time you need cash, put it on your grocery list. When you pay with a debit card, ask for cash back to avoid paying fees. But be careful — some stores might charge a fee for this, too. Ask the cashier before signing off on these transactions.

- Some banks will reimburse you for troublesome charges at the kiosk. Call your bank to see what your options are.

- Smartphone users can search out hidden ATMs or fee-free retail partners by down-loading the bank's mobile app.

DOLLARS & SENSE

Are you making this simple banking blunder?

A free checking account — like a free lunch — doesn't exist. Somebody has to pay for the upkeep, but those costs should be on your bank. In fact, you should never open a bank account that charges a monthly maintenance fee.

If you're paying $20 a month just to have a checking account, you're making a huge mistake. Take these simple steps to take control of your money.

> ▶ **Set up direct deposit.** When banks see that you have money regularly coming in, they're more likely to keep your checking account fee-free. So if you have a regular paycheck or Social Security benefits, look into linking them directly to your bank.

> ▶ **Maintain your minimum balance.** Another way to skip fees is to keep enough money in your account. Some places will only start charging you if you have less than, say, $1,000. Ask your bank how much you need in your account to avoid being charged.

> ▶ **Bundle your banking services.** You shop around to get the best deals on your loans, accounts, and credit cards. Banks don't like that, so they often tack on extra fees if you get your financial services à la carte. But if you get them all in one place, your bank might waive the maintenance fees. Read the fine print on your account docs to see if this applies to you.

Load up on savings with online banks

Your savings account is barely eking out enough to make it worthwhile. You might as well keep all your money under your mattress — at least that way you won't have to pay banking fees. But if you're ready to bite the bullet and take the plunge into online banking, you'll actually be excited to stash money in your savings account. Here's why.

Online-only banks don't have to pay for things like tellers or buildings, so they're cheaper to run. And that translates to low fees and high-yield savings for their customers. You can expect around 1.1 percent annual interest on savings accounts from internet banks, which dwarfs the measly 0.07 percent you might get from their brick-and-mortar cousins.

That means if you stowed away $10,000, you'd make $110 in a year with an online savings account, compared to $7 from the big bank.

Of course, swapping to online savings is a big step. Without actual buildings, it's easy to feel like you're turning over all your data to a faceless stranger. It doesn't have to be scary, though. If you know what you're getting into, you won't have any reason to fret.

Surf the web to catch your perfect bank. You have a lot of options on where to store your money, and it's tough to narrow them all down. Take these simple steps to start your online banking journey.

▶ Compare rates in a jiffy. Higher interest rates are one of the biggest selling points of internet-only banks, and you'll want to get your money's worth. It's easy to search for savings account rates with comparison tools like the ones at *bankrate.com/banking/savings/rates* or *nerdwallet.com/rates/savings-account*.

▶ Decide how often you'll need to cash out. Because online banks don't have physical locations, you may be wondering how you'll access your money. You can request transfers and checks over the phone or online. But keep in mind, savings accounts are limited to six transactions each billing cycle.

If you need more flexibility, you may want to go with a checking account.

Take the plunge to start saving. You couldn't waltz into a brick-and-mortar bank and open up an account without any identification, and the same is true online. You have to offer up some personal details. You shouldn't worry about security, though. These banks have robust online security systems set up, so all you have to think about is how to get the ball rolling.

▸ Apply online. You'll have to turn over your Social Security number and digital copies of your ID to most online banks. Be prepared to give out contact information, like your phone number, email, and street address, too.

▸ Make your first deposit. You'll need to put money into your new account to get it set up. Luckily, most online banks give you several ways to do this. Often the easiest option is to transfer money from your old account or simply mail a check.

> Choose an FDIC-member online bank so you know your money will be insured. Consider how long they've been in business, and make sure customer service is up to snuff. Since you can't just walk into a branch and chat with a teller, 24-hour phone service is a plus.

Stay alert to safeguard your cash. Don't hand over your info if you have concerns about security on your end of the net. Follow these tips to protect your data.

▸ Check the address bar at the top of the bank's web pages to make sure the URL starts with "https." That means the site is more secure.

▸ Don't do your online banking in public places. Coffee shops, bookstores, or anywhere else with free Wi-Fi might not have a safe, secure connection. Scammers could monitor your transactions and swipe your account info without your knowledge. Use password-protected Wi-Fi, and try to do your banking on your own network.

You don't have to dive into online banking headfirst. Most banks offer some online services, so check out your options. Start with paperless billing and other internet perks to get your feet wet.

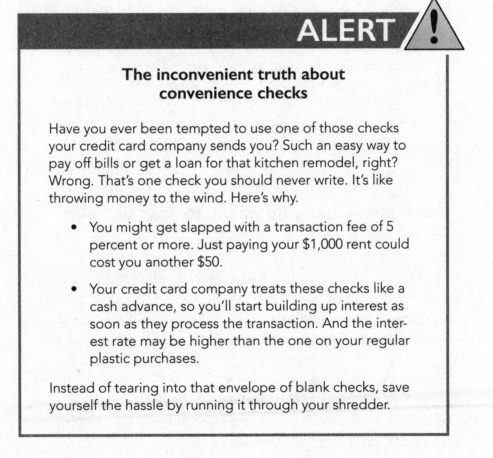

ALERT

The inconvenient truth about convenience checks

Have you ever been tempted to use one of those checks your credit card company sends you? Such an easy way to pay off bills or get a loan for that kitchen remodel, right? Wrong. That's one check you should never write. It's like throwing money to the wind. Here's why.

- You might get slapped with a transaction fee of 5 percent or more. Just paying your $1,000 rent could cost you another $50.

- Your credit card company treats these checks like a cash advance, so you'll start building up interest as soon as they process the transaction. And the interest rate may be higher than the one on your regular plastic purchases.

Instead of tearing into that envelope of blank checks, save yourself the hassle by running it through your shredder.

ALERT

Don't miss a beat with auto bill pay

Jerry set up automatic online bill pay so he'd never have to worry about missing a payment again. But a month later he got slapped with a late fee. So what went wrong?

Online bill pay isn't bulletproof. Sometimes, when you select the date you want to pay the bills it still takes a few days for the money to arrive. That's because the bank has to process the transaction.

To avoid surprise fees like Jerry's, set up your automatic payments to start processing about a week before the due date. You'll have ample time to catch any mistakes. And keep a close eye on your outgoing transactions, especially for the first few months you use these new features. You'll be able to deal with any problems on your end before they get too costly.

Get smart — use your phone to scan and sign important docs

Even if you do all your banking online, you'll still run across the occasional piece of paper. When you have to sign documents and send them in, snail mail isn't always the fastest, most secure option. But do you really want to go out and buy a scanner?

Smartphone users have the edge over their flip-phone counterparts. You can actually scan and sign all your documents without buying new hardware. Check out your phone's app store to search for handy options like these.

▸ Genius Scan uses your camera to turn paper documents into digital files like PDFs. The free version works well, but if you're concerned with security you can make encrypted PDFs by paying $5 to $8 for the premium version.

▸ Adobe Fill & Sign is a free app that stores your signature and lets you add it to any document on your phone.

Manage your money on the go

If you're smartphone savvy, don't pass up some simple money management apps.

- Cash apps, like Venmo, let you send money right from your fingertips. You can link credit cards or bank accounts and easily transfer money to other users. As a bonus, these apps have built-in fraud protection and alerts so you can monitor your spending.

- Mint and other budgeting apps help you keep an eye on everything from your petty cash to your savings account. You can even set up alerts that remind you when your bills are due. Take advantage of these tools to track your spending and create quick, convenient budgets.

DOLLARS & SENSE

Thwart hackers by bulking up your virtual protection

If you've invested in online banking, your computer is your bank vault. It stores precious passwords, personal data, and other keys to your accounts. But hackers might try to bust in and steal your hard-earned cash by tricking you into installing software that steals your files and holds them for ransom. You can fight back by beefing up your digital security.

Schedule regular updates to keep your computer secure. Do you regularly ignore update reminders that pop up on your computer screen? If you do, you're making a huge mistake.

Hackers and thieves take advantage of old, outdated software that's riddled with weak spots. When companies find vulnerabilities in their programs, they send out updates to patch these holes. But if you don't take advantage of them, you're not protected from future attacks. Set reminders to download new updates or see if your computer can install them automatically.

Fortify your defenses with anti-virus software. For extra security, it's a good idea to install programs that check your computer for harmful viruses and malware.

▶ Seek out a good, reputable program like those from Kaspersky Lab, Bitdefender, or Malwarebytes.

▶ Make sure you choose a software that will meet your computer's requirements. And look for one that automatically updates daily.

Have a backup plan ready. If your computer does get infected with a virus or malware, you'll need to be prepared.

▶ Make backups of all your files and store them on different devices.

▶ If you suspect your computer has a virus, disconnect it from the internet. This will keep the infection from spreading around to other machines in your network.

▶ You may be able to remove a bug by running a malware scan. But if hackers hold your data for ransom, go to the police and contact an expert to clean up your computer.

▶ Once you're in the clear, you can restore your old data with your backups.

ALERT ⚠

Secure your smart gadgets to combat computer threats

Are your lightbulbs letting hackers run rampant in your network? Smart devices that hook up to the internet — like thermostats, lights, or TVs — might be putting you at risk for computer viruses.

That's because they don't have the strong security measures your computer has. And since they're all connected to the same Wi-Fi network, hackers can slip in through the back door to steal info you thought was safe. But you can protect yourself by doing a security checkup.

- Make sure any smart devices in your home have strong passwords. And don't use the default codes they came with out of the box.

- Keep everything regularly updated so hackers can't exploit any known weak spots in your gadgets.

- If you can, use a second Wi-Fi network just for smart devices. That way your computer won't get hit if anything does catch a virus.

ALERT

Plastic pitfalls — are ATMs skimming off your savings?

You wouldn't let anybody look over your shoulder while you punch your PIN into the ATM, would you? But sneaky scammers can steal your info without hanging around the scene of the crime.

They hide devices called card skimmers on ATMs, gas pumps, and other card readers. When you swipe your card, it copies the data and the crooks get ready for a shopping spree. Take these steps to avoid getting the shaft.

- Wiggle the card reader before you insert your card. If it's loose, a card skimmer may be hidden inside.

- Avoid non-bank ATMs as well as gas pumps that are not in view of clerks and security cameras.

- Cover the keypad when you type in your digits. Thieves have been known to use tiny cameras, too.

Block ATM scammers by going cardless

Many banks penalize you for walking in their doors and getting cash from a teller. You have no choice but to make more trips to the ATM. But last year ATM card-skimming theft rose by over 70 percent.

What can you do to keep your money — and your identity — safe from hackers? If you're hip to mobile banking, you can add another layer of security to your ATM trips. A number of banks are debuting a new technology called cardless ATM access.

Instead of using your debit card at the ATM and risk getting your information stolen, you can use the bank's phone app to do your business. Simply request a one-time-use passcode that lets the ATM know you're verified to use it. Then you can punch your PIN in and get cash out, without worrying about skimmers.

Prepaid cards — pay ahead to save later

Gift cards are great when you'd like to treat somebody to a night out or give them a little stocking stuffer. Just load a specific dollar amount, and they're free to spend it however they want.

That's the idea behind prepaid debit cards, too. Put a set amount of money on the card, and you can only use what's available. A perfect way to control your spending, right? Maybe.

Make sure to read the fine print. Prepaid debit cards are touted as a good way to keep your finances on track because it's impossible to spend more than you have. The cards won't let you or a vendor process any transactions that go past the preloaded cash limit.

However, that's not always the case. Some prepaid cards, specifically ones sold by payday lenders, let you keep charging with your card even after you've reached your limit. At that point, they charge you a fee plus interest. So much for trying to keep your spending in check.

Fortunately, new laws are in place to combat sneaky "overdraft protection." But it's still up to you to check out the prepaid card terms and know what you're getting into.

Hunt carefully to find a fee-free card. Some prepaid debit cards are headache free, but others come loaded with fees. You might be charged to activate your card, reload money, or even just use it. Some companies charge you a whopping 20 percent to load cash into your account — meaning if you deposited $200, you'd only have $160 to spend.

You can hunt for the best cards at websites like *nerdwallet.com/prepaid* or *creditkarma.com/credit-cards/i/best-prepaid-cards*.

Use a prepaid card to combat credit crunches. The good news is, prepaid cards can be a practical option if you have bad credit. Like credit cards, you can use them to shop online or visit the ATM. But you don't need to go through a long credit approval process only to risk being denied a card or slapped with a high APR.

Just make sure you do your homework and find a reputable company that won't let you overspend. The best cards will let you load money with direct deposit, use ATMs, and even make cash deposits onto the card at certain stores.

> Prepaid cards have their place, but if you have solid credit, choose a debit card instead. Debit cards have more consumer protections in place and are more tightly regulated by the government.

It's important to remember that these cards won't help you build your credit rating. So it's best to use them sparingly and rein in your spending if you're trying to boost your credit score.

Swipe away safety concerns while paying with plastic. One of the biggest boons for a prepaid card is data safety. Unlike your debit or credit cards, nothing is tied to your personal data. That means if your prepaid card goes missing or gets stolen, thieves won't walk away with your Social Security number, bank account information, or other personal info.

Unfortunately, if your card goes AWOL, you may have to kiss your cash good-bye. You should report the loss as quickly as you can to your card issuer, but whether you recover any of the balance depends on several factors.

"Your rights to recover money taken from your prepaid card account depend on what type of card it is, what your contract promises, and how quickly you report the loss after you discover it," says a spokesperson for the Consumer Financial Protection Bureau. "You should check your card provider's website or your cardholder agreement to find out the specifics."

Should you cash in on the cryptocurrency craze?

You might have heard about bitcoin on the local news, but how much do you know about this digital money?

Bitcoin is a type of virtual money, or cryptocurrency, that is exchanged online, outside of traditional banking systems. It's popular with hackers and other internet-based criminals because it's hard to track and easy to use anonymously. But the currency is getting more mainstream recognition.

Recently many online retailers started accepting bitcoin, meaning you can use it to buy everything from gift cards to plane tickets. But does that mean you should swap your cash for a digital wallet? Not quite — cryptocurrencies have a lot of growing pains. The values swing wildly from day to day. One morning a single bitcoin might be worth as much as $7,000, but by that very evening it could have lost $500 in value.

4 common loan mistakes that will cost you a bundle

Whether you're trying to consolidate your debt or pay off medical bills, sometimes you need a bit of extra help. Borrowing money from your bank can give you the extra push to get your budget back in order. But it could also make your situation worse if you're not careful. Here are four risky blunders you don't want to make.

Settling for a bad loan. Hastiness can get you into a lot of trouble, especially when it comes to borrowing money. Shopping around is absolutely vital to getting the best interest rates and terms for your next loan.

> Be wary of upfront fees. A legitimate loan company will never ask you to pay for your application. There may be some fees after you're approved, but it's against the law to ask for cash before the loan is finalized.

Check out local banks, credit unions, and even the internet to see what sort of deals you can get. Make sure to avoid lenders who don't list a physical location. The Federal Trade Commission requires lenders to legally register in any states where they offer loans.

Rates will vary based on how much money you want to borrow and what your credit score looks like. You can compare different options and find reputable companies at websites like *loans.usnews.com* or *creditkarma.com/shop/personal-loans*.

Not asking about origination fees. There's no such thing as free money. You know you have to pay back your loan plus interest, but what you might not realize is that your personal loan comes with other fees, too.

One of the most common charges is an origination fee. Essentially, lenders charge you a percentage of the loan as a sort of processing fee, and they often take it out up front. So if you borrow $7,500 with a 5 percent fee, your take-home amount will only be $7,125. If they roll the fee into the loan instead, you'll owe $7,875 plus interest on the entire amount. That means you'll be paying more in the long run.

Relying on interest rates to make your choice. Don't get duped into thinking a lower interest rate automatically makes your loan better. Comparing interest rates won't tell you the whole story because they don't include the origination fee. A loan with a low interest rate may be a bad value if its fees are high, while a high-interest loan with low fees might prove to be a better deal. (See *A closer look* on page 108.)

Make sure you look at the loan's APR to get the big picture. The APR should reflect the total cost of the loan, including fees, so you can do an "apples-to-apples" comparison.

Glossing over the fine print. Believe it or not, paying back your loan too early can get you into hot water. Some lenders hide clauses in the fine print that let your bank charge you pre-payment, or exit, fees. When you pay off your loan before the due date, the bank will try to collect some of the interest it would have earned.

Carefully read all the details of your loan before you sign it, especially if you think you may pay it back ahead of schedule. Look for language that specifically says you won't have an exit fee or prepayment penalty. Otherwise it's likely you'll be slapped with an unwanted charge down the road.

A CLOSER LOOK

When sudden medical bills struck, Henry needed to get some cash fast. He set out loan shopping, and finally settled on one with a reasonable interest rate — but he made a major mistake. He forgot to calculate all the extra fees, so what looked like a decent offer actually wound up costing more.

When comparing two of Henry's choices, you'll see that Loan A's interest rate is 1 percent lower than Loan B. But after figuring in fees, Loan B ends up with a lower annual percentage rate (APR), which will save Henry money in the long run.

Before making a decision, check with your financial advisor or loan officer to make sure you understand what your total loan amount will be.

	Loan A ($20,000)	Loan B ($20,000)
Interest rate	5.25 percent	6.25 percent
Length of loan	10 years	10 years
Origination fee	$1,000 (5 percent)	$200 (1 percent)
Other fees	$1,000	$0
APR	7.37 percent	6.47 percent

Don't get trapped by zero-interest offers

Retail stores are loaded with flashy ads that promise financing for high-tech electronics and top-of-the-line appliances with no interest paid. And while you may think you're getting a great deal on that new refrigerator or flat-screen TV, if you take out a zero-interest loan you'll be falling into a classic retail trap.

Don't get duped into overspending. Stores partner up with third-party loan companies in hopes of pushing customers into buying things they can't quite afford.

You're more likely to spring for expensive items with all the bells and whistles when you're getting an interest-free loan. After all, what's a few hundred dollars more when you're saving all those dollars in interest? But it's still money you have to pay back, and once you add in all the fees you might not get the deal you expected.

Factor in the fees and fine print to see how much your loans really cost. Zero-interest loans may seem too good to be true — because they usually are. If you're a careful spender, they can be a great tool for buying pricey products with no extra cost. But there are still a few things you need to look out for.

  ▶ Make sure you know your final payment date. Some loans are only interest-free for the first year or two. If you don't pay back the loan on time, your wallet will suffer. The lender can now backdate the interest — at a very high rate — so you'll owe it on the entire amount, even if you have only one payment left.

  ▶ Read the fine print carefully so you don't wind up triggering a hidden fee. Some contracts make it easy for loan companies to walk back their no-interest promises. Make a payment one day late, and you may find yourself saddled with interest and charges that make your loan almost impossible to pay back.

Fight the pressure to spend — especially if you don't qualify.
The best no-interest loans are hard to get. You need an excellent
credit score to qualify, but that doesn't stop salespeople from
pitching them to everybody.

So what happens? You get hooked in by the amazing offer, only
to find the loan you qualify for comes with higher interest and
worse terms. By the time you get to that point, if you're like most
people, you'll feel pressured into going through with the deal.

You can avoid these mind games just by knowing ahead of time
what type of loan you'll qualify for. Check your credit score before
you start shopping for major purchases. And ask the salesperson
up front what score you need to get their zero-interest offer.

Home and auto loans

Pain-free steps to paying less

Discover the hidden perks of managing a mortgage in your golden years

Who hasn't dreamed of their perfect retirement home? Whether it's a cozy cabin in the mountains or a breezy beach bungalow, you're probably itching to kick-start your golden years in your own personal paradise. When it comes down to it, getting back into the mortgage game can be daunting — especially if your current home is already paid off.

But if you do decide to take the plunge and get a mortgage later in life, you're not alone. A recent study says 35 percent of seniors have home loans. Learn how joining their ranks might help you stack up your savings.

Take advantage of tax breaks by opting for a mortgage. A number of seniors choose the mortgage route so they don't have to splash out tons of cash to buy a house outright. They can put the extra savings toward investments, but they're also in it for the tax breaks.

An itemized deduction on your tax bill could save you a hefty sum — but it all depends on your retirement situation. That's because earning less in your later years drops you into a lower tax bracket. As a result, your mortgage deduction might not net the savings you anticipated.

"The tax benefits of having a mortgage debt have been reduced in the latest tax bill," says Barry Zigas, the director of housing policy at the Consumer Federation of America. "The savings people may see in their taxes, especially as their incomes decline, may not be as great as they hoped."

> The latest tax laws have changed how much mortgage interest you can deduct. It used to be $1 million, but if you signed your loan after December 14, 2017, that amount dropped to $750,000.

Crunch the numbers carefully to make sure you'll actually save money. To get a better idea of what the true costs will be, try out the online calculator at *bankrate.com/calculators/mortgages/loan-tax-deduction-calculator.aspx*. Be sure to adjust your federal and state tax rates based on your retirement income instead of what you earned while working.

Sizing down might mean moving up in price — but you can still save. As you age, you might find you don't need that suburban five-bedroom house anymore. Cleaning and caring for a big space can get tough, so downsizing seems like a good idea.

However, buying a smaller house doesn't necessarily mean it'll be any cheaper. A number of people find that their older homes don't fetch enough to cover the costs of a smaller, newer house.

But even if you do have enough to pay cash, it isn't always the best option. Some research has shown that getting a mortgage for part of the purchase can make more sense, but there's a catch. You'll have to invest the initial savings if you want to see any benefits to your bank account.

Still, consider your finances before you decide to get a mortgage in retirement. Carrying debt into your later years could be a burden if you don't plan carefully.

Cash out to get a better bargain

In the right market, a mortgage can be a smart choice. But what if you want to skip all the hassle and buy your house now? Splashing out the cash comes with a few advantages.

- You'll get a better deal. More often than not, paying for a home with cash puts you in a prime position to bargain. If you're savvy, you might wind up getting a much better deal than you could with a mortgage.

- Cash bumps up your buying power, too. Not only can you drive a harder bargain, but sellers are likely to take cash buyers more seriously. Plus, it cuts out the time-consuming hassle of the mortgage approval process.

But beware — putting a lot of your cash into one investment can tie your hands. Only consider going without a mortgage once you've considered all the costs.

An ARM might save you thousands if you're between homes

Francine and Ed decided to sell their old, big house after they retired, so they tracked down a perfect cottage to start their retirement years.

The only problem — they couldn't quite afford to buy the house outright until after they wrapped up selling their old home. And neither were interested in tying themselves down to a long, fixed-rate mortgage.

Fortunately, they found a solution that helped them transition to a new house while saving an arm and a leg on monthly mortgage payments.

An adjustable-rate mortgage (ARM) offered them the option to finance the home and keep their initial monthly payments low. So as soon as Ed and Francine recouped the cash from selling their old place, they paid off their home — and their bank account was none the wiser.

The low payments were possible because the initial interest rate on an ARM is usually below the market rate. You can take advantage of these savings, too.

But beware if you take on an ARM without a game plan. After the early fixed-rate period is up — anywhere from one month to 10 years — the interest rate can rise with market spikes, hiking up your monthly payments in the process. If you're not careful, you might find yourself in over your head.

May the fixed-rate be with you: Know when to stiff-arm an ARM

Like Anakin Skywalker in "Star Wars," ARMs can quickly cross over to the dark side if conditions are right. Before you apply for this type of mortgage, ask yourself how long you think you'll live in your house. If the market swings after the fixed-rate period ends and you still have a hefty balance, you'll wind up paying thousands more for your house. Check out how much you might pay if you went for a 30-year $203,700 fixed-rate or adjustable-rate loan.

	Fixed-rate mortgage	Adjustable-rate mortgage
Initial interest	4.5%	3.7%
Maximum interest	4.5%	8.7%
Initial monthly payment	$1,003	$937
Maximum monthly payment	$1,003	$1,434
Initial fixed-rate period	N/A	60 months
Total cost after 30 years	$371,562	$465,596

In this scenario, you'd save more than $94,000 with a fixed-rate mortgage. And that's no Jedi mind trick.

DOLLARS & SENSE

3 routes to finding a lender you can write home about

Getting a mortgage isn't a decision you should take lightly, but stats show that most buyers don't shop around. Sure, it's difficult to go from bank to bank and broker to broker, but you could be losing out on thousands in savings. Been a long time since you bought a house? Discover new options for finding a lender.

Surf the web to reel in some great savings. Because online mortgage lenders don't have to put up with expenses like brick-and-mortar buildings or hire as many staff members, they often have very low costs.

That's good news for you — online mortgage lenders typically offer much lower fees and interest rates than traditional banks or mortgage brokers.

And you get an added level of convenience, without the cost. With an online lender you don't have to go to an office, fill out paperwork, make copies, and deal with the traditional hassles of applying for a mortgage. You can do it all from the comfort of your own computer simply by filling out forms online.

If you do choose to go with an online lender, don't be blindsided by these common drawbacks.

▶ Customer service can be hard to reach, making it tricky to get fast, convenient help when you need it. Before you apply, explore the website to see how you'll get in touch if you have questions.

▶ Because online lenders offer services nationwide, chances are you'll lose a lot of local expertise by choosing to consult them instead of a bank or broker who knows the area.

Head straight to the source to score bona fide bargains in person. If you're not quite ready to trust an online company with your mortgage, you still have plenty of options. You can go to a direct lender, like a bank or credit union, to see what types of loans are available. These are usually great choices because they are reliable, offer great customer service, and know the community well. And if you already do your banking with them, you may bag even better deals.

On the other hand, just going to one bank limits your options. Though it takes time and effort, you can shop around to find the best deals.

Don't go it "a-loan" — team up with a mortgage broker to curb the confusion. When you need help with your taxes, you call up an accountant. So why wouldn't you seek out expert advice if you've got questions about buying your house? Mortgage brokers can help you fill out applications, apply to lenders, and ultimately find the right loan for your budget.

There was a time when mortgage brokers had a less-than-savory reputation, especially because they earned more money if they talked you into signing a bigger loan. But stricter laws and regulations make it easy to find a broker who's actually there to help you.

Still, you should do some homework to make sure you pick the best mortgage lender for you. Ask around, or better yet talk to your real estate agent, to find a few solid choices. You should also check out online reviews to see how they stack up against the competition.

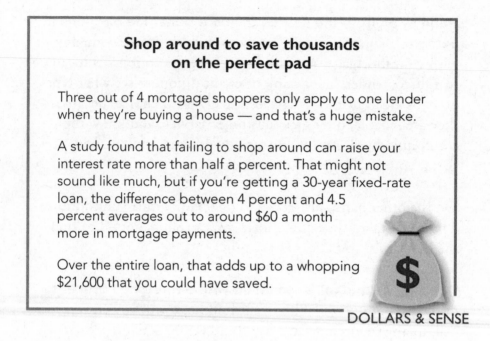

**Shop around to save thousands
on the perfect pad**

Three out of 4 mortgage shoppers only apply to one lender
when they're buying a house — and that's a huge mistake.

A study found that failing to shop around can raise your
interest rate more than half a percent. That might not
sound like much, but if you're getting a 30-year fixed-rate
loan, the difference between 4 percent and 4.5
percent averages out to around $60 a month
more in mortgage payments.

Over the entire loan, that adds up to a whopping
$21,600 that you could have saved.

DOLLARS & SENSE

Credit crunches curtailing your dream move?
Not anymore

You've dealt with all your debt and are finally ready to kick back
and enjoy retirement. Good for you. But guess what else may
have retired along with you? Your credit score.

After a few years without debt payments or open accounts, your
credit score may be low or even nonexistent. So when you
decide it's time to downsize or move to sunny Arizona, you
might run into a few problems getting a mortgage. Who would
have thought? Fortunately, there are a few solutions.

Tap into your portfolio to prove you can pay. One of the best
ways to get approved for a loan is show that you can stay on top
of the bills. Without a steady paycheck coming in, that can be a

bit difficult. But if you've been planning for retirement, you shouldn't worry.

- ▸ If you have some savings stored away, tap into those for your down payment. This can help assure lenders you're able to keep up with your mortgage payments.

- ▸ Proving you have a strong income can boost your chances of getting a better rate, too. Fortunately for retired loan seekers, banks will let you count withdrawals from your retirement funds as income, as long as you've been drawing from them for at least two months.

Reach out to find a helping hand. If your credit score isn't as high as you hoped and you don't have a lot of cash squirreled away, you might be able to get some government assistance.

- ▸ The Federal Housing Administration (FHA) offers some help for borrowers with low credit scores. For example, you only need to make a 3.5 percent down payment if your score is over 580. And you could get help with closing costs. Keep in mind the loan must come from an approved lender.

- ▸ If you're a veteran, talk to the Department of Veterans Affairs. The VA can help you buy a home with a competitive interest rate. And you won't shell out a down payment as long as the sales price isn't more than the appraised value.

4 costly mortgage mistakes you don't want to make

Complicated mortgage contracts make it easy for a few fees and penalties to fly under the radar. A good company will help you every step of the way, but if you don't know what you're looking for it can be hard to ask the right questions. Here are a few common mistakes you need to watch out for.

Don't get trapped by prepayment penalties and other unscrupulous fees. Most residential mortgages signed after 2014 come with perks for borrowers. Lenders can no longer charge you extra if you want to pay off your loan before its due date — whether you refinance, sell your home, or unexpectedly win the lottery. So read the fine print of your contract and watch out for tricky fees — they can really add up.

For example, if you tried to refinance a two-year-old mortgage with a balance of $220,000 and a 2 percent prepayment penalty, you'd owe an additional $4,400 to your original lender. Ouch.

Want to get clued in to how much you can borrow before taking the plunge? Get a preapproval letter. A lender will look over your credit report and financial history, then give you a letter letting you know the loan amounts and rates you qualify for. Having one of these also lets buyers know you're serious.

Biting off more than you can chew can land you in big trouble. While it's not your mortgage company's job to come up with your household budget, a good company is going to work your finances into the equation. The general rule of thumb is to spend no more than 28 percent of your gross monthly income on payments.

For example, somebody with about $3,500 coming in every month could afford to spend about $980 in housing each month. To get a better idea of how much you can afford to pay for a house, check out the online mortgage calculator at *nerdwallet.com/ mortgages/how-much-house-can-i-afford/calculate-affordability*.

Keep your eyes peeled for scammers or bad lenders who disregard your finances and try to force you into a mortgage that's way beyond your means.

Watch out for balloon payments — they might blow up in your face. Some loans include clauses that allow the lender to charge you a huge, one-time fee at the end of your loan. This lets them advertise low monthly premiums, but you could wind up with a huge final payment.

"Generally, a balloon payment is more than two times the loan's average monthly payment, and often it can be tens of thousands of dollars," says a spokesperson from the Consumer Financial Protection Bureau. "Most balloon loans require one large payment that pays off your remaining balance at the end of the loan term. If you're considering a balloon loan, you need to think about whether and how you can make the balloon payment when it comes due."

Credit matters, no matter what anybody says. A good credit score is one of the most important factors in getting a good deal on your mortgage. Advertisements or companies that claim they can get you a great mortgage deal regardless of your score should set off the alarm bells in your head.

These loans are almost always awful deals for the customers and are loaded with fees, penalties, and other tricks that can cost you thousands of dollars. Avoid doing business with anybody who claims they don't care about your credit history.

Trading equity for income — is a reverse mortgage right for you?

You love watching Tom Selleck light up the small screen in "Bluebloods" and the old "Magnum, P.I." Now you can see him in commercials as a spokesman for reverse mortgages. The American Advisors Group is counting on his reputation as an honest, upstanding guy to give you the confidence to make this somewhat scary financial move.

Reverse mortgages are loans that let you convert the equity in your home to cash. So instead of making monthly payments to your lender, your lender makes payments to you. And you won't have to pay it back as long as you still live in your home.

These loans used to get a bad rap from financial planners, but that's starting to change. New laws and safeguards mean they could be a great way to put thousands of dollars in your pocket. In the right situation, you'll get guaranteed, tax-free income for years. But how do you know if they're right for you?

When is a reverse mortgage an option? The most common reverse mortgages are known as Home Equity Conversion Mortgages (HECMs), which means they are federally insured. Before you consider a HECM (pronounced heck-um), make sure you meet all these criteria.

▶ You're over the age of 62. It's a good idea to think about your spouse's age, too. If they're too young to meet the requirements, you can still get money by borrowing under your name. But if you pass away first, you might leave your spouse homeless.

▶ Your home is completely or mostly paid off, and you live in it.

▶ You will receive government-approved counseling before you get the loan. "Reverse mortgages are best used by people who have a relatively sophisticated understanding of how they work and who have had extensive counseling about their features, their benefits, and their pitfalls before they commit to one," says Barry Zigas, director of housing policy for the Consumer Federation of America.

▶ You plan to stay in your home for a long time. Reverse mortgages often come with higher upfront costs. If you sell your house within a few years, not only will the debt kick in, but you've just chosen an expensive way to borrow money.

▶ You can afford to look after your house and pay other expenses. Reverse mortgages will take care of your monthly mortgage payment, but you're still on the hook for other things like property taxes, insurance, and maintenance.

When is a reverse mortgage the wrong choice? Reverse mortgages aren't for everybody. They still pose some risks, even with all the new regulations. Here are a few signs that a reverse mortgage might get you into hot water.

▶ You want to leave the house to your heirs. If you're not living alone, or you'd like to keep the house in the family after you pass away, a reverse mortgage isn't the best choice. Once you pass away, lenders will come to collect on the house. And if other family members aren't on the loan, they could be left without a home.

▶ Poor health or plans to move? Forget about it. It's tempting to use your reverse mortgage to help deal with medical expenses, but remember that as soon as you move out you're on the hook for the loan. So in the event that you need to move to a nursing home or assisted living facility, you could find yourself short on cash.

What happens if you leave behind a HECM?

If you leave behind a HECM reverse mortgage, the debt kicks in when you pass away. That doesn't mean the home is going to hit the market, though. In most cases, the lender will contact your heirs explaining the terms of the loan and these options moving forward.

- They can keep the house, but they're on the hook for the loan. They'll owe a maximum of 95 percent of the home's value, even if the loan balance exceeds that.

- They're allowed to sell the home, and they can keep the profit as long as it sells for more than the amount of debt still owed.

- If they don't want to keep the home and the debt outweighs the value, they can sign it away with a deed in lieu of foreclosure.

3 ways to pocket your reverse mortgage money

Do you want your reverse mortgage payout as a lump sum or a line of credit? Think carefully, because your choice is going to make a big difference.

Take a lump sum. If you want a bit of extra breathing room in your budget, you might want to consider using the loan to pay off the rest of your home and put a little extra cash in your pocket. And one way you can do that is to get a big, one-time cash windfall.

▸ You'll get all your available funds at once, but this option usually offers the lowest total payout.

▸ It costs more, too. You'll face a lot of upfront expenses and lender fees that add up.

▸ There's a higher chance you'll outlive your money, especially if you're a younger borrower.

Open up a line of credit. You might want to take a reverse mortgage, but you don't need all of the money right away. Fortunately, you can draw from the credit line on your house and take a bit of money out whenever you need it.

▸ You can only tap into some of your available money in the first year. After the second, though, you'll be able to access all your funds.

▸ Because you only take money out when you need it, the fees won't be nearly as expensive as the lump-sum option.

▸ The line of credit increases with time, too. Unused money builds interest, giving you more funds if your home value rises.

Get a monthly payment. You can also opt for a plan that puts cash in your pocket every month. Just choose to get payments for a set number of months, or until you've received the full loan amount. And, as an added bonus, you can combine this with a line of credit for a bit more versatility.

▸ Because you'll be responsible for fees as you get money, this can be a low-cost option.

▸ You'll also continue to build interest on unused credit.

▸ The amount you can get is limited in the first year, though.

2 surefire strategies to fight foreclosure

Those unexpected medical bills mean you just can't meet your mortgage payments anymore. And with foreclosure looming in the background, you don't have anywhere to turn. But don't panic — help is out there.

Talk to your lender to fend off foreclosure. The worst thing you can do is stop making payments without any explanation. It's stressful and often embarrassing to reach out for financial help, but your mortgage provider doesn't want to deal with a lengthy, ugly foreclosure any more than you do. Call them up to see what your options are. You can help move the process along by having a few things in mind before you pick up the phone.

▸ Why did you start missing mortgage payments? Whether it's an unexpected surgery or a problem with your pension, lenders need to know why you're suddenly not paying your bills before they can start working with you.

▸ Are you dealing with a short-term financial crisis or will you likely never be able to make your payments again?

Lenders need to build a personal timeline that helps you avoid foreclosure.

▸ What type of payments can you afford? And do you even want to stay in your house? Sometimes it might make sense to scale down and find something cheaper. It's not an easy decision, but a good lender will help you every step of the way.

Call on Uncle Sam to hold on to your house. The government offers free, certified counseling for people who are having trouble making ends meet. Find an approved counselor near you at *apps.hud.gov/offices/hsg/sfh/hcc/fc/.*

Your counselor will help you examine your financial situation, build a budget to get your money under control, and work with your lender if you're still not sure you can make your payments. And counselors will let you know if you're eligible for any government assistance that could help you keep your home.

Stay a step ahead to stop mortgage scammers

A sudden slash in Fred's pension left him unable to pay his mortgage on time. The threat of an impending foreclosure was hanging over his head. So when a letter arrived in his mailbox that promised easy relief, he was overjoyed. What he didn't know was that the letter came from a fraudster who would leave him worse off.

Scammers often target people who are in financial trouble. Some even go through public foreclosure notices so they can craft personalized letters and emails designed to take advantage of homeowners like you. Here are a few ways to sniff out these scams and keep yourself safe.

Beware of people who are asking to help. Scammers often approach you, promising to help get your mortgage back under control — for a fee. As soon as you send the money their way, they'll disappear and you'll be out of luck.

And sometimes these scammers will ask you to send your mortgage payments to them while they deal with your lender. But they're not smoothing things over at all. Instead, they pocket the cash and let your lender foreclose on you.

Avoid this by ignoring unsolicited advice. Only work on mortgage relief through approved counselors or directly with your lender.

Rebuff any rent-to-buy schemes. Other thieves might ask you to hand over the title to your home to help you avoid foreclosure. In return, you just have to pay rent until you can buy it back later. But these deals are loaded with fees, loopholes, or other tricks that let them kick you out and keep your house.

Or sometimes they'll just wait until you sign over the deed and then do nothing at all. They pocket your money, and your old mortgage lender will evict you for not making any more payments.

3 red flags that should sound an alarm. Remember these common warning signs to spot a phony company or scammer who will over promise and under deliver.

- Don't deal with companies that ask you not to talk to your lender or get other mortgage help.

- Steer clear of companies that tell you they only take payment in cashier's checks or wire transfers. They're definitely scams.

▶ Avoid upfront fees. In fact, it's illegal for mortgage relief companies to even ask for money before they deliver on their promises. Only lawyers can charge beforehand, and you can make sure you're getting good legal advice by researching them online at your state bar association.

3 common car-leasing myths you need to bust

Car leases get some bad press, but in the right situation they might actually be a great deal. You'll get low monthly payments, a warranty for the length of the lease, and — if you're the type of person who trades in your car every few years — some big savings. Here are a few ways your next car lease could surprise you.

Myth 1: You can't get any tax incentives. While only businesses can deduct monthly leasing expenses from their taxes, there are still savings in it for you — if you live in the right state. In most cases you only have to pay taxes on your monthly lease payments, not the whole sale price of the vehicle. This could be a pretty significant saver, but you'll need to check local laws to see if you can reap the benefits.

Myth 2: You can't swap your car out early. You might have heard you're stuck with a leased car, no matter what. After all, a lot of contracts come loaded with hefty penalties and fees if you bring the car back too soon.

That might not be true, depending on your contract. But even if it is the case, you're not necessarily out of options. Websites like *leasetrader.com* or *swapalease.com* let you find a customer to take over the rest of your lease for you.

Myth 3: Negotiations are a lost cause. You can definitely haggle over a car lease, but it helps to know a few business terms before you go toe-to-toe with the dealer.

▶ Capitalized cost essentially means vehicle price. You can try to talk them down from here just like you would if you were buying a new car.

▶ Money factor is a tricky way of describing the interest rate. It's usually given as a decimal, but if you want to get an idea of what your APR will be just multiply the number by 2,400. So if the money factor is 0.003, the interest rate would be 7.2 percent. The percentage should be pretty close to the APR on a new-car loan. If it's higher, try talking them down or take your business somewhere else.

▶ Residual value is an estimate of what the car will be worth after the lease ends. Though your dealer doesn't set this number, he will use it to determine your monthly payment. Higher numbers mean lower monthly payments, but they also make it harder to trade your car in early or buy it at the end of the lease.

One of the best things about leasing a car is getting a brand new ride every few years without fretting about maintenance. Do your research and look around for the very best deals to make sure you're getting the most out of your car lease.

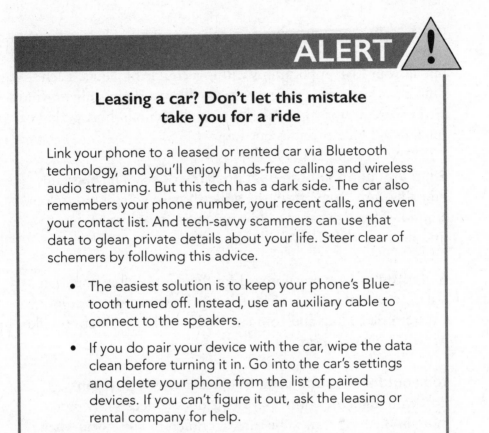

ALERT

Leasing a car? Don't let this mistake take you for a ride

Link your phone to a leased or rented car via Bluetooth technology, and you'll enjoy hands-free calling and wireless audio streaming. But this tech has a dark side. The car also remembers your phone number, your recent calls, and even your contact list. And tech-savvy scammers can use that data to glean private details about your life. Steer clear of schemers by following this advice.

- The easiest solution is to keep your phone's Bluetooth turned off. Instead, use an auxiliary cable to connect to the speakers.

- If you do pair your device with the car, wipe the data clean before turning it in. Go into the car's settings and delete your phone from the list of paired devices. If you can't figure it out, ask the leasing or rental company for help.

Auto loan checklist: How to get the best deals

Paying cash for your next car might not be an option, but getting a loan from the dealership could be a huge mistake. Here are a few things you need to do next time you're searching for an auto loan.

Check your credit early to be prepared. Your credit rating is a huge factor when it comes to getting a good deal on an auto loan. If you know where you stand before you start shopping, you'll have a decent idea of what kind of deals to expect.

Get a credit report to help you catch any mistakes before they cost you big bucks on your next loan. And do your best to submit all your loan applications within a couple of weeks. Each time a company runs your credit, you'll get a slight ding on your credit score. But if you apply for several within a short period of time, it will only count as one inquiry.

Shop around to get the best possible deals. The best rates probably won't come from the dealership, so you'll need to look around. Compare banks, credit unions, and online lenders to find the best loans for your budget.

And if you can get preapproved for financing before you even walk into a dealership, you'll be in a prime position to negotiate a better price. Shop and compare deals online with websites like *bankrate.com/auto.aspx.*

Look out for the total cost, not just monthly payments. A loan with higher monthly payments doesn't necessarily cost more in the long run, so be sure to crunch the numbers when you're comparison shopping. You'll need to consider the big picture if you don't want to overspend by thousands.

For example, a five-year $20,000 car loan with 7.5 percent interest will have cheaper monthly payments than the same loan shortened to three years, but you'll wind up paying almost $2,000 more in interest. Plus, most lenders raise the interest rates if you opt for a longer loan.

Compare prices yourself using an online calculator like the one found at *bankrate.com/calculators/auto/auto-loan-calculator.aspx.*

Refinance your auto loan to stuff your wallet

Were you so eager to get a brand new car that you signed up for a loan right there at the dealership? Those costly payments sting, especially because you could have gotten a better deal if you'd just shopped around. Fortunately, it's not too late to do something about it.

Start fresh to put hundreds of dollars back in your pocket. You probably know you can refinance if your mortgage gets out of hand, but your car loan might be a prime candidate, too. Even better — getting a new auto loan is easier and cheaper than reworking your mortgage. Here are a few questions to ask yourself before you consider an updated loan.

▸ Can I get a lower interest rate? A refinanced auto loan is usually treated like a loan for a used car, which means the rates are generally higher. But if the market is right, you can still save.

A mere 2 percent difference could save you thousands over the course of your loan. Say your monthly car payment is $550 and you still owe $25,000 over the next five years at 7.5 percent interest. If you can find a loan to drop the interest to 5.5 percent, you'll save more than $4,300.

▸ Is your credit score better than when you got the loan? Your score is a huge factor in determining what a loan is going to cost. If you've raised your score or paid down big chunks of old debts since you bought your car, you might be a prime candidate for refinancing.

▸ Can you keep up with your monthly payments? Sudden expenses or a loss of income might mean you can't afford the luxury sedan anymore. But rather than defaulting on your loan, you might want to consider refinancing. See if you can extend the final payment date and get a lower monthly payment. You'll probably wind up paying a bit more in the long run, but it's better than tanking your finances by not paying back your loans.

3 signs refinancing won't be worth the time. If you're not careful, getting a new loan will hurt you more than it will help. So how do you know if it's the wrong move?

▸ Your car is close to being all paid off. A new loan will have upfront fees and costs, so you'll be wasting time and money trying to refinance it.

▸ Your car is worth less than what you owe. Lenders aren't likely to give you any deals if you have an upside-down loan. If you're not sure what the value of your car is, check it out at *kbb.com* or *edmunds.com/tmv*.

▸ You'll need your credit score in tiptop shape soon. Looking for a new mortgage or shopping around for credit card offers? Think twice before refinancing. You'll take a little ding to your credit score, so it might be best to hold off.

Home and auto insurance

Clever ways to safeguard your property

10 ways to save a heap on home coverage

Watching paint dry. Waiting for the well-known pot to boil. Measuring your lawn to see if that blade of grass has grown a fraction of an inch. Just a few of the dull pastimes that are still more interesting than reading about insurance.

But here's something that might make you sit up and take notice. Check out this list of 10 home insurance discounts you must ask your agent about. Nothing boring about saving money every month for the rest of your life, is there?

Be the early bird. Ask your agent for a 10 percent discount when you sign up for a new policy before your current one expires. Are you a brand new customer? You may qualify for a 10 percent discount for your first two years. Check with your agent for details.

Generate your own discount. During the winter months, power outages can be especially disastrous and costly. If you lose power, your pipes could freeze, causing a whole flood of problems. An automatic generator that kicks on when the electricity goes off keeps your important appliances running, too. Ask your agent if your generator purchase generates a delightful discount.

Set it and forget it for savings. Pay your bill through an automatic deduction from your bank account, and save 5 to 10 percent on your premiums. Simple, easy, and stress free. Ask your agent for details.

You better shop around. It may take a little time and effort, but comparing rates could save a chunk of change. Check consumer guides and online insurance quote services for the best deals. Don't forget to look for complaints, too. Quality service and a fair price go hand-in-hand. The National Association of Insurance Commissioners can help you choose a company in your state. Visit *naic.org*.

Raise your deductible. The deductible is the amount of money you're required to pay towards a claim before your insurance kicks in. Raise your deductible to $1,000, and you could save up to 25 percent off your annual premium.

Tighten your security. Knock off up to 5 percent of your bill by installing smoke detectors, a security system, or deadbolt locks. But ask your agent for advice before you invest in a high-tech, state-of-the-art system. You want to make sure you get the most bang for your buck.

Enjoy this benefit of retirement. Are you at least 55 years old and retired? Talk with your agent about a 10 percent discount on your homeowners insurance. You've earned it.

Do a credit check. Many insurers are now using your credit score to figure out the price you'll have to pay for premiums. A high credit score tells the insurers you pay your bills on time and you probably take good care of your home, too. Make sure your credit report is up to snuff.

No butts about it. Smoking accounts for 23,000 residential fires every year. Ask your agent for a discount if no one in your home smokes.

Keep disaster from your door. Think about steps you can take to protect your home from natural disasters like windstorms or earthquakes. You may get a discount if you have professionals add storm shutters or stronger roofing materials. Modernize your heating, plumbing, and electrical systems to protect against fire and water damage, too.

Bundling up means cool savings for you

Buying your home and auto insurance from the same company — known as bundling — is a cost-cutting option that's available to everyone. Insurance giant Allstate says you could save up to 35 percent off your insurance premiums by bundling home and auto.

"Bundling is a great strategy to save money on your insurance," says Laura Adams, senior insurance analyst at InsuranceQuotes. "However, the amount you save depends on the state where you live and the types of policies you have."

For example, bundlers in Louisiana save 20 percent, or close to $600. But folks in Florida save around a third of that — about $200. To find out how your state fares, go to *insurancequotes.com*, and search on "bundling."

DOLLARS & SENSE

Coverage checkup: 3 questions you need to ask

Here's a surprising little insurance fact for you. A recent survey said close to 6 out of 10 homeowners don't know how much coverage is included in their homeowners policy. And 4 out of 10 weren't sure their coverage was enough to protect them against future disasters. How about your policy? Does it fit the bill?

If it's been more than a year since you took a nice, long look at your homeowners coverage, it may be time to set up a sit-down with your agent. But first, get a copy of your policy. You can get one from your account online, or ask your agent to mail a copy. Once you've reviewed it, ask your agent these three questions.

Is there coverage I may need — but don't have? For example, if a hurricane hits, you might be protected from damage caused by the rain and wind. But guess what? Flood damage is covered separately.

So what else could you be missing? Your agent should be able to advise you about the types of coverage needed for your area.

Do I have the right amount of coverage? Experts say you should have enough insurance to cover rebuilding your home, replacing your possessions, and protecting yourself from liability if you're sued. Make sure your policy will provide you with the funds you need to pay for a place to live until you can move back into your home.

Am I paying too much — or too little? It's time to tweak your policy if any of these statements apply to you.

▶ You decided to give a pound puppy a forever home. Good for you, but call your agent and adjust your coverage. Dog bites breed expensive liability claims.

▶ You remodeled your home. Did a professional upgrade your wiring, windows, or roofing materials? Cha-ching. Discount time.

▶ You purchased some expensive items like jewelry, firearms, or state-of-the-art electronics. Or, you've gotten rid of some pricey stuff.

▶ You installed a security system or upgraded other safety features in your home. Woohoo! Ask for a discount on your premium.

▶ You added a swimming pool or a trampoline for the grand-kids. Uh-oh. Insurers aren't real fans of outdoor fun. Your premium may go up, but you'll need the correct amount of coverage in case of injuries.

▶ Did you get married? Have an aging parent move in with you? Retire? To help you find the best coverage, your agent needs to know about all these important life changes.

Check your homeowners coverage: What you don't know could cost you

Ann Hodges was hit by a meteorite that burst through the roof of her Alabama home in 1954. She was just relaxing, taking a nap on her sofa, when the softball-sized black rock crashed through the ceiling and hit her on the thigh, leaving a pineapple-shaped bruise.

Interesting, right? But what does that have to do with insurance? Turns out the roof damage caused by the meteorite — classified in insurance-speak as "falling objects" — would be covered by a standard homeowners insurance policy. Surprised? Wondering what other benefits you may not know about?

You'll save money — and some sleepless nights — if you know what perils your policy covers. Here are a few you may have missed.

▸ **People-made messes.** These include riots, vandalism, theft, and home damage caused by vehicles and airplanes. Nuclear accidents? War? Sorry. Not covered.

▸ **Planet Earth's dirty work.** Think fire, lightning, hail, windstorms — even volcanic eruptions. And, of course, falling objects like meteorites. But earthquakes, sinkholes, floods, and mudslides require their own coverage. Go figure.

▸ **Plumbing and other homegrown perils.** Frozen pipes? Probably covered. Air conditioner or household appliance leaking? Should be included in your policy, along with lots of other homemade disasters. Just be sure to check your policy, or call your agent for details.

Personal liability coverage — usually built right into your homeowners policy — is designed to help protect your assets when you find yourself facing one of these situations.

▸ **Dog bites.** This is a big problem. Dog bites cost homeowners about $400 million a year and account for one-third of all liability claims.

▸ **Libel and slander.** Many homeowners policies protect your assets if you're accused of libel or slander, aka defamation of character. But you still need to be careful what you post on Facebook or Twitter.

▸ **Food poisoning.** Uh-oh. Something in Grandma's recipe turned your guests' faces green — and not with envy. Your liability coverage should cover medical bills and lawsuits, if anyone decides to sue. Be sure to check the wording of your policy for details.

A CLOSER LOOK

California resident Janet Ruiz says she carries a 50 percent upgrade benefit on her 1970s home — just in case she needs to comply with new building codes and expensive materials if she ever has to rebuild. And as a representative for the Insurance Information Institute, she knows just how important that is.

Here's why. On a $200,000 home, her 50 percent building code upgrade coverage provides Ruiz with a total of $300,000 to rebuild her home according to today's higher standards.

"Code upgrades are super important because the more resilient our homes are, the more affordable we can keep insurance and building costs," she says.

So do you have enough coverage to rebuild your home according to updated safety codes? Not sure? Ask your agent about adding a building code upgrade to your policy. Your homeowners coverage may come with a standard 10 percent benefit, but that might not be enough — especially if you have an older home.

An umbrella policy keeps your assets covered

Accidents happen. In fact, injuries around the house — everything from slips and falls to electrical shocks — result in an average of 21 million medical visits each year. And that adds up to a whopping $220 billion in medical costs.

Big numbers for sure, but what do they mean for you? Let's suppose your elderly Aunt Jane comes for a Christmas visit. She slips on your icy front porch and breaks her hip. She is hospitalized for surgery, followed by a lengthy stay in rehab. And she's counting on you to pay her medical expenses.

Standard liability insurance might not be enough. Your homeowners insurance probably includes about $100,000 in liability coverage. This means if someone gets hurt on your property — like poor Aunt Jane — your policy will pay up to that amount in medical bills, legal judgments, and lawyers' fees. But Aunt Jane's bills topped $800,000. Now what?

Don't forget your umbrella. Insurance Information Institute rep Janet Ruiz says she'd never own a home without investing in an umbrella policy. "They're one of the best deals out there," Ruiz says. "Umbrella policies are not that expensive, and it's just like taking an umbrella out when it rains. You don't get soaked since the policies have coverages that might not be included in your homeowners insurance."

This type of policy is particularly important for seniors who have built up their nest eggs and may even have a second home. "Generally speaking, in your senior years you have the most assets of your lifetime," Ruiz says. "The last thing you want to do is lose them because of something you're liable for."

Get protection for pennies. Umbrella policies are budget-friendly. In fact, for about $200 a year, you can purchase a $1 million personal umbrella liability policy that will provide the extra coverage you need.

Check with your agent about your policy's liability limits and to find out if an umbrella policy is right for you. A smart way to protect yourself and your wealth from a rainy-day disaster.

Slam the door on scammers with these savvy tips

Ruthie was heartbroken when her favorite magnolia — the one her late husband planted on their 10th wedding anniversary — toppled during a terrible spring storm. To make matters worse, the enormous tree destroyed her front porch.

Thank goodness her homeowners insurance would cover the repairs. And she's already had a nice young man approach her about fixing her house, and at a great price, too.

Wait a minute, Ruthie. Better batten down the hatches. Because once the rain stops, you could be hit by another storm. Scammers.

The most common homeowners insurance scams involve fraudsters known as storm chasers. After disaster strikes, these people go door-to-door, posing as roofers, carpenters, or electricians. They promise to quickly repair your home – if you're willing to pay them upfront.

Some will just take your money and run, while others will do some quick, shoddy work that may not be covered by your insurance.

How to spot a scam a mile away. Here are some clues to recognize storm chasers.

▸ Beware of door-to-door salesmen with out-of-state license plates. Scammers rush into disaster areas, trying to make a quick buck.

▶ Look out for contractors who don't have business cards or company flyers. Make sure they have a street address, too — not just a post office box. A local phone number is a good sign.

▶ Be there when they inspect your property. Crooked contractors could add bogus storm damage to your home using hammers or golf balls, just to make your insurance claim higher. Some may even use dimes to scrape roof shingles and cause indentations — known as dime spinning — to fake roof damage.

▶ Professionals get the right permits to do the job. Slam the door on contractors who offer to save you money by working without a contract or permits.

As the song says, only fools rush in. Be smart with your time and money, and you won't be a victim.

▶ Get at least three estimates before you make a decision. Scammers will push you to make a decision immediately.

▶ If you don't have a regular repairman, get a recommendation from your neighbors or insurance agent. Ask for references from their former clients. And check out your prospective repairman online. The Better Business Bureau at *bbb.org* is a good place to start.

▶ Be careful what you sign. Dishonest contractors may ask you to sign a repairs contract on a digital tablet. But when the paper is printed out, the bid is actually thousands of dollars higher.

▶ Don't be in a hurry to pay. Your deposit or upfront fees should be no more than 25 percent of the job estimate.

Pay it only after the building materials are on site and work has begun. And pay the rest in installments. Wait until the work is finished to your satisfaction before you make the final payment.

A CLOSER LOOK

"We have a saying here at NICB. If you didn't request it, reject it." So says Frank Scafidi, director of public affairs for the National Insurance Crime Bureau (NICB), an organization that helps combat insurance fraud and theft.

In other words, don't trust contractors that just show up at your door. Instead, Scafidi recommends you call your insurance company and ask them for a list of pre-qualified and pre-cleared workers who can repair your home correctly.

"Slow down. Take your time," he advises. "Don't be in a hurry to get something done, especially if you don't know who you're dealing with."

5 ways to put the brakes on rising car insurance costs

To cover any injuries or damage he might cause while driving his self-built car, Gilbert Loomis bought the first-ever auto insurance policy way back in 1897. He paid the then-outrageous amount of $7.50 so he could get $1,000 in liability coverage.

Fast-forward over 100 years, and you'll find Loomis' great-great-grandson paying a whole lot more for his policy — a whopping annual average of $1,200. Of course for that hefty price tag, the younger Loomis also gets liability, collision, and comprehensive coverage for his medium sedan, all required to protect today's drivers and their more expensive cars.

Looking for ways to pay less and get more protection? These little-known tips could slash your insurance costs by as much as 50 percent. Pay close attention as insurance insiders spill the beans about how you can keep more bucks in the bank.

Drive down your premium by hooking hidden deals. Rev up your savings with these discounts your insurance agent may never tell you about.

▸ Save 5 to 10 percent on your premium by paying your renewal bill in full instead of using a payment plan. You could slash your bill by $120. Cha-ching.

▸ Butcher, baker, candlestick maker? Can't help them, but if you're a firefighter, police officer, EMT, or teacher, you could save up to 10 percent on your premiums. Another $120 in your pocket every year.

▸ University alums will tip their mortarboards to this discount. In one study, college grads with bachelor's degrees paid 15 percent less in Seattle than people who didn't graduate from high school. And advanced degrees saved drivers even more — up to 17 percent. That's like saving $200 every year.

Ask your alumni association about a group plan. It may help you trim 5 percent off your bill. That'll tuck $60 back into your wallet. Sis boom bah.

Listen up, seniors! Don't pay too much for your car insurance. Check into these savings for older adults. They can add up fast.

▶ You're never too old to learn something new, right? Especially if it can save you up to $240 a year. Sign up for a defensive driving course and hone your highway skills. When you finish, take proof of your course completion to your insurance agent and request a discount.

Experts say you could save 5 to 20 percent on your premiums, depending on your location and insurance provider. Check with your agent for discount details.

▶ Giving up that long commute now that you're retired? One study found that someone who drives around 5,000 miles a year pays an average of 8 percent less for car insurance than someone who racks up 15,000 miles. That's about $100 off the average yearly premium. Not bad, right?

Back-to-school savings:
Slash $800 off your insurance tab

Hazel, 65, pays $142 each month for her car insurance. When she decided to brush up on her driving skills, she paid $40 to take a defensive driving course. After she finished the class, the insurance company rewarded her with a 10 percent discount on her monthly premium.

With the discount, Hazel's premium dropped $14, making her new payment $128 per month. She saved almost $170 after just one year.

But her 10 percent discount keeps rolling in for three to five years, letting the savings really pile up. After five years, Hazel will have saved more than $800, all because of that one $40 investment. But more importantly? Her trip back to school made her a safer and smarter driver.

DOLLARS & SENSE

Here's the bottom line on car coverage rollbacks. You could save more than 50 percent by taking advantage of these discounts. If you're paying the national average for auto insurance, that might add up to more than $600 a year. What are you waiting for? Call your agent right now.

Time to review your auto coverage? Follow these signs

Has your life's road recently taken some unexpected twists and turns? Then it may be time to take a good look at your auto insurance — just to make sure it's still got you covered. It is especially important to check your policy if any of the following apply to you.

▸ You sold your car, or you're no longer driving it. Or maybe you got a new car.

▸ You moved to a new state — or even to a new ZIP code. A small move can make a big difference in your premium.

▸ Your annual mileage has changed because you retired or shortened your commute. Perhaps you joined a ride-sharing group, for example.

▸ You added or dropped a driver. An empty nester at last?

▸ Your car is paid off and old enough that you wouldn't repair it. Might be time to drop collision and comprehensive coverage.

▸ Your credit score improved. Paying off your debt can pay off in lower premiums.

▸ You've gotten married. Congratulations! Celebrate with a nuptial discount.

▸ You haven't updated your policy in a long time. Chances are you're not getting the best coverage for the best price. Make a plan to update your insurance at least once a year.

The spy in your dash can drive down your premiums

Telematics. Tele-what-ics? Yes, you read it right. Telematics. It's a kind of technology that's changing the face of auto insurance by keeping an eye on your driving habits. Here's how it works.

Gentlemen, start your engine tracking. First, contact your insurance agency, and they'll provide you with a special device called a dongle.

A dongle? Who comes up with these words?

A dongle is about the size of a USB flash drive. You install it in a special port in your dashboard that connects with your car's computer system. Once in place, the dongle monitors your driving habits including your speed, the length of your trip, and the time of day. It even records your accelerating and braking habits, so hold back on those jackrabbit starts and tire-screeching stops.

British actor Rowan Atkinson is best known for his comic character Mr. Bean. But in-the-know insurance folk recognize him as the recipient of the largest auto insurance payout of all time. The accident repair bill for his McLaren F1 supercar hit almost $1.3 million. You can bet his premiums took a turn for the worse!

Next, the dongle sends a report to your insurance company about your safe driving. And you wait for your discount to roll in.

Technology that saves you money. Sounds a little like science fiction, right? But dongles and telematics could be the keys to unlocking cheaper premiums for good drivers like you.

So says Jonathan Hewett, Global Chief Marketing Officer for Octo Telematics, a leader in the tech industry. Hewett says drivers can save big with this technology. "We see up to 30 percent discounts for consumers who are able to demonstrate they drive safely and they drive well."

Accident not your fault? You may still pay more

While leaving a shopping center on a busy Saturday afternoon, Gail stopped for a red light. An enormous pickup truck came out of nowhere and barreled into the rear of her small sedan. Thank goodness no one was hurt. She called the police, and the pickup driver was found to be at fault. So why did Gail's premiums shoot up a whopping 15 percent?

Sometimes car insurance — like life — isn't fair. "Most people know that if they cause an accident or get a ticket, they could face a premium increase," says J. Robert Hunter, director of insurance for the Consumer Federation of America (CFA). "But they don't expect to be punished if a reckless driver careens into them."

The CFA is trying to make things right by convincing legislators to get rid of not-at-fault penalties. It's already the law in California and Oklahoma.

You use it, you lose it. So don't use it? Hunter points out another problem with these rate hikes. Penalizing drivers for being hit by another car discourages them from filing legitimate claims. "Lawmakers and regulators need to protect consumers from being punished when they've done nothing more than use the policy they have already paid for," he says.

Who's really on your side? Find out where your insurance company stands on this issue. Start by talking with your agent. If you find out that your premiums could climb — as Gail's did — you may want to consider changing to a company that won't charge you for an accident that's not your fault.

Policies vary. Of the five companies reviewed by the CFA, State Farm did not raise the rates of not-at-fault drivers, while other insurers charged up to 16 percent.

Crash for cash: Dodge these common highway cons

The Swoop and Squat. The Drive Down. They sound like positions you might learn at your yoga class, right? Wrong. These are just two of many staged highway scams aimed at unsuspecting drivers like you. Read on to find out how you can protect yourself — and your wallet — from fraud on the open road.

Accidentally on purpose? Staged auto accidents can be very expensive for everyone. According to the FBI, the total cost of non-health insurance fraud is more than $40 billion every year.

But what does that mean for you? In a nutshell, it means your family gets stuck paying between $400 and $700 in hiked-up premiums every year. All because a few bad guys are out to make some fast cash. Here are a few of their favorite cons.

▶ **The Drive Down.** You're trying to merge onto a highway. The criminal spots you and politely motions for you to merge in front of him. As you move into his lane, he speeds up and causes a collision. When questioned, the criminal insists he didn't motion for you to merge. And you're held liable.

▸ **The Wicked Waver.** In a twist on the Drive Down con, a criminal waves for you to turn left in front of him into a shopping center. When you do, he hits the gas — and smacks into you. You're found at fault because the person turning left must yield to oncoming traffic.

▸ **The Panic Stop.** An older car packed with passengers pulls in front of you. In this scam, a backseat passenger acts as the crook's lookout. When he notices that you're distracted by something — your cellphone, the radio, the car's air conditioner — he tells the driver to slam on the brakes. You panic and try to stop your car, but it's too late. You rear-end the criminal's car, and your insurance company ends up paying for damages and any injuries, real or imaginary, suffered by the passengers.

▸ **The Swoop and Squat.** This con involves three drivers — two criminals and you. The "squat" car pulls in front of you. The "swoop" car quickly pulls in front of the "squat" car, causing him to slam on brakes. You have no time to react and end up crashing into the "squat" car. The "swoop" vehicle vanishes in traffic. And you're left holding the bag for injuries and damages.

> If an accident happens, snap pics with your cellphone, or carry a disposable camera in your car. NICB's Frank Scafidi says, "Take pictures of your car, their car, and the damages. And particularly people who show up as occupants of the car you hit or as witnesses. They may all be part of the scam."

Put the skids on scams. Staged accidents can be very complicated and could include lots of fake witnesses, doctors, and legal advisors willing to give false testimony. Here are a few tips to help you protect yourself.

▶ Avoid tailgating. Always leave yourself plenty of room to stop your car.

▶ Don't get distracted. Keep your eyes on the road, not on your phone.

▶ If an accident happens, immediately call the police.

▶ Report the accident to your insurance company. Don't try to make a financial settlement at the accident scene by handing over cash.

▶ Shield yourself from identity theft. Be careful giving out your personal information.

▶ Use medical staff, lawyers, and auto mechanics you trust.

Steer clear of costly tow-truck scams

Most tow-truck companies are honest and responsible, but some untrustworthy operators could be out to scam innocent drivers. Be on the lookout for these three common cons.

Steering. You've had an accident, and a tow truck appears — seemingly out of nowhere. Actually, the trucker heard about your wreck while monitoring a police scanner. Now he insists on taking you to a body shop where he's in cohoots with the owner to defraud your insurance company.

You don't have to go with a tow truck that rolls onto the scene uninvited. Call a company yourself. And demand to have your car towed to the shop you choose.

Spot 'n scam. A tow-truck driver has an accomplice who spots a car parked — legally or illegally — on the side of the road. He calls the trucker, who hooks up the car and heads to a body shop or impound lot. The trucker, body shop, and impound lot, who are all in on the con, profit from inflated and unnecessary fees.

Towing companies must take pictures of the car's location to prove it was illegally parked. And they must contact the police to be sure the car hasn't been stolen. If you suspect a scam, ask to see copies of the photos. And don't be afraid to call the police.

Pocket-picking prices. The towing company inflates its prices far above what your insurance will pay, and you're stuck with hefty out-of-pocket fees.

Know in advance what your insurance will cover in regard to towing. Don't give out your insurance information to a towing operator. And request a price list that shows all the charges, including towage and daily storage fees.

In most states, the towing company must release your vehicle if you cannot — or will not — pay the towing fee. After that it will be left up to local courts to decide what payments need to be made.

If you dent a rental, are you sure you're insured?

It's finally here. The vacation of your dreams on a lovely tropical island, your woes and worries far, far away. Your hair blowing in the breeze as you zoom down the beach highway in your rental car, a cherry red convertible. Just you and the sea, the sand, the sun — and suddenly — the smashup?

Don't let your dream vacation take a turn down the road to disaster. Make sure your insurance has you covered.

Rental insurance is similar to regular insurance. When you sign the papers at the car rental counter, you'll be offered these policies.

▸ Collision Damage Waiver and Loss Damage Waiver. These policies waive your responsibility for damage or theft. Expect to pay $9 to $19 a day.

▸ Supplemental Liability Coverage. This policy increases your liability coverage up to $1 million. You'll pay $7 to $15 each day.

▸ Personal Accident Insurance. If you or your passengers are injured or killed in an accident, this policy will pay medical and accidental death benefits. And it'll cost you $1 to $7 a day.

▸ Personal Effects Coverage. If your laptop, luggage or any other personal property is stolen from your rental, this insurance will reimburse you. But be prepared to plunk down $1 to $5 per day for this policy.

If you opt for all the coverage, rental car insurance could tack on almost $50 to your bill every day.

Want to save but still stay covered? Try these tips to pile on protection and watch out for your wallet.

▸ Don't double up your coverage. If you own or lease a car, check with your insurer about your coverage before you pay for rental insurance. In most cases, whatever coverage you have on your own car will apply when you rent a car. Deductibles, too.

▸ Do you still have collision and comprehensive coverage? If you dropped these because you drive an older car, or just to save money, you may not be covered if the rental is stolen or damaged. Check your policies.

▸ Does your homeowners policy — not your car insurance — provide coverage if your possessions are lost or stolen from your car? If so, the same kind of coverage should apply to your rental.

Don't forget about your credit card coverage. The card you use for your rental might provide some protection for you. It may only cover your deductible, but it's worth checking into.

▸ Card colors matter. Higher level cards like platinum or onyx may offer more benefits than, say, standard green or blue. Coverage also depends on the company or bank that issues the card.

▸ Credit card benefits are usually secondary, too. In other words, your credit card coverage won't chip in until after your personal insurance pays up.

▸ Contact your credit card company to find out what's covered. Ask a representative to send you the details in writing.

Personal insurance

The best protection at rock-bottom prices

5 smart reasons to use a health savings account

Ah, retirement. You've been saving for years, preparing for this moment. So what if you've been a little nutty about squirreling away every dollar you could get your hands on. Your IRA and 401(k) are almost bursting at the seams, ready to pay your way through the golden years.

Or so you think. But did you know the average 65-year-old couple retiring today will need $280,000 to cover their health care costs in retirement? Yikes. Don't let medical bills drain your cash stash. Keep your golden years green with a health savings account (HSA).

An HSA is sort of like your personal savings account — but it's just for medical expenses. You deposit money in, and you take it out when you need to pay a qualified medical expense. And if you're lucky, your employer may contribute, too.

Sounds great. But there's more. Your HSA offers a few perks you might not expect.

You'll profit from a trio of tax breaks. First, the contributions to your HSA are not taxed. Secondly, the withdrawals you make to pay for qualified medical expenses are also tax-free. And finally, the interest earned on the money in your HSA is — you guessed it — tax-free, too.

It's yours to keep. In other words, you own it. And an HSA is portable. So if you change employers or retire, the account goes where you go.

You don't lose what you don't spend. If you don't spend all the cash in your account during the year, your balance just rolls over to the next year, earning interest all the while.

Your spouse is covered, too. You can use your HSA money to cover your spouse's and dependent's medical expenses — even if they're not listed on your health plan.

Time is on your side. Pay a qualified medical expense with cash rather than dipping into your HSA, and you have an unlimited amount of time to reimburse yourself. Just hang on to your receipts. You can withdraw the money for those costs tax-free at any time — even years down the road.

To open an HSA, check with your employer's human resources department to find a participating bank or credit union. Or search online for "HSA providers." Next, complete an application and start funding your account. You can contribute up to $3,450 individually or $6,900 for a family per year. Over 55? Tack on $1,000 to those numbers.

ALERT

Steer clear of this taxing HSA mistake

Chomping at the bit to sign up for Medicare, but still paying into your health savings account? Hold your horses. If you want to keep contributing to your HSA, you'll have to delay your Medicare enrollment — or you'll face a tax penalty.

The reason? In order to contribute to an HSA, you can't have any health insurance other than your high deductible health plan (HDHP). So hold off on Medicare if you expect to keep your employer's HDHP as your primary coverage.

Here's something else you need to know. If you're 65 and still contributing to your HSA, put off those Social Security checks. Starting your Social Security automatically signs you up for Medicare Part A — and it's retroactive for six months. If you pay into your HSA during those six months before your Social Security starts, you'll end up paying tax on those contributions.

Qualify for an HSA: It's as easy as 1, 2, 3

More than 22 million people already reap the benefits of health savings accounts. "More than ever, patients want value from their coverage, choice in their health services, and control of dollars they spend on care," says Jeanette Thornton, senior vice president of America's Health Insurance Plans, explaining why these accounts are so popular.

So do you qualify for an HSA? Here are the three basic requirements, according to the IRS.

▶ You must be covered by a high deductible health plan (HDHP) on the first day of the month. For example, your minimum insurance deductible should be about $1,350 for individuals or $2,700 for families.

▶ You have no other health coverage, including Medicare.

▶ You can't be claimed as a dependent on someone else's tax return.

Stretch your health care dollars with a flexible spending account

In the 1700s, William Shippen ran a profitable medical practice in Philadelphia. How did the common folk pay the good doctor for his services? Ledgers show payments of tea, silk stockings — even a lottery ticket. But the days of bartering coffee for cough syrup are long gone. How will you pay the rising costs of today's health care? A flexible spending account (FSA) might just fit the bill.

An FSA allows you to save money to pay for qualified medical expenses, just like health savings accounts do. And, like an HSA, flexible spending accounts are tax-free — and that leaves you with more money in your pocket. But there are a few differences you need to know about.

▶ Your employer has to set up your account. You can't do it yourself.

▶ Contributions are limited to $2,650, but that amount can change annually.

- The full amount of your FSA is available to you at the beginning of the year — or as soon as you make your first deposit.

- You can use an FSA with any health insurance plan, not just a high deductible plan.

- If you don't use up your savings by the end of the year — or in some cases, March 15 of the following year — you may lose any money left in your account.

- Some employers may allow you to roll over $500 to the next year.

Personal finance expert Manisha Thakor is a big fan of FSAs. "As consumers' out-of-pocket health costs continue to creep upward, a flexible spending account is one of the best ways to reduce the impact of these high costs on your family's budget," she says. "The bottom line is that an FSA will help you to keep more of your hard-earned money."

HSA and FSA: Your heath plan's one-two punch

The jab and right cross are two of the most powerful punches in a boxing match. Land them just right, and it's lights out for your opponent. Wish you had a surefire way to KO your mounting health care costs? Pair up your HSA with a special FSA for a combo that will have those bills down for the count in no time.

Special FSA picks up the slack for your HSA. The IRS doesn't usually let you contribute to a health savings account (HSA) and a flexible savings account (FSA) in the same year. But if your employer OKs it, you may be able to pair your health spending account with an HSA-compatible flexible savings account, also known as a limited-purpose account (LPFSA).

You can contribute up to $2,600 to your LPFSA, just like a regular FSA, but you can only use the money for eligible dental and vision expenses. That's where the term "limited-purpose" comes in.

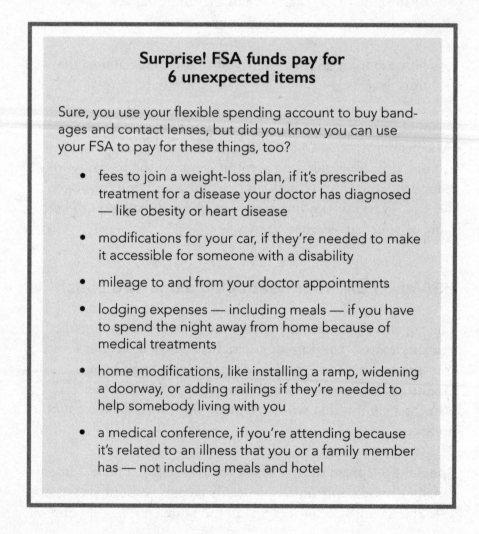

Surprise! FSA funds pay for 6 unexpected items

Sure, you use your flexible spending account to buy bandages and contact lenses, but did you know you can use your FSA to pay for these things, too?

- fees to join a weight-loss plan, if it's prescribed as treatment for a disease your doctor has diagnosed — like obesity or heart disease

- modifications for your car, if they're needed to make it accessible for someone with a disability

- mileage to and from your doctor appointments

- lodging expenses — including meals — if you have to spend the night away from home because of medical treatments

- home modifications, like installing a ramp, widening a doorway, or adding railings if they're needed to help somebody living with you

- a medical conference, if you're attending because it's related to an illness that you or a family member has — not including meals and hotel

Your LPFSA helps your HSA grow. So why pay those expenses with a LPFSA instead of your HSA? First, the money in your LPFSA doesn't earn interest. But your HSA does. Secondly, you don't own your LPFSA. That means if you change jobs or retire, the money in your account goes back to your employer. But an HSA is yours to keep no matter what — all the way through retirement.

Special benefit is up to the boss. If your employer is willing, you may be able to use your LPFSA money for regular qualified medical expenses — not just vision and dental — after you've met your health care deductible for the year. All you have to do is roll your leftover funds into a regular FSA. Then you can use the extra money for any other eligible health costs you have that year. Thanks, Boss.

Making sense of Medicare and Medicaid: Your benefits in a nutshell

July 30, 1965. A great day to be a senior adult in America. On that day, President Lyndon Johnson signed the Medicare and Medicaid health plans into law. Harry Truman was on hand to receive the very first Medicare card — rather appropriate since the former president was the first to propose national health insurance way back in 1945.

But now it's your name on that red, white, and blue card. So what benefits are you entitled to? Read on to find out.

The ABCs of Medicare. The four parts of this health care plan cover medical expenses for people who are over 65 or have special health conditions.

▶ Part A will pay for expenses like inpatient care in a hospital, hospice, or a skilled nursing facility. If you paid into the Medicare system for at least 10 years while you were working, Part A coverage is premium-free. But don't forget about the annual deductible.

▶ Part B covers outpatient care like doctor visits, flu shots, and some screening tests. You'll pay an annual deductible as well as monthly premiums. If you receive Social Security, your Part B premiums will be deducted from your check. If you don't get Social Security yet, you'll get a monthly Medicare Premium Bill instead.

▶ Part C includes Medicare Advantage plans. These are managed-care plans that pay for everything covered by traditional Medicare, which includes parts A and B, along with extra benefits like vision, dental, and hearing. You can choose either a Medicare Advantage plan or traditional Medicare — but not both. Want traditional Medicare but still need extra coverage? You can always add a Medigap policy, also known as Medicare supplement insurance, to help fill in the gaps.

> If you qualify for both Medicare and Medicaid, you are "dual eligible." This means most, or perhaps all, of your health care costs will be covered. Medicaid will pay for your Medicare Part A and Part B premiums, copayments, and deductibles — even some Part D drug costs. To find out if you're eligible for Medicaid, contact your state's program.

▶ Part D is your prescription drug coverage. Harry Truman didn't have the option to sign up for this part of Medicare, but you do. You can choose from a number of different drug plans, but you'll have to pay an average premium of $34 per month.

Medicaid — a safety net for those at risk. This program provides health coverage to millions of low-income Americans, including children, the elderly, and people with disabilities. Your state has its own eligibility standards, but the primary oversight of the program is in the hands of the feds.

Medicaid covers the following services — and many more — for eligible people.

▶ inpatient and outpatient hospital services

▶ physician services

▶ nursing facility services for people 21 and older

▶ home health care for people eligible for skilled nursing services

▶ lab and X-ray services

To find out more about your benefits and what you're entitled to, visit *Medicare.gov* and *Medicaid.gov*.

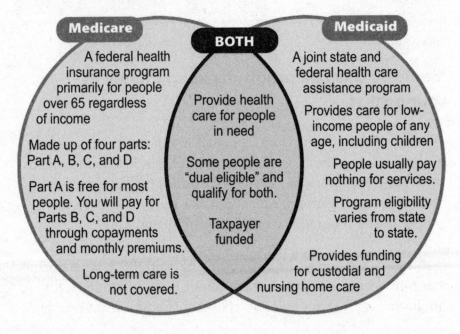

Medicare

A federal health insurance program primarily for people over 65 regardless of income

Made up of four parts: Part A, B, C, and D

Part A is free for most people. You will pay for Parts B, C, and D through copayments and monthly premiums.

Long-term care is not covered.

BOTH

Provide health care for people in need

Some people are "dual eligible" and qualify for both.

Taxpayer funded

Medicaid

A joint state and federal health care assistance program

Provides care for low-income people of any age, including children

People usually pay nothing for services.

Program eligibility varies from state to state.

Provides funding for custodial and nursing home care

Got Medicare questions?
Go here for answers

Has the whole Medicare process got you stymied? Are you addled by Part A? Baffled by Part B? And you don't even want to get started on the whole Medigap versus Medicare Advantage muddle. Befuddling, to say the least.

Fortunately, the National Council on Aging offers an online assessment tool to help you figure out all you need to know about Medicare.

To get started, go online to *mymedicarematters.org/take-an-assessment.* Answer a few basic questions, and you'll get personalized advice on how to get the health care coverage that's right for you. The site will even spell out what enrollment periods you need to keep an eye out for. And you'll find lots of videos, easy-to-understand infographics, and a helpful glossary of Medicare terms — all designed to make signing up for Medicare muddle-free.

Medicare savings programs keep money in your pocket

"Who's FICA and why does he get all my money?" demanded Rachel Green of "Friends" fame as she stared at her first paycheck. Most American workers know FICA stands for the Federal Insurance Contributions Act, a law that funds Social Security and Medicare programs through payroll deductions.

If you're 65, worked at least 10 years, and paid FICA taxes during that time, you don't have to worry about paying premiums for Medicare Part A. They're already covered. And for most people, your Part B premiums will be automatically deducted from your Social Security check every month.

But if you haven't worked long enough to be eligible for Medicare, you can still enroll when you turn 65 — or in certain cases, if you are disabled before age 65. Just be prepared to pay the Part A and Part B premiums yourself. Here are four programs that could help you pay those bills.

Qualified Medicare Beneficiary (QMB) Program. The QMB program provides financial assistance for Part A and Part B premiums, deductibles, coinsurance, and copayments. To qualify, you must have a monthly income below $1,032 if you're single, or $1,392 if you're married. Your resource limit must be below $7,560 for an individual or $11,340 for married couples.

Qualified Disabled and Working Individuals (QDWI) Program. QDWI assistance pays for your Part A premiums only. To qualify, you must be a disabled working person under the age of 65, and you can't be receiving medical assistance through your state. Your individual monthly income must be less than $4,132 for an individual, or $5,572 for a married couple.

Specified Low-income Medicare Beneficiary (SLMB) Program. This program is designed to pay for Part B premiums only. If your individual monthly income is below $1,234 — or $1,666 for married couples — you may qualify. But your resources must total less than $7,560 for an individual or $11,340 for a married couple.

Qualifying Individual (QI) Program. This is another program that will pay Part B premiums only. You must have a monthly income below $1,386 for individuals and $1,872 for married couples in order to qualify. And resource limits are the same as for SLMB.

However, you must apply every year for QI, and you can't receive benefits if you qualify for Medicaid. QI applications are granted on a first-come, first-served basis, and people who got QI benefits the previous year are given priority.

Need more information? These savings programs are available through your state. You'll find the contact information you need at *medicaid.gov/about-us/contact-us/contact-state-page.html*.

ALERT

Hit the sign-up sweet spot or pay the penalty

Approaching 65? The way you sign up for Medicare depends on your Social Security status.

- You're already getting Social Security benefits. The Social Security Administration will automatically enroll you in Medicare Parts A and B. But because you have to pay a premium for Part B coverage, you can turn it down.

- You're not getting Social Security benefits. You can apply for Medicare starting three months before and up to three months after the month of your birthday.

Beware. If you miss your sign-up window for Part A, you may have to pay a penalty premium for twice the number of years you were eligible for Part A but didn't sign up. And if you don't enroll in Part B when you're first eligible, but decide later that you want it, you may have to pay a late enrollment penalty for as long as you need coverage.

Make the most of annual Medicare freebies

When it comes to text messaging, teenagers certainly have their own language, don't they? For example, there's LOL for "laugh out loud" or BTW for "by the way."

Time to learn some text speak just right for the senior set — CBM stands for "covered by Medicare." You'll be texting that one to all your friends when you discover the free benefits you get as part of your health care plan. THX, Medicare!

Here's a list of some of the yearly screenings and tests covered by Medicare Part B that are absolutely FFA — that's "free for all" in text speak — as long as your doctor agrees to accept the Medicare-approved amount as full payment for his services.

▸ a seasonal preventive shot for the flu, and vaccines for pneumonia and hepatitis B

▸ a screening mammogram

▸ a visit to talk with your doctor about your risk for cardio-vascular disease

▸ a prostate-specific antigen (PSA) blood test that screens for prostate cancer

▸ a wellness checkup that will likely include a review of your prescriptions, along with personalized medical advice to keep you healthy

▸ a screening for depression that should take place in a primary care setting — like your doctor's office — where you can get follow-up treatment and referrals if needed

Scammers use new card to swindle seniors

Your bright new Medicare card has probably popped up in your mailbox by now. You love its snazzy look and its smart, computer-generated numbers specially designed to protect your info. No more Social Security number on display for the world to see.

But beware. Your new card still comes with the same old crooks and ne'er-do-wells looking to make a bundle at your expense. Keep an eye out for these scams.

The refund rip-off. In this swindle, you get a phone call from someone identifying himself as a Medicare representative. The caller explains that with a new card, you're eligible for a refund of premiums or drug costs. The scammer asks you for your banking information so he can set up a transfer to wire you the money.

Stop! Don't ever give your bank account numbers over the phone. If you were really entitled to a refund, you'd get a check in the mail.

> Look closely. Your brand-new Medicare card will be sporting a newfangled 11-character code where your Social Security number (SSN) used to be. It's officially called your Medicare Beneficiary Identifier, or MBI for short. Guard it just like you do your SSN. Give it only to doctors, pharmacists, and health care providers you trust.

The fee fleecer. Scammers call to tell you that a small fee is required to pay for your new Medicare card. They may insist that you verify your identity — in other words, give them sensitive information like bank account details and your Social Security number.

Don't fall for the fee fleece. Your new card is completely free. And Medicare will never ask you to give your personal information over the phone.

The health care hustler. A scammer calls you, claiming to be from your insurance provider. He wants to verify your personal information over the phone so he can send you a new Medicare card. When you refuse to give him the information, he gets very angry and threatens to cancel your health care coverage.

Yikes! Don't give in to his threats. Hang up and reach out to the folks at Medicare to report the scam. Call 800-633-4227.

New law sure to perk up your ears

A federal law just turned expensive hearing aids on their, um, ears. The Over-the-Counter Hearing Aid Act allows adults with mild to moderate hearing loss to buy over-the-counter (OTC) hearing aids without first seeing a hearing care professional like an audiologist. Under this law, the FDA will regulate OTC hearing aids, making sure they meet high standards for safety and manufacturing.

According to *Consumer Reports*, people who purchase hearing aids face an average out-of-pocket expense of more than $2,700. It's still unclear how much cash this new law will save you.

But Barbara Kelley, executive director of the Hearing Loss Association of America (HLAA) says, "This legislation offers hope that the cost of all hearing aids will go down with the anticipated market innovation and competition it will bring. Everyone who needs hearing aids should be able to have them to stay connected to family, remain on the job, and enjoy a high quality of life."

Take the quiz: How Medicare savvy are you?

You think traditional Medicare's got you covered for things like eyeglasses, dentures, and hearing aids, but are you sure? Take this quiz to see just how benefit-savvy you really are.

Eyeglasses. The print in your favorite cookbook has gotten so small you're dragging out a magnifying glass to read the measurements. Time for new glasses. That's OK, though, because your Medicare Part B will cover the entire cost of your new specs. True or false?

False — unless the glasses are required as a follow-up for a type of cataract surgery. Then you'll pay 20 percent of the Medicare-approved amount for one pair of glasses. Your Part B deductible applies.

Hearing check. You've always liked to crank up the volume on your Fleetwood Mac CDs, but your neighbors have started complaining that the thumping bass is knocking their pictures right off the walls. Maybe it's time to get your hearing checked. Thank goodness Medicare Part B pays for a hearing exam. True or false?

True. But the exam must be ordered by your doctor and must be performed by a qualified audiologist. If you need a hearing aid, though, you're out of luck. They're not covered by traditional Medicare Part B.

An out-of-the-country emergency. You're driving home from a dream vacation — a cruise along the Alaskan coast. Still miles away from the U.S. border, you run into some fierce weather and end up in an accident. An ambulance rushes you to a local Canadian hospital, where you're treated in the emergency room for a broken arm. Thankfully, your medical care is covered by Medicare. True or false?

True. But only if you're traveling through Canada by the most direct route between Alaska and another state — and the Canadian hospital is closer than the nearest U.S. facility that can treat you. And that's a very special situation. Most medical care outside the United States will not be covered by your traditional Medicare.

Dental care. Pearly whites lost their sparkle? Just flash that Medicare card at the dentist office, and you'll be treated to a free cleaning. And while you're at it, might as well update those X-rays. It is free, after all. True or false?

False. Unless it's an emergency or a complicated dental procedure, traditional Medicare will not cover your dental work. You're on your own for dentures, too.

Did you know all the answers? Good for you. If not, you can check out the Medicare website at *medicare.gov/coverage/is-your-test-item-or-service-covered.html.* Just click on the service or condition you have a question about, and you'll be guided to the information you need.

Buying medical supplies: A little hassle, a lot of savings

Debbie's mom needed a new walker. No problem. Medicare's got this, right? So with the doctor's prescription in hand, Debbie headed to the nearby medical supply store to pick out a sparkling red rolling walker.

Hold on, Deb. Did you check to see if Mom lives in a Medicare competitive bidding area? If so, getting that shiny new walker just went from a simple stroll in the park to a hike through the Medicare maze.

So what is Medicare's competitive bidding program? Its official title is Durable Medical Equipment, Prosthetics, Orthotics, and Supplies (DMEPOS) Competitive Bidding Program. Leave it to the Feds to come up with a name like that.

Under this program, medical equipment stores submit bids to the government to provide traditional Medicare beneficiaries with certain durable medical supplies like wheelchairs, walkers, oxygen tanks, and other items. Medicare then awards contracts to the suppliers who offer the best price and meet their quality and financial standards.

Here's how the pricing works. If you live in a competitive bidding area and you don't buy your supplies from an approved store, you'll pay full price. For example, at a local discount store — not an approved supplier — the price for the walker was about $150. But when Debbie took her paperwork to the approved supplier in her area, the price dropped to 20 percent of the $150, or around $30 — as long as Mom's Part B deductible of about $130 was already paid for the year.

> To buy your item at a Medicare-approved store, your doctor's order must include a detailed description of the item you need, your full name, the date of the order, and your doctor's signature and date. And you may need an additional written order that includes an ICD-9-CM diagnosis code, too. Questions? Ask your doctor's staff for help.

An easy fix for your Medicare denial

Medicare is notorious for denying claims. In fact, out of the nearly 5 million claims filed every day, a staggering 10 percent are denied. And out of those, 2 percent — that's about 92,000 claims — are turned down because of missing or incorrect information like faulty medical codes. Oops, wrong number.

Are you facing a Medicare denial? Well, before you begin the exhausting appeals process, try this simple solution. Call your doctor's office to make sure the proper codes were used when the staff filed your paperwork. An easy-peasy solution that could save you time and trouble.

How do you know if you're in a competitive bidding area? It all depends on your ZIP code. Most of the competitive bidding areas are in highly populated urban areas. From California to the New York island, as the song goes.

But some states have no competitive bidding areas — namely Alaska, Maine, Montana, North and South Dakota, Vermont, and Wyoming. If you live in those states, or in an area without competitive bidding, you can buy your supplies from any store that accepts Medicare. Generally, you'll pay 20 percent of the Medicare-approved price, as long as your Part B deductible has been paid.

To find out if you live in a competitive bidding area, go to *medicare.gov/supplierdirectory/search.html*. Enter your ZIP code and click Go. Check the box next to the product you're interested in, and then click Search at the bottom of the page. You'll see a list of Medicare-approved suppliers in your area where you'll get the discounted price.

How does it work with Medicare Advantage (MA) plans?

The competitive bidding program only applies to traditional Medicare beneficiaries. Medicare Advantage should cover the same items as traditional Medicare, but your costs will depend on your MA plan. If you need durable medical equipment like a wheelchair or walker, call your plan representative to find out how much you'll have to pay.

Plugging the gaps: Pick a plan that's right for you

Decisions, decisions. There's the very complicated kind — get married or stay single? Or the very simple ones — paper or plastic? But now it's time to make some important decisions about your Medicare coverage. For example, what plan offers the best bridge to get you across that financially fearsome Medicare gap? A PPO? An HMO? A Medigap plan? Let the info below guide you into making one of your best decisions yet.

Medicare Advantage plans and Medicare Supplement plans, also known as Medigap, are designed to help you pay the deductibles and copayments not covered through Medicare parts A and B. These charges include things like the $1,300 hospital deductible you'll pay each time you're admitted to the hospital. And the 20 percent copayment you'll foot for outpatient treatments, including doctor visits.

A Medicare Advantage (MA) plan with no monthly premium? Sounds great, but before you sign on the dotted line, know that zero-premium MA plans aren't really free. Many of these plans include higher copayments or other out-of-pocket expenses. And you'll still have to pay your Part B premium, too.

Check out this side-by-side comparison to see how Medigap and Medicare Advantage plans measure up.

	Medicare Supplement (Medigap)	Medicare Advantage (Part C)
Purpose	• Private health insurance plans • Helps you pay Medicare's out-of-pocket expenses	• Private health insurance plans, usually HMOs and PPOs • Alternative to traditional Medicare
Plans	• Only available to people enrolled in traditional Medicare • Benefits of each policy type are the same across different insurers, but prices vary	• You cannot have traditional Medicare and a Medicare Advantage plan at the same time • Must have all the same benefits covered by traditional Medicare
Coverage	• Covers Part A hospital deductibles and some Part B costs • You must buy a Part D plan if you want prescription drug coverage	• Often includes vision and hearing benefits • Prescription drug coverage often included at no extra cost
Premiums	• Monthly premiums range from less than $100 to more than $400 • You pay Part B premiums as usual	• Monthly premiums range from $0 to more than $300 • You're still responsible for Part B premiums
Networks	• You can go to any health care provider that accepts Medicare • You don't need referrals to see specialists	• Most require you to see health care providers in an assigned network • You may need referrals to see specialists

The official Medicare website makes it easy for you to compare plans and pick out your best options.

▶ For Medigap policies in your area, visit *medicare.gov/find-a-plan/questions/medigap-home.aspx*.

▶ To view Medicare health plans, visit *medicare.gov/find-a-plan/questions/home.aspx*.

Sick of medical bills? 3 tips to make you feel all better

Are your sky-high medical bills causing you to toss and turn from dusk till dawn? Debt may be costing you more than just sleepless nights. Studies show people with health issues get sicker if they're also dealing with money problems. And researchers at the University of Michigan and Northwestern University now know that losing three-fourths of your hard-earned nest egg over the course of two years — perhaps as you try to pay off whopping health care bills — makes you more likely to die within the next 20 years. Yikes.

So how can you lower those bills and reduce your stress? After all, insurance companies get a discount. Why shouldn't you? Hang on. Help is on the way. Here are three tips that can help you lower your medical bills by as much as 30 percent.

▶ **Dicker with your doctor.** Schedule some time to talk honestly with your physician about your financial situation. Feel a little awkward? Then bargain with the billing manager instead. Some medical offices, including specialists, may offer up to 30 percent off your bill — but you have to be willing to ask.

▸ **Set up a payment plan.** Many medical offices will allow you to make payments at a very low interest rate, or even interest-free. That's a real savings boost to your bottom line.

▸ **Pay with cash on the barrelhead.** Before heading off to the doctor's office, check online at *healthcarebluebook.com* to find a fair price for a doctor in your area. In some cases, Healthcare Bluebook will even list the local providers who will offer discounts if you pay cash ahead of time. Something to keep in mind, especially if you're uninsured or have a plan with a high deductible.

Take the pain out of prescriptions — get your meds for free

When Barbara saw the price tag for her elderly mother's new prescription, she did a double take. More than $450 for just one month! Did the pharmacist add a digit to the price by mistake? And to make matters worse, this medicine wasn't covered by her mom's Medicare plan.

But instead of pulling out her credit card to foot the bill, Barbara pulled out her cellphone — and ended up getting the medicine for free. How did she do that? Read on to discover her secret.

Don't pay for prescription drugs — get them free. In a survey of more than 2,000 seniors, nearly 30 percent said paying for their meds put them in a financial bind. So is it surprising that many seniors decide not to fill a prescription — or cut down on the dosage — just to save a little cash?

But nearly half of the folks who couldn't afford their meds hadn't taken the time to talk to their doctors about the high cost of their prescriptions. There's good news for those who did, though. Two-thirds of the people who went to their doctors for help got their high-priced drug swapped for a less expensive one.

And some folks even walk out of the doctor's office with free samples. Take Barbara for example. Calling her mom's doctor netted her a month's worth of free pills. And here's something else to consider. Trying a medicine before you buy it helps you and your doctor decide if it's the right option for you.

Table the cost of pricey prescriptions. Still on the hunt for a better deal? Head over to your supermarket and ask the pharmacist about free medicines they offer. It's a great way to stretch your budget. Here are just a few of the freebies you might find at stores near you.

Free medication	Store
Certain antibiotics	BI-LO, Harveys, Meijer, Publix, Winn-Dixie
Certain blood pressure meds	BI-LO, Harveys, Publix, Winn-Dixie
Certain diabetes meds	BI-LO, Harveys, Meijer, Price Chopper, Publix, ShopRite, Winn-Dixie

Rx for a secure ID: Take steps to keep your privacy in the pink

You never go online or use a credit card, so you think you're safe from identity theft. But wait — the prescription you just filled at the local pharmacy could place you at risk. Pharmacies store tons of data about your medical history. And while they're not technically allowed to give out those details, your personal info may still end up in the clutches of con artists.

Your pharmacy might be selling you out — literally. Pharmacies can remove personal details from your prescription records and sell the profiles to companies known as data miners. These agencies then send junk mail and emails about new drugs to folks who match your profile.

The scary part is some companies have even found ways to link your profile to you, allowing them to target you directly. Read the fine print to see if your pharmacy participates in data-sharing programs. If they do, ask to opt out.

Guard your health history to keep records in fine fettle. Even if a pharmacy doesn't share your data, computer hackers and garbage thieves could still get their hands on medical records and financial details. They may use the info to buy insurance, drugs, or expensive medical treatments in your name — unless you take steps to keep your secrets safe.

▶ Avoid giving out personal information over the phone or email unless you kick off the conversation. Scammers often claim to work for pharmacies, doctor's offices, and insurance agencies.

▶ When you finish a prescription, black out the label or tear it up before you throw the bottle away or toss it in the recycling bin.

▶ Review your medical and insurance documents on a regular basis to make sure that all the claims match your treatments. If you catch a mistake, report it before it costs you big.

In the works: Surprising new benefits from Medicare Advantage plans

A lift to the doctor? Home-delivered meals? Air conditioning to help your asthma? Just a few of the unexpected benefits that could soon be available through your Medicare Advantage (MA) plan.

Many MA plans already include vision, hearing, and dental benefits not covered by traditional Medicare. But under the new guidelines proposed by the Centers for Medicare & Medicaid Services, your MA plan may also pay for additional services and equipment to help with physical impairments or certain health conditions. For example, your new perks could include home modifications, like bathroom grab bars, or aides to help you with the daily activities of dressing and eating.

That's great news for the 20 million Americans enrolled in Medicare Advantage programs across the country. Keep your eyes peeled for updates.

Turn that frown upside down with a great dental deal

Four-year-old Billy was fascinated by the sight of his grand-mother cleaning her dentures. He sat spellbound as she carefully took them out, scrubbed and rinsed them, and then popped them back in place. "Cool, Nana!" he exclaimed. "Now take off your arm!"

Little Billy didn't know that in today's world, proper dental care could cost his beloved Nana an arm and a leg. But take heart. You can find dental care you can actually afford.

Tooth trouble? Don't just grin and bear it. Dental care is pricey, no doubt about it. And the cost depends on where you live, too. For example, in the Southern U.S., your dentist may charge between $88 and $105 for a cleaning. Dentists out on the West Coast, however, could charge you upwards of $140. And in New York City, you may have to shell out close to $200.

No matter where you live, you'll be pleased to know that you can keep your pearly whites whiter — and pay a whole lot less to keep them that way — through a little-known govern- ment program that does what most Medicare plans can't. Find the help you need at the Bureau of Primary Health Care (BPHC), a part of the U.S. Department of Health & Human Services.

> To find a BPHC health center, go to the website *bphc.hrsa.gov* and type in your location at the bottom of the page. Or give them a call at the BPHC helpline, 877-974-2742.

No need to put your money where your mouth is. The BPHC works with health centers around the country to offer quality health care — including dental — to low-income people on a sliding fee scale. You'll receive care even if you can't pay at all.

But what kind of services will you receive? Everything you'd expect from a traditional dentist. Cleanings, fluoride treatments, fillings, and extractions, just to name a few. Nana can even get her dentures checked. And don't worry. All services are per- formed by licensed dentists and hygienists.

Give yourself a little financial TLC with LTCi

You're getting old, America. In fact, by 2030 over 60 million people will be part of the group called the "young old" — folks aged 66 to 84. That's you, baby boomer.

And the costs of the long-term care you may need are staggering. Some $40,000 for a year in an assisted living facility, and up to more than $91,000 annually for a private room in a nursing home. Maybe it's time to think about paying for your old-age TLC with LTCi, aka long-term care insurance.

"Americans generally live long past retirement, but all too many do so without adequate financial security," says Sharona Hoffman, author and law professor at the Case Western Reserve University School of Law. "Meager savings make it extremely difficult for retirees to cover their out-of-pocket medical costs, often reaching thousands of dollars each year."

Long-term care insurance is designed to help you pay for the services you might need down the road, including things like dressing, bathing, and eating. In insurance speak, these are known as the activities of daily living.

But do you really need long-term care insurance? Let these four questions help you decide if LTCi is right for you.

Are you working hard at staying healthy? That's great. Live long and prosper. But your healthy lifestyle probably means you'll be celebrating birthdays far into your 90s. And more birthdays can add up to more care. It's time to start pricing LTCi.

What's the ideal age to begin your search? Premium prices are best for shoppers between the ages of 52 and 64, the sweet spot in LTCi. After that, expect to pay more for your coverage.

Want more information? Remember, long-term care policies vary in the amount and type of services they cover. Contact a licensed insurance agent, broker, financial planner, or insurance company for advice about choosing the policy that's best for you.

Anything shaking in your family's health tree? Take a look back at your parents, grandparents, aunts, and uncles. Did they need help from family members later in life? Having insurance means you won't be a burden to your family if you need extra care as you age.

How do your numbers add up? If you don't have a lot of income, and you haven't saved a lot over the years, you'll probably count on Medicaid to help with your senior care. On the other hand, if you're a millionaire with a healthy pension, you'll likely be able to handle your own expenses. If you're in the middle of these two examples, LTCi might be just what you need.

Are the odds in your favor? Close to 7 out of 10 people over age 65 suffer cognitive problems or are unable to complete two activities of daily living, reports the American Association for Long-Term Care Insurance. But for you personally, the odds of needing long-term care are pretty simple. Either you'll need it or you won't. But if you do end up needing it, you'll be glad you have it.

5 clever ways to beat skyrocketing premiums

The numbers say it all. In the past decade, long-term care insurance (LTCi) premiums have jumped a colossal 60 percent. Those surging prices can be a bitter pill to swallow. But if you've been making the premium payments for years, it might be a mistake to quit now — just when you're getting close to needing the coverage.

Before you pull the plug on your policy, try these cost-saving tips.

Lower your daily benefit amount. Check the average costs for nursing home or assisted living care in your area, and decide how much you could afford to pay out of pocket for their services. Making a simple switch from a benefit of $250 per day to $200 per day could really impact your premium — for the better.

Shorten your coverage period. If your policy provides benefits for a lifetime, switch to a three- or four-year benefit period instead.

Reduce your inflation protection. This option is designed to help your policy keep up with rising health care costs. Lowering your inflation protection from 4 to 2 percent could make a nice dent in that pricey premium.

Make the switch to a paid-up policy. Your insurer may let you stop paying premiums altogether. Instead, you'll have a paid-up policy that will equal the amount you've already shelled out in premiums over the years. But this means if you've paid $20,000 in premiums so far, that would be the maximum you could get in benefits if you need care later on.

Cancel extra riders. A rider is an optional benefit you may have added to your policy when you bought it. Riders might include special benefits for your spouse or perhaps a provision for home health care. If you cancel a rider, your premium goes down. But you lose that special coverage, too.

Before you make changes to your LTCi, review your options carefully. Talk about your choices with family members, your financial advisor, or an insurance agent.

Solve your life insurance dilemma — love it or lose it?

For the "if" in life. Like a good neighbor. You're in good hands. Catchy tag lines from well-known insurance companies, all designed to make you feel warm and fuzzy about protecting your loved ones with generous life insurance payouts.

But after you retire and the kids are grown and gone, is it time to stop shelling out big bucks for that pricey policy? Try this out. Put yourself in Will and Wendy's shoes. What would you do about life insurance? Would you love it, or lose it?

Don't get caught in a pension pickle. Will and Wendy are enjoying their retirement, thanks to Will's generous monthly pension. But if something happens to Will, Wendy will lose his pension, and her income will be reduced to a meager Social Security check. Should Will and Wendy love or lose their life insurance?

▸ Love it. Hang on to that insurance if someone is financially dependent on you — your spouse, an elderly parent, or a disabled adult child, for example. "If anyone depends on you, if anyone would be hurt without your income or assets, then you need life insurance to protect those people," says Laura Adams, personal finance expert and host of the top-rated *Money Girl* podcast.

And by naming multiple beneficiaries, you can give a certain amount to several people — without buying multiple policies.

Look for a long-term solution. When Will was 30, he bought a life insurance policy to provide for his family in case something happened to him. But now the kids have all finished college and moved away to launch their careers. Will is well into his 60s and is considering long-term care insurance (LTCi), but it costs a small fortune. Is it time to lose the life insurance in favor of LTCi?

▸ Will could cancel his policy and put the payments toward a new long-term care policy. But it's possible he could convert his life insurance to a long-term care plan in the future, so he may want to "love" it a while longer. According to the U.S. government's Administration on Aging, you can only apply for a conversion if you have an immediate need for long-term care. For more information, go to *longtermcare.acl.gov*, and click on Costs & How To Pay. Or talk with an insurance agent about your options.

Make the house their home. Wendy would like to leave the family home to her kids. But it still has a mortgage that may be more than her family can pay. And her life insurance premiums aren't really that expensive. Love it or lose it?

▸ Love it — if it's not posing a financial hardship for you. Your life insurance policy may be just what your family needs to pay off that mortgage.

So when is it time for Will and Wendy to drop their life insurance? Financial experts say when both partners have enough assets and income to be financially secure through retirement — and the children are self-sufficient adults — there's no need for life insurance. Talk with a financial advisor for guidance about your particular situation.

Lost policy? Here's how to track it down

Trying to find a loved one's missing life insurance policy may leave you begging for an assist from Sherlock Holmes. Or maybe Nancy Drew. Or even Encyclopedia Brown. But with a little smart sleuthing, you can solve the mystery of the dearly departed documents on your own — without calling in the Scooby Doo gang for backup.

Start your search with these tips. All it takes is good detective work, plain and simple.

- Contact advisors like bankers, financial planners, attorneys, and accountants — anyone who might have information about insurance policies.

- Talk to the benefits departments at previous and recent employers. Don't forget to check with company union representatives, too.

- Scour bank statements and canceled checks for signs that a premium has been paid. Look for automated payments, too.

- Keep an eye on the mail for up to one year. You may find some information about the status of the missing policy, like a request for payment or a dividend notice.

▶ Review tax returns for the past two years. Is there any mention of interest income? How about interest paid? Insurance companies pay interest on permanent policies and charge interest on loans.

No luck? All is not lost. You still have options.

Try a locator service. Go online to the free NAIC Life Insurance Policy Locator Service at *eapps.naic.org/life-policy-locator/#/welcome*. You'll be asked to enter your loved one's birthday, social security number, past addresses, and other important information. But be patient. It may take 90 days for the service to complete the search.

Maybe someone's looking for you. Many companies check their records against the Social Security Administration's death records. If they find an in-force policy left behind by a policyholder who passed away, they'll come looking for you, the beneficiary.

Real estate wisdom

How to buy, sell, remodel, or age in place

Get moving: How to sell your home in any market

Timing is everything, especially when it comes to real estate. And to get the most money for your home, you want to sell at the perfect time — when the market is at its peak. So should you time it to sell in a buyer's market or a seller's market? For a sale that will raise the roof in either market, try these tips.

Figure out which market you're in. Check the inventory of available homes in your area. How? One way is to drive around town and count the number of homes for sale. Then go back in a month and see how many of them have sold. Take the original number of homes and divide it by the number of sales to find out how much inventory is available.

For example, if you found six houses for sale, and only one sold last month, that's six months of inventory — a buyer's market.

But if all six houses were sold, there's a smaller inventory. And that's a sign of a seller's market.

Another way to find out about local home sales? Visit the website *realtor.com/soldhomes*. It's a great place to find lots of information about home buying and selling in your neighborhood.

Once you've determined your market, it's time to try out some selling strategies.

Selling your home in a seller's market. In this market, there are more buyers than homes for sale. That means you'll have a lot of people looking at your house.

▸ Plus. Expect a speedy sale. You'll sell your home faster in a seller's market. And you may even receive multiple bids that could trigger a bidding war for your house. In a seller's market you hold the power, especially when it comes to negotiations.

▸ Minus. In this market, the best houses go quickly. If yours doesn't spark buyers' interest right away, your listing could lose appeal. And if a deal falls through because of a higher-than-expected appraisal, buyers may wonder what's wrong with your home.

Selling your home in a buyer's market. In a buyer's market, homes for sale outnumber the people looking to buy.

▸ Plus. In this slower market, you'll have more time to prepare for moving. More time to pack and get organized. And you may see lots of short sale properties and foreclosures flooding the market. That's good news for you. When house hunters compare those properties being sold "as-is" with your well-maintained home, you'll be sure to attract the more qualified buyers.

▶ **Minus.** You'll have lots of competition. That means putting in more effort — and maybe more money — to make your home stand out in a crowded market. And it may take a little longer to find the right offer. Patience is a must when you're selling your home in a buyer's market.

How to get huge savings on your mortgage

Did you know you can pay some of your mortgage interest in advance in exchange for a lower interest rate on your new home? That's basically what you do when you buy discount points, also known as mortgage points. They lower your monthly payments by letting you buy down — or discount — your mortgage interest rate.

It's not cheap though. According to the Bank of America, one point costs 1 percent of your mortgage amount. Or $1,000 for every $100,000 of your mortgage.

Here's how one scenario would work. On a $200,000 home, you'd likely have a monthly mortgage payment of around $1,000. If you buy one discount point at closing, an upfront cost of $2,000, your interest rate would drop a quarter percent. And so would your monthly payment — around $30. It may not seem like much, but on a 30-year loan your savings would add up to more than $10,000. Score.

DOLLARS & SENSE

Test drive your dream home before you buy

You expect to try on shoes before you buy them. And you take a car for a spin around the block before you sign on the dealer's dotted line. Some mattress makers even let you test their product to see if it brings you the sweet dreams they promise. But a house? Who gets to test out a house? You do, if you sign on with Home Partners of America.

Home Partners' Lease with Right to Purchase program lets you choose a home from metro areas in 20 different states. Thinking about making a move to California or Tennessee? How about Florida or Texas? For a list of all of Home Partners' approved communities, go to *homepartners.com/how-it-works/communities*.

Once you've picked your new community, it's time to find your new home. With the help of a real estate agent, you'll choose a qualified house in a neighborhood that feels like home. But keep in mind your Home Partners' home must meet certain requirements.

▸ The house must be located in an A-rated school district.

▸ It must be priced below $550,000.

▸ You can't opt for a condo or townhome.

▸ Age-restricted communities are not allowed.

▸ No homes built over 100 years ago or those in need of lots of renovations will be considered either. In other words, fixer-uppers need not apply.

Go to *s3.amazonaws.com/hhstatic/flyers/HPA_auto_property_disquals.pdf* to find the complete list of Home Partners' standards.

After you pick a house that meets all the requirements, what's next? Home Partners buys it and rents it back to you. You'll have five years to decide if you want to buy. After the first year is up, you can walk away at any time — no questions asked.

With Home Partners, you'll know the monthly rent and full purchase price of the home before you move in. You can expect your rent to go up no more than 3.75 percent every year. That's about $75 on a $2,000-a-month lease. And the purchase price of the house will increase every year by 3 to 5 percent.

How does Home Partners differ from rent-to-own programs? When you rent to own, you usually make two monthly payments — one to cover the lease and another that's set aside for your purchase. With this program, you only make one payment, and none of your monthly rent goes toward the future purchase of your house.

Make the right move: Should you buy or sell first?

Which came first, the chicken or the egg? Debated for centuries, this classic brain teaser has lots of real-life applications. For example, which came first — ketchup or mustard? Oven or grill? How about in sports — baseball or basketball? Or, if you want to get the best real deal when you're planning a move, which should come first — buying or selling? For the answer in a nutshell, or eggshell if you prefer, keep reading.

You've decided to sell first. You're ready to leave your old nest behind. Fly the coop, so to speak. Not so fast. This strategy has its pros and cons.

▶ Pros. You'll have a nice nest egg from your sale to pay down on your new house. You won't have to juggle two mortgage payments. And you won't be tempted to lower your price in order to make a quick sale.

▶ Cons. Where will you live after you sell? You'll feel rushed and pressured to make a decision about a new house. And, are you sure you're ready to move twice — first out of your old home, and then again into your new one?

If you decide to sell first, talk to your buyers about setting up a longer closing period, say 60 days instead of 30, to buy yourself some home shopping time. Or ask your buyers if they'd be willing to rent your home back to you for a month or two after you close.

You've decided to buy first. Are you in a hot housing market where homes are going fast? Or are you in a slower market where sellers are willing to bend over backwards to make a sale? Either way the buy-first strategy can be a little scary — definitely not for chickens.

▶ Pros. You'll only have to move once. And you'll have plenty of time to select your perfect new nest.

▶ Cons. You may find yourself scrambling to find a buyer for your old home. Will you be able to come up with the down payment for your new home? And finance offers, if you already have a mortgage, may be pricey — and scarce as hen's teeth.

If you decide to buy first, one option is to talk to your seller about a contract contingency plan. In other words, you'll buy their home, but only if you sell yours first. Sounds good, unless the sellers receive multiple offers. Then your offer gets stuck at the bottom of the pile.

You could also use your home equity line of credit or apply for a bridge loan to get the money you need for your down payment. But you'd need to have enough savings or income to cover payments on three loans — your old mortgage, your line of credit, and your new mortgage.

So, buy or sell first? The choice is yours, but consider your options carefully. And just in case you were wondering — mustard, ovens, and baseball all came first. The chicken or the egg? The world is still trying to decide.

A CLOSER LOOK

When buying a house, don't skip home-owner's title insurance. It's designed to protect your equity in your new home, just in case someone challenges your ownership to the property.

Take the case of Jack and Janet. Just months after closing on their dream home — a remodeled 1920s farmhouse surrounded by acres of rolling pasture — they were notified that a distant relative of the original owner had made a claim on the property. Fortunately, their title insurance covered court costs to resolve the claim, and they were able to keep their home.

"Title insurance is very important," says Jo Shepherd of Keller Williams Realty in Newnan, Georgia. She explains that a real estate lawyer will search a title for claims and liens, but they can make mistakes. "Someone from 50 years ago could say they own that property, and you have no right to it. Title insurance covers the legal expenses to fight their claim."

Seal your lips to seal the deal

Loose lips can sink ships. And in some cases, real estate deals. Here are some things experts say you're better off keeping to yourself.

"We won't sell for less than our asking price." Putting a price on your home that's too high — or refusing to negotiate — may discourage buyers from making an offer. It's a good idea to have a few realtors give you prices on your home, and pay attention to their estimates.

Remember, just because you've added costly upgrades like a spa shower and granite countertops doesn't mean you'll get your money back — especially if you're the only home on the block with those improvements. You might have overpriced your home for the neighborhood.

"I've always wanted to knock down this wall to bring more light into the living room." When you list all the things you might like to change, you're just pointing out more ways the buyers might have to spend money. Not a good idea.

"I can't understand why our house has stayed on the market for so long." Length of time on the market is generally listed on the home's information sheet. Why mention it to potential buyers? They may wonder why you're having a hard time selling. Or they may figure out you're anxious to sell and drop their offer from "above market value" to "dirt cheap."

"I meant to fix that, but I just never got around to it." The porch step is loose. The front door sticks. A bathroom faucet is dripping. If sellers are greeted with a handful of items that need repair, they may wonder how well you've kept up the things they can't see.

Pretend you're a prospective buyer, and do a walk-through of your home. Make a list of repairs that need to be done. Then spend a few afternoons catching up on your honey-do list.

Senior experts make housing decisions a breeze

Maybe you've decided it's time to downsize. Or maybe you're getting ready to sell the old home place and move closer to the kids. Tough decisions. But you can get the help you need from a Seniors Real Estate Specialist (SRES).

Specifically trained to help older adults with their housing decisions, these agents have studied all about Medicaid, Medicare, and Social Security, and they know how these programs can impact your real estate decisions. They've even been trained in federal housing laws that affect senior adults.

Adam Shamus, a realtor with Keller Williams in Newton, Massachusetts, has been an SRES for nearly a decade. He describes his job as being part detective and part psychologist. "The qualities of a good SRES include patience, listening, and really understanding and empathizing with your client and the situation they're going through," he says.

Whether you need an estate planner or a financial advisor familiar with reverse mortgages, an SRES can help, Shamus says. Here are five ways they can assist with your buying, selling, and aging-in-place decisions.

Put you in touch with friendly faces. An SRES is familiar with senior care groups and agencies within your community that can provide in-home assisted living services. A little help from your friends might be all you need.

Recommend helpful financial programs. Money a problem? Programs are out there that provide financial aid for seniors. You just need to know where to find them.

"One of the jobs of a seniors real estate specialist is to be aware of local specialists or companies that can help seniors with a variety of different tasks," Shamus says. These tasks may include finding government, community, and private programs that can help you save money.

Refer you to stay-at-home specialists. You'd like to stay in your own home, but you realize you need to make some modifications. An SRES will refer you to an aging-in-place specialist who can evaluate your home for trouble areas and suggest ways to make your home safe and comfortable.

"A lot of people don't want to move and that's understandable," Shamus says. An SRES can work with home modification companies to widen doorways and install ramps and grab bars. "It's about identifying what the client wants and making sure we can achieve that for them."

Guide you through a reverse mortgage. Want information on a reverse mortgage? An SRES can put you in touch with financial counselors who know all the ins and outs.

Help you organize your life. Ready to move but need help getting things organized? Ask an SRES to point you toward declutter specialists, landscapers, and stagers who can get your house market-ready.

Making these housing decisions — especially after living in the same home for 30, 40, or even 50 years — can be overwhelming. An SRES can help you decide what's right for you. To find an agent in your neighborhood, go to *seniorsrealestate.com/Find-SRES/find* and enter your information, or call 800-500-4564.

Secret to selling your home fast — and for more money

You've heard location, location, location is key where real estate is concerned, but a recent study finds timing is crucial, too.

According to the experts at Zillow, a leading real estate and rental marketplace, you should pick a spring date to get the best deal on your home. Overall in the U.S., houses listed in late spring, especially May 1 through May 15, sell about 19 days faster. They also earn about 1 percent more on average than other listings — a boost of $1,700.

Timing affects the number of views your listing gets, too. Zillow says the best day of the week to list your house is Saturday, with Friday coming in a close second. Makes sense. Prospective buyers are searching online during the weekend, trying to choose houses they want to see.

DOLLARS & SENSE

Get an appraisal that's right on the money

What does the appraiser's wife say to her husband when she just can't get to sleep? "Honey, tell me about your day at work." Funny, but true. To the average homeowner, an appraiser's job might seem a little dull. But if you're buying or selling a home, and there's a mortgage involved, that lackluster appraiser may quickly become the star of the show.

What can you do to get the very best appraisal? An appraiser's job is to figure out the current value of your property, so make sure you've finished all the repairs your home needs before he gets there.

The appraiser will check out the interior condition of your home by doing a room-by-room walk-through. Then he'll tour the outside of the house to evaluate its condition. He'll look at things like your swimming pool or finished basement. He'll search for health or safety code violations. And he'll compare your home with others in your neighborhood to decide how much your property is worth.

An appraiser's report will include lots of details about your house, including a street map that pinpoints your location, a sketch of the outside of the house, and photos of your home's surroundings. An appraisal can cost several hundred dollars, but the buyer usually pays the fee.

You think the appraisal is wrong. What now? Lower-than-expected appraisals are common in some housing markets where comparable home sales — known as "comps" — aren't available to help appraisers figure out the actual market value. Local foreclosures and short sales play a role, too. But you have ways to protect yourself from an inaccurate appraisal.

▸ If you're the buyer. Ask your lender to hire a local appraiser, someone who knows your area well. Make sure the appraiser has a residential appraiser certification and professional designation. You might see initials like SRA for senior residential appraiser, or MAI — Member of the Appraisal Institute — by his name. And plan to be there when the appraiser inspects the home. Tell him what you know about the sales and foreclosures in the neighborhood.

▸ **If you're the seller.** Get an appraisal before you put your house on the market, and use that number to set a realistic price for your home. Give a copy of your appraisal to the buyer's appraiser. And don't hesitate to question a low appraisal.

Step up curb appeal for less than $200

To find true love, the saying goes, you have to kiss a lot of frogs before you find your prince. Same could be said for finding a new home. Don't let prospective buyers head off in search of more appealing options. Make sure it's love at first sight with these five simple — and inexpensive — outdoor updates.

Give your house a good scrubbing. Professionals say washing the outside of a house can add $10,000 to $15,000 to the price of a home. Find a pressure washer that's powerful enough to remove last year's collection of bugs and grime, but not strong enough to blast off paint or splinter wood. You can rent a gas-powered one for about $80 a day.

Spiff up the entry. A resin planter, some potting soil, and a few bright blooms say "welcome home" to prospective buyers. A sure-to-please front-porch upgrade for around $50.

A new mailbox really delivers. You can go high-end with a die cast aluminum mailbox for $100 to $350. Or you can pick up a simple, but attractive, mailbox for about $50. Even cheaper? Give your old box a new look with a fresh coat of paint. A can of spray paint can cost you less than $4.

Make sure your number's up. While you're sprucing up your mailbox, go ahead and update your house numbers. A package of stick-on numbers for your mailbox can range from $6 to $15 depending on size and style. For your home, choose something big and bold to catch a buyer's eye. Four brass or iron house numbers will run you around $30.

Brighten their path with a new porch light. Black, brushed nickel, and brass are all popular finishes right now. You can choose your favorite for as little as $30. Too much for your budget? Make your old light sparkle with restoring wipes that polish up faded or dirty metal. A pack of five wipes from companies like Rust-Oleum or Rejuvenate costs less than $20.

Choose these hues to score higher profits

You know those picky buyers. Their must-haves include a beautiful bath that bowls 'em over. A bright, sunny kitchen with all the fixin's. A chic dining room that dishes out style and sophistication.

Sounds expensive, right? Doesn't have to be. Just choose the colors those picky buyers will gobble up. And with any luck, you'll be stuffing lots of green in your pocket.

Moody blues? Not any more. In fact, homes with blue bathrooms — think light periwinkle or powder blue — sold for $5,400 more than the owners expected. Paint your dining room in shades of slate blue or pale bluish-gray, and watch your profits soar nearly $2,000. And a light blue kitchen or cadet blue bedroom can send your profits up more than $1,800.

"Color can be a powerful tool for attracting buyers to a home, especially in listing photos and videos," says Svenja Gudell, chief economist at real estate giant Zillow. "Painting walls in fresh, natural-looking colors, particularly in shades of blue and pale gray not only make a home feel larger, but also are neutral enough to help future buyers envision themselves living in the space."

But stay away from blue in your living room. Research shows light beige, taupe, or oatmeal are the moneymakers there. A great way to boost your profits by a cool $1,800.

Greige? What's greige? It's the color you should paint the outside of your house — if you want to up your profits by almost $3,500. Greige is a soft mix of gray and beige that brings in the buyers, especially when compared with houses painted a medium brown. In fact, studies show tan stucco or brown homes can lose you nearly $2,000.

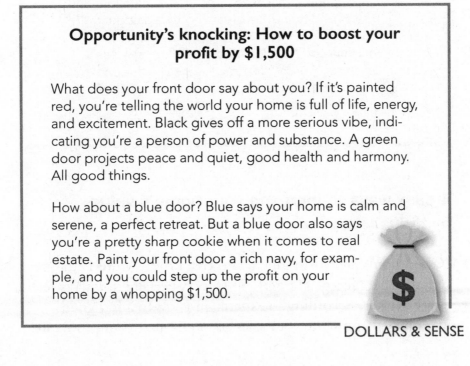

Opportunity's knocking: How to boost your profit by $1,500

What does your front door say about you? If it's painted red, you're telling the world your home is full of life, energy, and excitement. Black gives off a more serious vibe, indicating you're a person of power and substance. A green door projects peace and quiet, good health and harmony. All good things.

How about a blue door? Blue says your home is calm and serene, a perfect retreat. But a blue door also says you're a pretty sharp cookie when it comes to real estate. Paint your front door a rich navy, for example, and you could step up the profit on your home by a whopping $1,500.

DOLLARS & SENSE

Keep your hardwoods glowing with these steps

You'll floor prospective buyers with gleaming, upscale hardwoods. Just follow these simple steps to keep your floors open-house ready.

- Every day. Floors should be swept or dusted daily with a dry microfiber mop.

- Once a week. Vacuum using the bare floors setting on your vacuum cleaner. This will help get the hard-to-reach corners and spaces between each piece of wood.

- Once a month. Clean with a product made just for hardwood floors. Good Housekeeping Institute's top three choices are made by Bona, Libman, and Pledge.

- Every three to five years. Consider giving your floor a sand and refinish, a great way to repair deep gouges and scratches. For helpful tips, go to *us.bona.com/articles/hardwood-floor-sand-and-finish.html*, or try YouTube videos like this one produced by Lowe's at *youtube.com/watch?v=xQtjCu87zWY*.

4 easy ways to increase your home's value by thousands

"Good words are worth much, and cost little," wrote 16th-century poet George Herbert. So true. Especially in today's real estate market. According to experts, just toss in a few good words when you write your sales ad, and watch your profits soar.

For example, using "luxurious" ups your home's sale price by more than 8 percent. "Impeccable" can boost your bottom line by around 6 percent. Even "basketball" brings in more cash — almost 5 percent more. Who knew? So what else can you do to easily increase the value of your home?

According to *Remodeling* magazine's "2018 Cost vs. Value report," these home improvement projects will bring you the biggest bang for your buck when you get ready to sell your home.

A beautiful new garage door. *Remodeling* lists a new garage door as the most profitable improvement you can make to your home. Paid $3,500 for the door? Expect a payback of 98 percent on your investment — around $3,400 when you get ready to sell.

And even though "beautiful" may seem like an odd way to describe your garage door, using it in your ad could hike your profit by more than 2 percent.

Captivating stone veneer. Adding manufactured stone veneer to the outside of your home came in second on *Remodeling's* list. Get ready for a payback of almost $8,000 — or 97 percent — on a typical $8,221 investment.

Try using the word "captivating" in your ad. Don't be surprised if it boosts your profits upwards of 6 percent.

An updated wood deck addition. Look to recoup around 83 percent of your $11,000 investment on the cost of a wood deck addition. That's a hefty $9,000. Tack on the word "updated" to your sales ad, and you could raise your profit by almost 1 percent.

An upgraded kitchen with stainless and granite. A value finale. Invest $21,000 in a kitchen remodel, and you can expect to get back around $17,000. That's a spectacular 81 percent.

Looking to make even more profit? Plug "upgraded" into your ad, and watch your profits shoot up almost 2 percent. Add upscale descriptors like "granite" to pull in a 1 to 4 percent boost and "stainless" to bring in a skyrocketing 5 percent hike.

Make your house safe — and stylish — for your golden years

Oh, the signs of your times. Your e-reader is set on an extra-large font so you can read without your specs. The new night light you installed gets you in and out of the bathroom with ease, even in the midnight hours. And who knew orthopedic sandals — sans socks — really are stylish and comfortable? Well, sort of.

As you age, little adjustments like these can make your life easier and safer. Some changes to your home can make you safer, too. Read on for some high-end and low-cost renovations that will have your house golden-years ready.

A grand entrance for one and all. Make your front door more welcoming — and accessible — by adding a ramp. But not necessarily the unsightly wooden ramp that wipes out your home's curb appeal. Instead, make your ramp look like a sidewalk by using slate or other high-end materials. Attractive landscaping will really seal the deal. A pricey project for about $8,000.

For a lot less — say around $400 total — you can provide easy access to your front door for folks with wheelchairs or walkers. Just remove the metal bump on your front door threshold and install a retractable bottom on your door. It lifts up when you open your door, but drops and seals tight when the door closes. No more threshold hurdles for visitors to get over.

Take a step toward safer stairs. How about a jazzy stair solution that will leave you feeling like the Jetsons? If money were no object, you could treat yourself to a pneumatic vacuum elevator — straight out of George and Jane's condo in the sky. The elevator works like the teller tube at your bank, but with a seat for you to ride on. A cool $60,000 to $80,000. Talk about a wow factor.

For a more practical alternative, consider a stair lift. Depending on the staircase in your home, and the lift model you choose, you'll probably end up footing a bill between $2,000 and $5,000. Not nearly as much fun for the grandkids, but a more cents-able solution for you.

Tips for a stretch-proof, stress-free kitchen. Reach all your kitchen essentials without pulling a muscle. Make your kitchen an easy-to-use dream for senior chefs by installing pullout shelving in your cabinet and pantry. These shelves are pricey, though. A pullout system including 24 custom-made shelves — with installation — could cost you up to $5,000.

But you don't have to pull out all the stops to make your kitchen more senior-friendly. Change out the drawer and door handles with easy-to-grip lever-style pulls that are longer and wider. A budget-friendly tip for around $300.

Keep your shower safe and stylish. Worried about a slip-and-fall in the bathroom? Experts suggest installing a curbless shower that lets you get in and out without stepping over a big threshold. Makes it super simple to get a rolling shower chair in and out, too. The shower floor is sloped so water goes right down the drain. Add a chair or bench if you like. Cost to go curbless? Around $8,000 to $11,000.

Properly installed grab bars can provide a budget-friendly bathroom safety net. Priced between $200 and $600 — that's including three bars and installation — today's grab bars can add style and safety to your bath.

Can't afford to renovate? Help is closer than you think

Every 11 seconds an older adult is treated in the emergency room for a fall. A scary statistic, right? You can protect yourself from falls and other in-home injuries by making safety modifications to your home. But everybody knows those renovations can cost a bundle.

Wait, here's some good news. There's more help than ever for seniors who want to safely live out their golden years in their own home.

More than 400 federal, state, and local programs provide financial assistance for seniors who need help aging in place. And that's not even including all the nonprofits, private organizations, and other agencies just waiting to make your house a safe place for you to call home.

But finding the assistance you need can be challenging. Here are a few programs on the next page to check out — just to get you started.

▸ **Government loans and grants.** Some government organizations offer low-interest loans for home modifications. For example, the Rural Housing Repair Loans and Grants program provides funds to low-income folks age 62 and over. To get more information, go online to *rd.usda.gov/programs-services/single-family-housing-repair-loans-grants*.

▸ **Free materials and labor from nonprofits and charities.** Need a ramp to get you out your front door? Go to the web page *ramps.org/free-ramps.htm* and click on your state. You'll get a list of organizations near you, ready and willing to build your ramp for free.

Another nonprofit, Rebuilding Together, has several programs available to help low-income families, veterans, and seniors stay in their own homes by providing free remodeling services. Get more information online at *payingforseniorcare.com/home-modifications/rebuilding-together.html*.

▸ **Medicaid home and community based services.** Most states have Medicaid programs that help people avoid nursing homes by paying for home modifications. But eligibility requirements differ from state to state. Click on *payingforseniorcare.com/home-modifications/medicaid-waivers.html* to find out what's offered in your hometown.

▸ **Medicare benefits for home modifications.** Unfortunately you won't find much help available here. Medicare and most private insurers won't usually pay for the home renovations you need to age in place. In some rare situations, Medicare may pay for bathroom modifications or stair lifts. Explore your options at *payingforseniorcare.com/homemodifications/how-to-pay-for-home-mods.html*.

Detailed records show your home's been in good hands

If your walls could talk, they would tell potential buyers they just got a fresh coat of paint last month. But what about the roof you recently replaced, or the air conditioner checkup you schedule every year?

Providing detailed records of maintenance and renovations shows prospective buyers you've taken good care of your home. Include dates of repairs and improvements, the materials used — including paint and stain colors — and costs. Add some before and after pictures, too. List names and contact information of the professionals you hired to complete the work.

Your record could be as simple as a spiral notebook tucked in a desk drawer or as high-tech as a digital logbook stored in the Cloud.

Live mortgage free: The money-saving secret smart homeowners should know

Remember Fred Mertz, the penny-pinching sourpuss of "I Love Lucy" fame? Known for being frugal — well, cheap — Fred made at least one good investment during his lifetime. That brownstone where he and Ethel collected around $125 rent each month from the Ricardos. Probably just enough to make a nice little dent in his 1950s-era mortgage payment.

Take a page from Fred's bankbook. He knew the smart secret that helped cover his home mortgage payment every month. He became a landlord, and with a little help, so can you.

Start with the right property. Experts recommend starting with a single-family house, priced around $150,000, that's not far from your home. Look for a safe neighborhood with great schools and popular amenities like parks and shopping centers. It's a good idea to find an area that provides plenty of job opportunities for your tenants, too. And be ready to invest $250 to $450 in a thorough home inspection. It's worth its weight in gold.

Make sure you're fiscally fit. Need a mortgage to buy your rental home? You'll need to make a down payment of at least 20 percent. Spend some time researching lenders online to find the best deal. And you'll need homeowners insurance. Since you won't be living in the home, expect to pay more for coverage — like 25 percent more.

> Thinking about tackling a fixer-upper to rent out? Not so fast, Bob Vila. Unless you have a contractor who does great work on the cheap — or you have some serious handyman skills — experts say you'll spend too much on renovations. Instead, buy a well-maintained house that needs just a few inexpensive repairs.

Be a legal eagle. Study up on legal ways to handle security deposits, safety codes, and even how to evict a tenant. The Fair Housing Act was created back in the 1960s to protect everyone's right to rent or buy a home or get a mortgage without worrying about discrimination. Brush up on this law's basics at *hud.gov/ program_offices/fair_housing_equal_opp/FHLaws*.

Pick a winner. Choosing a tenant may be the most difficult decision you'll make as a landlord. Have an applicant you're considering? After an initial interview, request a consumer report from a qualified agency before you make your final decision. The Federal Trade Commission (FTC) has important advice about using these reports at *ftc.gov/tips-advice/business-center/guidance/using-consumer-reports-what-landlords-need-know*.

You can also contact an online tenant screening service like *entprep.com* or *myrental.com* to help you with your decision. These services are not free, but in the end, their advice may save you valuable time — and money.

This rule of thumb makes figuring rent a snap

Now that you've picked your rental property, are you struggling to decide what you should charge for rent? The 1 Percent Rule says your monthly rent should be at least 1 percent of the price of your property.

For example, a house that costs you $100,000 should be rented for around $1,000 per month. A $200,000 property? Go with at least $2,000 per month. And the rent you charge should include any upgrades or repairs you're planning. Keep routine maintenance costs in mind, too.

Here's the best part about the 1 percent rule. If a property meets the rule, it will take 100 months to pay for itself. In other words, a $100,000 property bringing in $1,000 every month will be paid off in 100 months. That's just a little over eight years. A nice return on your smart investment.

DOLLARS & SENSE

Are you ready to be a landlord?

Think you're ready to take on the challenge of a rental property? Here's a checklist to help you decide.

1 You're available to take care of tenant repairs and emergencies 24 hours a day. That's including vacations.

2 You're willing and able to make mortgage payments during the months when you'll have no tenants in your rental.

3 You've studied the state, local, and federal laws about landlord and tenant relationships. And you've considered the cost of hiring a lawyer should legal problems pop up.

4 You're willing to spend your time and money to make sure your rental property is kept in good repair and is habitable.

5 You're prepared to keep detailed records of your rental expenses and income, or you've hired a bookkeeper to take care of that for you.

6 You've contacted a tax accountant to help you with tax returns and other accounting issues.

7 You've considered all the risks of investing in rental property, and you're willing to take on the challenge.

House or condo: Make the move that's right for you

Now that they're retired, Jay and Lorna can't wait to pack up and leave the cold, snowy North. But the couple has a tough decision to make. Should they choose a condo or a house?

Lorna likes the condo idea, pointing out that Jay's days of grass-cutting will be over once and for all. But Jay is leaning towards buying a house, reminding Lorna how much she dislikes noisy, nosy neighbors.

How will they decide? How will you? The answers to these questions may help you make up your mind.

What's your price point? According to the National Association of Realtors, the average price of a single-family home in the United States is around $245,000. You can pick up a condo for an average of $14,000 less — about $231,000. Of course, these prices depend on your location. In the West, you'll likely save $12,000 if you choose a condo. In the South? A whopping $44,000.

Don't forget to factor in those homeowners association (HOA) fees that come with a condo. They could boost your monthly payments by as much as $700. But homeowners won't get off scot-free. They can expect to pay more in monthly electric and water bills.

What's your style — city slicker or country folk? If a condo that's close to restaurants and shops in town appeals to you, expect to pay more than you would for a single-family home in a quieter suburban neighborhood.

And then there's privacy. With shared walls, ceilings, and floors, it may be hard to tune out noisy neighbors in a condo. Not usually a problem with a house in the 'burbs. But there you'll have to deal with yard work and cleaning gutters.

Are you in it for the long haul? Both condos and single-family homes can be great long-term investments, increasing in value as time goes by. And both kinds of properties can be rented out if you want to make extra money to help pay down your mortgage.

But a house will have the edge when it's time to sell. Condo owners must check with their HOA before they can make any renovations to the property that could increase its market value. You'll also need to talk to your HOA before you rent out your condo to make sure you're not breaking any rules.

Get professional help. Still not sure what to buy? An experienced realtor can help you figure out your next move. Go to *realtor.com* and click on "Find Realtors" to locate a professional real estate agent near you.

Upsize or downsize — how to right-size your life

As you get closer to retirement, conventional wisdom says it's time to clean out all the stuff you collected over the years and move to a little condo near the beach. Or the mountains.

But according to a Merrill Lynch survey, lots of baby boomers aren't interested in going smaller. In fact, when the time came to move, retirees were split almost 50-50, with 49 percent heading off to a larger or same-sized home, and 51 percent opting for a place with less square footage.

So should you size up or size down? Here's how to find the perfect fit for you.

Downsize to the right size. Are you tired of climbing stairs or spending your weekends cleaning house? A smaller home might be just what you need if:

 ▶ you don't want to invest the time and money to furnish, clean, and maintain your large home.

 ▶ you want to save money. Downsizing could reduce or eliminate your mortgage payment. You could lower your property taxes and insurance costs. And cut that utility bill, too.

 ▶ a small ranch-style house or a ground-floor condo would be more comfortable and easier for you to manage, especially if you have health issues. Just think — no more stairs.

Sizing up your perfect retirement home. Maybe you've always dreamt of having a gourmet kitchen or a spa bathroom. If you can afford it, now may be the right time to pick out your dream home. More square footage might fit you to a T if:

 ▶ you're expecting lots of visits from friends and family members — especially those grandkids — and you need more room for guests.

 ▶ you've cleaned out cabinets and closets, but you still don't have enough storage space for your essentials.

 ▶ you want a designated place for an office or craft room, and your present home is just too small.

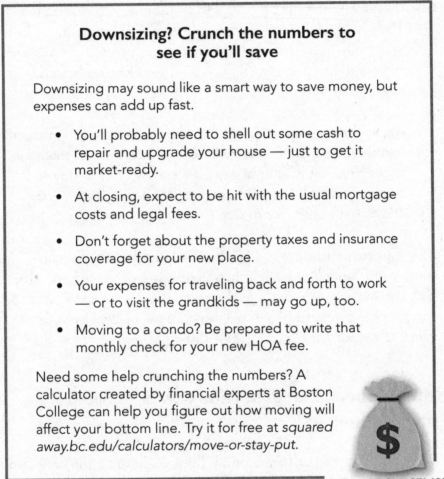

Downsizing? Crunch the numbers to see if you'll save

Downsizing may sound like a smart way to save money, but expenses can add up fast.

- You'll probably need to shell out some cash to repair and upgrade your house — just to get it market-ready.

- At closing, expect to be hit with the usual mortgage costs and legal fees.

- Don't forget about the property taxes and insurance coverage for your new place.

- Your expenses for traveling back and forth to work — or to visit the grandkids — may go up, too.

- Moving to a condo? Be prepared to write that monthly check for your new HOA fee.

Need some help crunching the numbers? A calculator created by financial experts at Boston College can help you figure out how moving will affect your bottom line. Try it for free at *squared away.bc.edu/calculators/move-or-stay-put*.

DOLLARS & SENSE

Not too big, not too small. Be like Goldilocks and find the one that's just right. Here are some things to think about to get you on the right track.

▸ Consider your future needs. Suppose an aging relative moves in and you need an extra bedroom. Or you start a new business that requires a home office. Choose a home that will adjust to changes in your life.

▸ Think about your lifestyle. How often do you entertain?
Do your travels take you away from home frequently? Do
you really need that chef's kitchen, or are you fine with take-
out several nights a week? Maybe you'd like a dedicated
space for your hobbies.

▸ What about outdoor space? You like the look of a manicured
yard with colorful flower beds. But do you want to maintain
them? Are you willing to pay for a lawn service to do the
mowing and trimming if you can't do the work yourself?
Maybe you'd just like to skip those lawn worries altogether.

Use your current home as a guide. Take a walk through your
house, and think about the function and size of the rooms. Are
they too large or too small? Make notes about each space, including the changes you'd like to see in your new place. Use your
notes as a guide for choosing your just-right retirement home.

HOAs: Check the 'dues' and don'ts to avoid
pricey penalties

The condos at Sierra Towers in Hollywood have all the bells and
whistles you could imagine. A state-of-the-art fitness center and
spa to keep you movie-star trim. A sparkling swimming pool to
beat the West Coast heat. Round-the-clock staff — including
concierge, valet, and doorman — at your beck and call.

Think all these luxuries are free? Not quite. Perks like these will
set you back around $4,000 every month in homeowners associ-
ation (HOA) fees. Ouch.

Remember, though, that's a pricey California condo. According to a national study, the average HOA fee is around $331 per month. But fees can range anywhere from $100 to $700, depending on your location and the services provided. So what might be covered by your HOA?

▸ trash removal, water, and sewage

▸ lawn care and snow removal

▸ community security

▸ building maintenance like roof leaks, exterior painting, and driveway repairs

▸ insurance protection for any damage to the outside of your building. You'll still need your own policy to cover your personal possessions.

Sound good to you? That's great, but be careful. Before you sign on the HOA's dotted line, there are some things you should look out for.

Double trouble. "You could end up paying two home-owners association fees," warns Georgia realtor Jo Shepherd. "You could have a main HOA for all the buildings in your complex and then another one for your own building. Just

> Part of your HOA fees go into a reserve fund — a savings account for long-term projects or repairs. So when the pool needs a new liner or the clubhouse needs repainting, the HOA has the funds to pay for it.

be aware how much those fees are going to be." Falling behind on your dues could lead to foreclosure by your HOA.

Proper "manors." The HOA sets the standards for your home. From how you decorate your house for the holidays to where you park your car — all of these things may be regulated by your HOA. If you're more of a free spirit, those rules and regulations may feel too restrictive.

Assessment mess. Suppose your community has some unexpected — and expensive — maintenance problem, like a flood in the clubhouse due to a broken water pipe. Sure, homeowners insurance will pick up part of the bill, but the HOA will foot the rest.

And if there's not enough money in the HOA reserve fund to cover repairs and clean up the mess, watch out. Your HOA board may require you to pay a special — but usually temporary — assessment bill over and above your monthly fee.

Intelligent investing

Smart moves to make your money grow

Pay taxes up front to save thousands later

"Why do today what you can put off till tomorrow" is the motto of procrastinators everywhere. And who doesn't love to push back unpleasant tasks like paying taxes?

With a traditional 401(k), you get to do just that. Your money goes straight to the bank before Uncle Sam gets his share. Unfortunately, you're just delaying the inevitable — the money is taxed when it comes out of your account.

However, if you have a Roth 401(k), you can stock your savings with post-tax contributions. In the right situation, you could stand to save thousands. Here are a few things to consider.

- ▸ Does your employer give you the option? Not all companies offer a Roth 401(k). Make sure you talk to your manager or human resources representative to see what your choices are.

▶ Will fees eat away at your savings? Some 401(k) plans come with high fees, so you'll need to crunch the numbers to make sure you're getting a good deal. A Roth 401(k) with high fees might cancel out any post-tax savings.

▶ What does your tax situation look like now and in the future? If your current tax bracket is higher than the one you think you'll retire in, experts usually recommend a traditional 401(k). Otherwise, you won't save any money by paying your taxes ahead of time. If it will be the same or higher at retirement, you're better off with a Roth.

For example, let's say you're in the 22 percent tax bracket and expect the same during retirement. You stock your traditional 401(k) with $10,000 each year for the next 15 years. At a 7 percent return rate, that $150,000 will net you $253,954 after taxes are taken out. But if you put the same amount into a Roth account, which is taxed beforehand, you'll end up with $260,720 — almost $7,000 more.

It's important to remember any money your employer matches for your Roth 401(k) is a pretax contribution. You'll still have to pay some taxes when you tap into your retirement account.

Simplify your 401(k) swap in a few easy steps

Remember those colorful Now and Later saltwater taffies that promise long-lasting flavor? Roth accounts aren't nearly as delicious, but they do allow you to pay taxes now so you can get long-lasting, tax-free perks later. If you stand to benefit from a post-tax retirement fund and your company gives you the option to make the switch, follow these steps.

▸ First, calculate your taxes. This can be a complicated equation, so it might be worth it to talk to a financial advisor. But a good rule of thumb is to figure out your tax bracket and then multiply that percentage by the amount you're rolling over.

▸ Second, make sure you set aside money to cover the costs of taxes without drawing down your retirement stash. You don't want to take a bite out of your 401(k) to fund the conversion. Remember, if you convert the account at the beginning of the year, you'll have until next April to scrape the money together.

▸ Finally, start the conversion process. This is going to vary depending on the company you work for and the plans they offer, so consult your human resources department to see what steps you need to take.

> Planning on converting your traditional retirement plan to a Roth IRA? If the new tax changes have landed you a lower tax rate, now is a great time to make the switch, especially if you'll be in the same or higher tax bracket in retirement.

Even if you're not in a position to convert your 401(k), you can start putting money into a new Roth account. Talk to your HR department or check with your 401(k) providers to see what options you have.

Super savings plans for the self-employed

Company-sponsored retirement plans are the lynchpin of so many people's savings, but what do you do if you're self-employed? Fortunately, you have some great options. It all depends on your situation.

Solo 401(k). Ned owns a small business and he's the only employee, so his best bet is to go with a solo 401(k). This retirement plan lets him contribute $18,500 each year, and next year when he hits 50 he can add $6,000 in annual catch-up contributions.

Plus this plan lets him put in an additional 25 percent of his earned income, with a total cap of $55,000 each year, not counting catch-up contributions.

SIMPLE IRA. Nellie, who runs a little ice cream store, isn't eligible for a solo 401(k) because she has employees. Instead she stocks her savings away in a Savings Incentive Match Plan for Employees (SIMPLE) IRA.

She can contribute up to $12,500 yearly. And since she's already 50, she can make a $3,000 catch-up contribution each year. Nellie can offer her employees great retirement packages, too.

401(k) rollover: 3 deadly don'ts could cost you dearly

Converting your old 401(k) to an IRA often gives you a wider selection of investments, fewer tax burdens, and more withdrawal loopholes. But if you make these dangerous errors you could wind up torpedoing your retirement savings.

Transfer mistakes bring about unwelcome taxes. When you move money from a 401(k) to an IRA, you need to do it the right way. Otherwise, you could wind up paying taxes before you need to.

Make sure you transfer the funds through a trustee-to-trustee transaction, which means it will go directly from one account to the other. It's a good idea to set up your IRA before you begin the transfer process to avoid this mistake.

The important thing is to keep the money away from your personal account. If you transfer the funds there first, the IRS will think you're making a withdrawal and send you a not-so-nice tax bill.

Fiendish fees take a bite out of your nest egg. Changing jobs or retiring might make switching to an IRA seem like a good option, but read the fine print. Some IRAs come loaded with fees and commission costs that eat away at your hard-earned cash. Be on the lookout for contracts that push you towards high-fee accounts.

Gambling on your investments will leave you high and dry. Moving your money to a self-directed IRA puts you at the helm of your financial boat so you can invest in anything your heart desires. But think carefully about this option. Although the high returns may sound enticing, retirement isn't the time to take chances with your cash.

Are fees draining your retirement fund?

Investment fees can take a big bite out of your retirement. Check out how much your 401(k) would lose after 10 years if you contributed $5,000 per year and got a 7 percent return.

Fee	What's left for you	Lost money
0%	$134,440	$0
0.5%	$128,576	$5,864
1%	$122,994	$11,446
2%	$112,617	$21,823

The investments in self-directed IRAs are diverse and exotic, and often haven't been vetted by financial advisors. Experts recommend staying away from these unknowns, and instead sticking with lower-yielding, safer investments.

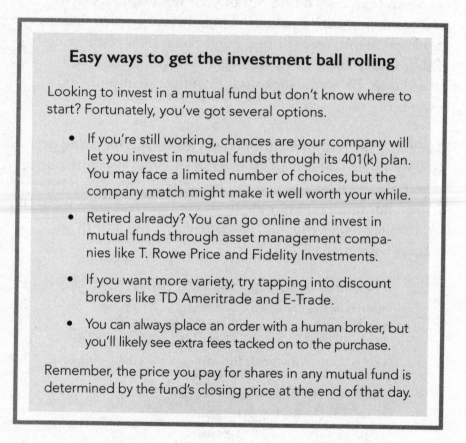

Easy ways to get the investment ball rolling

Looking to invest in a mutual fund but don't know where to start? Fortunately, you've got several options.

- If you're still working, chances are your company will let you invest in mutual funds through its 401(k) plan. You may face a limited number of choices, but the company match might make it well worth your while.

- Retired already? You can go online and invest in mutual funds through asset management companies like T. Rowe Price and Fidelity Investments.

- If you want more variety, try tapping into discount brokers like TD Ameritrade and E-Trade.

- You can always place an order with a human broker, but you'll likely see extra fees tacked on to the purchase.

Remember, the price you pay for shares in any mutual fund is determined by the fund's closing price at the end of that day.

Get Wall Street advice for a Main Street price

It's easy to wave away anyone who tells you to consult a financial advisor, especially if you think you could never afford investing help. But not all advisors sit behind mahogany desks and service clients with multimillion-dollar portfolios. If you know where to look, you can find some great options for every budget.

Seek an advisor who caters to the middle class. If you have friends or family members who use a financial advisor, don't be afraid to ask for recommendations. Or you can search online to find an advisor willing to work with your budget. Go to *napfa.org/find-an-advisor* to track down advisors who meet your needs. Here are a few important questions to help narrow down your search.

▸ How do you get paid? Some financial advisors get money by taking a percentage of your investing portfolio over time, while others will consult with you for a specific fee. A fee-only advisor is usually a better choice, especially if you don't have a lot of assets.

▸ Are you a fiduciary? A fiduciary must work for the best interest of the client, but other advisors only have to recommend a suitable product — even if it's not necessarily the best option for you.

▸ What services do you offer? Some advisors offer more investing advice and strategies while others are tailored toward retirement planning. You'll need to find an advisor whose specialties and services line up with your needs.

Search out savings on the world wide web. Internet-based financial advisors can cater to clients from anywhere in the world. Couple that with the low costs of running an online business, and you have a formula for affordable financial advice for any situation.

You'll lose out on the face-to-face connection, but most online advisors still give you personalized planning sessions over the phone or email. Just make sure you take steps to protect your data by following basic online safety.

Let a computer crunch the numbers for a fraction of the price. Robo-advisors are computer programs made for the sole purpose of managing your portfolio. They examine market trends and your personal finances, then develop investing strategies tailored to your needs.

This comes at a cost, but it's still much cheaper than a human advisor. Fees usually range from 0.25 to 0.5 percent per year. That means if your robo-advisor manages an account with $20,000, you'll pay $50 to $100 annually. The money is taken straight from your account either monthly or quarterly, depending on the service you're using.

Some companies have hotlines you can call for human advice, but their computers will still be your primary portfolio managers. Robo-advisors may be a good choice if you're willing to try out new technology and want a low-cost, hands-off way to manage your investments.

Don't derail your investments with these blunders

Your investments are supposed to pay off when you're ready to retire, so even small mistakes can throw you off course. Certified financial planner Debra Morrison compares it to traveling cross-country.

"If we're starting in New York City and heading to San Diego and we're off by one degree at the outset of our journey, it could take us to San Francisco," says the president of Empowered Retirement, a financial planning firm. "I always like to get a person on the right trajectory as early as I can."

Here are some of the blunders that may take you off your financial course.

Thinking it's too late to catch up to your retirement goals. Your 401(k) or IRA is a great tool to save for retirement, but what if you haven't been making the most of your options? Lucky for you, the government gives you a break. Once you hit 50 you can put extra payments toward your retirement accounts over and above your normal contributions. So don't give up.

"These catch-up contributions are really valuable because it allows you to go backwards and tuck money under that pretax umbrella and give yourself a whole lot more 401(k) balance to compound," says Morrison.

A single-minded portfolio could sink your savings. You wouldn't waltz into a casino and bet your whole retirement on red, would you? You're taking that same gamble if you don't have a diverse portfolio. If all your money is in the same type of stocks, bonds, or mutual funds, one slip could leave you without a back-up plan. Experts recommend a portfolio with assets spread across different investments to help you make it through market ups and downs.

Investing in the past could mean losing out on the future. The hottest pharmaceutical company had a banner year at the stock exchange. Should you rush out to buy up all the stock you can? Not so fast. Experts warn against investing in something just because it did well in the past.

The stock market is subject to the theory of mean revision, which holds that abnormally high or low returns will eventually even out and revert to a normal pattern. So that high-priced stock will eventually drop. Make sure you do your research and weigh your options carefully before you buy.

Bad advice from so-called experts could cost you a fortune. A friend introduced you to a financial advisor who pitched you a great annuity. You'd be crazy not to take advantage of his financial expertise — right?

Some advisors get commissions on products they sell, so your best interests might not be the first thing on their mind. It's better to get investing strategies and advice from a fiduciary advisor who is legally obligated to put your interests first. Do some research upfront to find an advisor you feel comfortable with.

Morrison recommends fee-only financial advisors, which is what her firm offers. "Fee-only planners have one agenda, and it's each individual client's particular goals," she says. "We have a fiduciary responsibility to each and every client to serve them only."

Choosing an advisor is a big decision, she says. "But with a little bit of due diligence you can seek out someone you can trust."

4 can't-miss tips for getting your mutual funds on the right track

Want to buy stock but fear putting all your eggs in one or two baskets? If that's the case, a mutual fund — a pool of shareholder money professionally invested by a fund manager — may be the answer.

That's because the average mutual fund holds hundreds of different securities, downsizing the risk if one of them loses value.

Let's say, for example, you invested $10,000 in Company A. If the business goes under, you lose your money. But if you invested $10,000 in a mutual fund that held only a small portion of Company A, your loss would be balanced out by the securities that perform well.

Before you jump in the pool, though, be sure to find a fund that fits your investment strategy. A smart plan includes a mixture of bonds and stocks along with investments in the U.S. and abroad. And don't forget to follow these tips.

Diversify your portfolio picks. Check if the fund is limited to a specific industry or sector. You wouldn't want to purchase, say, a transportation sector fund that invests in dozens of trucking companies or airlines. Your portfolio could take a beating if fuel prices soared.

Buy no-load funds. Some mutual funds charge a fee — called a sales load — that is pocketed by whoever sells the fund. The commission is often around 5 percent of assets. Imagine you invest $10,000. That's $500 skimmed off your account balance on day one.

Consider the expense ratio. Don't get sidelined by the high fees charged to run the fund. Just think — a $10,000 investment will grow to $46,610 over 20 years, assuming an 8 percent annual return. Add a 2 percent expense ratio into the mix and you'll have to hand over $15,493.

To find out if you're paying too much, compare the funds offered by your broker. You might find a similar fund with a lower expense ratio.

Look at management. Before you invest, go behind the scenes to learn the ins and outs of your favorite funds.

▸ Be sure your fund's manager has a large portion of his net worth invested in the fund. That makes it more likely he'll take an active interest in how it performs.

▸ Find out if the fund's returns over the last year were consistent with the general market.

▸ See if there was a high amount of turnover. That's the per-centage of the portfolio that was bought and sold. High turnover means higher taxes if your fund is not in a tax-deferred retirement account.

▸ Read the fund's documents — called a prospectus — and its shareholder reports filed with the Securities and Exchange Commission (SEC). They'll give you a good idea of the fund's risks, performance, fees and expenses, and management. You can find all of this legal information online at *sec.gov*.

Kick-start your investing with these surefire steps

Take a trip to the local ice cream shop and you'll see lots of options beyond vanilla and chocolate. That's a good thing. But when it comes to investing, too much choice can be bad. Take mutual funds, for example. There are nearly 8,000 up for grabs. How do you identify the right one?

Create a road map. You wouldn't bake a cake without a recipe. Similar reasoning applies to investing. Before buying into a mutual fund, think about your goals, risk tolerance, and time horizon.

▸ Are you seeking long-term capital gains over 20 years or are you looking for income right now?

▸ Can you hold on during a bear market or are you likely to sell at the drop of a hat?

▸ When will you need the money? If you're planning on retir-ing in five years, for example, you'd probably want to weigh your portfolio to less risky securities.

Check your wallet. Some mutual fund companies require a minimum investment of $3,000 or more. Others have much lower minimums of $100, $500, or $1,000.

You may be able to begin investing at lower amounts if you agree to an automatic investment plan of at least $100 each month.

Pick a style and fund type. Several types of mutual funds exist. Which one suits your fancy?

- Equity funds, which invest in stocks, usually seek long-term capital growth.

- Income funds, or those that generally invest in bonds, might work best for a retiree needing a steady stream of income.

- And if you're somewhere in between? A balanced fund investing in both stocks and bonds could be the ticket.

Consider low-cost funds. When you buy into a mutual fund, you pay extra for the manager to research, buy, and sell the securities. Want to save a bundle? Take a look at some less expensive alternatives.

- Index funds try to match the performance of an index like the S&P 500 or the Dow Jones Industrial Average. You won't beat the market, but you'll save on operating expenses and trading fees.

- Money market funds invest in short-term debt securities like U.S. Treasury bills. They provide a steady, but low, rate of return. Expect higher returns than you'd get from an interest-bearing bank account but less than you'd get from a certificate of deposit.

▶ Exchange-traded funds are essentially collections of securities that track an index. Unlike mutual funds, you can buy and sell them during market hours. Exchange-traded funds typically have lower fees than mutual funds.

ALERT ⚠

Stick with it or ditch it? 4 signs it's time to walk away from a mutual fund

So your mutual fund isn't performing as well as you hoped. Does that mean you should sell off the assets?

Not necessarily, experts say. Mutual funds are geared toward long-term results, so you don't want to hop in and out of funds just because they experience short-term fluctuations.

But of course, a buy-and-hold strategy won't work forever. Here are some situations that should raise red flags.

- The fund has lagged its benchmark index or similar funds for two years or more.

- Annual expenses increase significantly.

- Management turnover is high, hiking up taxes and transaction costs.

- The fund's investment strategy no longer matches your goals.

Want to hit the target? Consider this mutual fund

Experts advise you to rebalance your portfolio as you get older. But what if you don't want the hassle? Target-date funds might be for you. Here's how they work.

You choose a fund with a target year that's closest to when you plan to retire — say "2030 Fund." As you get closer to that date, the fund steadily swings toward safer investments so your exposure to risk goes down.

Be aware, though, that different target-date funds grow more conservative at varying rates. So if you're in the market for one of these funds, be sure to complete this checklist.

- Assess your tolerance for risk.

- Pick a fund that best matches your investment strategy.

- Compare fees and expenses using the Financial Industry Regulatory Authority's tool at *tools.finra.org/fund_analyzer/*.

Unscrambling annuities — the pros and cons of buying in

Annuities. Either you love 'em or hate 'em. Truth be told, an annuity can be a great investment or a terrible one. It depends on your circumstances. Of course, the best way to know what you're getting into — or running from — is by covering the basics.

So what's an annuity? It's a contract between you and an insurance company. Here's the lowdown — you invest a certain amount upfront, and then you get a steady stream of income later. You can either begin collecting payments immediately or at a future date.

Several factors determine how much you get each month, including your age and the length of your payment period. You can choose between receiving payments for the rest of your life or for a specific period of time, say, 10 or 20 years.

The size of your payments also depends on your tolerance for risk. Are you conservative? A fixed annuity, which acts like an interest-bearing savings account, might be more your speed. A bit of a gambler? Then consider a variable annuity. Your rate of return will hinge on how well the annuity's underlying investments perform.

An annuity might be right for you if you fit the following bill.

▶ You're looking for guaranteed income.

▶ You don't like to play the stock market.

▶ You don't qualify for life insurance and want to leave money to family.

▶ You're bad at managing money.

If you're thinking about buying one, be aware of these drawbacks.

▶ Early withdrawals carry high surrender charges.

▶ Annuities tend to come with lots of expenses, including commissions and investment-management fees, that reduce your rate of return.

▶ You won't get a tax break for buying an annuity like you will when investing in a traditional IRA.

▶ Guaranteed returns can be well below what you'd get with other investments.

Still interested? Before signing the bottom line, be sure you understand what you're buying. Compare the annuity with no-load mutual funds, which don't carry sales commissions or surrender charges.

And remember, most annuities have a "free look" period of about 10 to 30 days in which you can review your contract and terminate it without penalty.

Just the facts: Why an annuity won't make your kids rich

Would you rather inherit a $100,000 annuity or $100,000 in stock? You'd be wise to choose the latter.

Let's say Uncle Lou paid $20,000 for stock that was worth $100,000 when he left it to you. You sell the shares a couple of years later for $115,000. The IRS will tax you on the $15,000 you earned from the sale. You get a free pass on the $80,000 the stock earned when Uncle Lou owned it.

That's not so when inheriting an annuity. All the investment gains stay with the policy, and you'll generally pay taxes as if you were the original owner.

And inherited stock has an added bonus. Your profits are taxed at lower capital gains rates, while annuities are taxed as if they are ordinary income.

DOLLARS & SENSE

QLACs — upgrade your retirement with guaranteed income

Do you fear outliving your savings? If so, you're not alone. Two out of 3 Americans believe their money may run out before they die, according to a Northwestern Mutual survey.

What's a senior to do? See if a Qualified Longevity Annuity Contract (QLAC) is your cup of tea. It's a type of longevity insurance that guarantees future income and maybe even a longer-lasting nest egg. Here's how.

▶ You buy it with funds from your IRA, 401(k), or other retirement accounts, using up to $130,000 or a quarter of the total savings, whichever is less.

▶ The annuity amount is excluded from required minimum distribution (RMD) calculations, so you can withdraw less and save more.

▶ You can hold off on receiving the annuity payments until you're 85, ensuring you'll have a steady income in your later years.

Let's say, for example, you turn 70 1/2 after using $130,000 from a $300,000 IRA to buy a QLAC. Your first RMD, based on the $170,000 left in the IRA, would fall from $10,949 to $6,204.

You'd not only delay paying taxes on $4,745, but you'd also get to see that money continue to grow tax-deferred in your IRA. Remember, though, you'll pay income taxes on QLAC payments when they kick in.

Would buying a QLAC be a good deal for you? There are lots of things to consider, including your life expectancy, future inflation rates, and whether or not you want to include spousal or death-benefit riders. Be sure to consult a financial advisor before signing on the bottom line.

Taking stock: Avoid the perils of probate

Paul drew up a will several years ago, leaving his energy stocks to his daughter, Susie. When Paul died, the shares were worth

$200,000. But as his will sat in probate, crude prices tumbled. Susie watched helplessly for months while the value of her father's portfolio dropped 30 percent. When she finally was able to sell the stock, it was worth just $140,000.

Don't let a similar experience happen to your loved ones. Register your shares with a transfer-on-death (TOD) form while you're still alive. This way your stocks, bonds, and mutual funds will avoid probate and directly transfer to your chosen beneficiaries. Here's the scoop.

Get the ball rolling. Contact your account's administrator, whether it's a broker or the transfer agent of the company that issued your stock. Ask for a registration form and fill it out. You'll need the beneficiary's date of birth and Social Security number. Make a copy and send the form back using certified mail with a return receipt so you'll get proof the document was received.

Next, check that your TOD registration is actually on file. The new stock registration will look something like, "Paul Jones, TOD Susie Jones."

You can name several beneficiaries if you want. Just designate the percentage of your portfolio you want to transfer to each one.

Know the facts. You retain control of the securities and can change beneficiaries if you wish. And remember, beneficiary designations trump any requests you make in a will.

Have a joint account? The beneficiary can inherit the funds only when both owners are dead. Until then, the surviving co-owner has complete control over the shares, including changing the beneficiary.

Avoid a minor problem. If you plan on leaving stock to young grandchildren, you'll have to go an extra step. That's because minors can't legally control investments. The solution? Name a custodian or guardian when filling out the registration form.

But before doing so, consider this. Your grandchildren might not be responsible enough to manage a stock portfolio when they reach legal age. If that's the case, consider setting up a living trust. You'll have a lot more control over when the grandkids get the securities.

Build your portfolio drip by drip

Want to sit back, not spend a dime, and watch your stock portfolio grow? Dividend reinvestment plans, or DRIPs for short, help you do that very thing.

In a nutshell, they're plans that allow current shareholders to automatically purchase additional stock by reinvesting dividends — shares of the company's profits, often

> Not all companies offer a DRIP. If you own stock in a company, call its investor relations line to see if the plan is available. You may also find information on the company's website, as well as a link to enrollment instructions.

paid quarterly. The secret to the program's success? A long holding period and compounding returns. Here's an example.

Let's say Tom and Joe each buy 1,000 shares in Company XYZ. The stock trades at $25 a share. Fast forward a few months and the company issues a 30-cent quarterly dividend. Tom gets a check for $300. His portfolio is still worth $25,000.

Joe, however, enrolled in the company's DRIP. Instead of mailing him a check, Company XYZ reinvests the $300 and issues Joe 12 shares of stock. Guess what? The additional shares boost the value of Joe's portfolio to $25,300.

That means his next dividend will increase to nearly $304, while Tom will get just $300. That might not seem like much of a difference. But look what happens after 10 years if the company's stock price and dividend payments haven't changed in all that time.

Tom will have received $12,000 in dividend checks, based on the $1.20 annual dividend on his 1,000 shares. His portfolio will still be worth $25,000. Total gain on Tom's original investment? A solid 48 percent over a decade.

And Joe? He's been reinvesting his dividends the whole time. His portfolio is valued at $40,287. Total gain on his original investment? An impressive 61 percent.

Selling stock? Save on taxes with this tip

About to sell some stock? Before you place the order, consider how long you've owned the shares. If it's a year or less, Uncle Sam will take a bigger bite of your profits.

For example, Helen invested $4,000 in stock in July. She sold it the following June for $4,700. Helen, who reports $50,000 in taxable income, is in the 22 percent tax bracket. She'll owe $154 of her $700 profit to the IRS, which taxes short-term gains like hers as ordinary income.

But if Helen had waited a month, she'd pay just $105. The IRS would classify the sale as a long-term capital gain and tax it at a 15 percent rate.

And don't forget about dividends. You'll have to pay taxes on them, too, whether you've cashed them out or reinvested them. Come tax time, a 1099-DIV tax form will tell you which rate you qualify for.

DOLLARS & SENSE

How to build a bulletproof bond portfolio

You want to create a well-balanced, profitable bond portfolio, but where do you begin? Fortunately, bond buying can be easy — if you have a little know-how.

Take advantage of online expertise to kick off your fund. The internet is one of the best places to start building your bond portfolio. Online brokers make it easy to buy and sell bonds, and some of the best companies — like Fidelity, Charles Schwab, and TD Ameritrade — offer advice to help you get started. All you have to do is set up an online account, and a few mouse clicks later you're in the bond market.

Some bonds have hidden markups used to pay the broker's fees. Make sure you shop around and compare prices at *www.investing inbonds.com* or *emma.msrb.org*. You can search for a fair market price using the bond's information. If you can't find the exact same bond online, just compare it to another one with a similar rating, yield, and date of maturity.

Visit your bank to make bond-buying easy. Most local banks and credit unions are great places to pick up bonds. Your options depend on what's on hand, but they should have a host of corporate bonds, federal bonds, and maybe even municipal bonds.

Get your treasury bonds straight from the source. While you can buy most government-backed bonds from your bank or

If you don't want to buy bonds à la carte, an exchange-traded fund (ETF) lets you buy bonds as a bundle. Think of them a bit like mutual funds for bonds. As an added bonus, you won't have to research dozens of companies and pay transaction fees for each individual bond.

broker, treasury bonds come straight from the government. You can buy them at a regional federal reserve bank or online at *www.treasurydirect.gov*. The best part? You bypass fees and other transaction costs.

Decipher the financial jargon to get the best deals. The best way to avoid getting duped by a bad deal is to learn to speak the seller's language. Here are a few bond terms you'll need to know before you start shopping.

▶ Issuer — the company or government entity who is offering the bond.

▶ Coupon — the interest rate paid by the issuer to you, the lender.

▶ Maturity date — the date on which the bond will be fully paid back to you.

▶ Yield — what the annual return will be until the bond reaches maturity. Some bonds are listed with a "c" next to them, which means they're callable bonds. These bonds can be recalled by companies and reissued at lower interest rates if the market takes a dip.

▶ Rating — the safer a bond is, the higher its rating. Experts generally recommend sticking with AAA rated bonds, which are the highest rated, safest bonds.

▶ Bid price — market value, or what people are willing to pay for bonds. Don't be deceived by the low amount. It's quoted as a percentage of the bond's face value of $1,000. So a bid price of 150 means a buyer is willing to pay $1,500 for the bond.

Climb the ladder to financial stability

Think of a bond like an IOU. Whenever the government or a company needs money, they ask you to lend them some cash. In exchange, they promise to pay your money back with interest.

But when you buy a bond, you're kissing your cash goodbye for a few years while the bond matures. Building a bond ladder is a way to stagger your investments so they don't all come due at once. Instead, you'll have a steady stream of income spaced out over a number of years.

A big plus is that spreading out your bonds helps minimize your risk if the market falls. If one bond comes due, you may have to reinvest it at a lower interest rate, but in the meantime the rest are still making money at the higher rates.

Of course you can always choose to keep your profit and reinvest when the market is on the upswing.

Experts recommend starting your ladder with at least $10,000. You should keep all the "rungs" of the ladder about the same size — meaning bonds should cost the same and mature at even intervals. Look for higher-quality bonds, and avoid those that can be called in before their maturity date.

When it's time to cash out one rung, you can either pocket your money or turn around and reinvest it to keep the ladder — and your profits — going.

Check out the graphic on the next page to see how you can build a simple bond ladder.

How to build a bond ladder

Gretta wants to put $10,000 of her savings into bonds. She invests $2,000 into five different bonds that mature at regular intervals. This creates a simple bond ladder that will pay off every two years for 10 years.

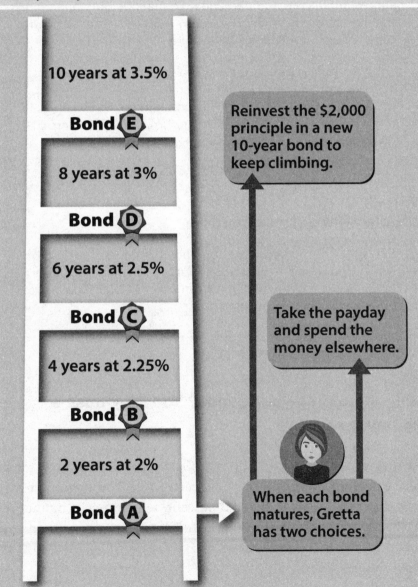

10 years at 3.5%

Bond E

8 years at 3%

Bond D

6 years at 2.5%

Bond C

4 years at 2.25%

Bond B

2 years at 2%

Bond A

Reinvest the $2,000 principle in a new 10-year bond to keep climbing.

Take the payday and spend the money elsewhere.

When each bond matures, Gretta has two choices.

A CLOSER LOOK

Casey bought a 10-year, $3,000 bond at 5 percent interest three years ago. By multiplying the number of years, the value of the bond, and the interest rate he can see he's earned $450 already (3 x $3,000 x .05 = $450). But the market value of the bond today is $3,750. He's tempted to sell now, but will he be better off?

Use the holding period return yield (HPRY) formula to find out. The formula says HPRY = [(market value – purchase price) + payments received] / purchase price. So selling the bond would net him a 40 percent return, or $1,200. Here's the breakdown:

- HPRY = [($3,750 – $3,000) + $450] / $3,000

- HPRY = ($750 + $450) / $3,000

- HPRY = $1,200 / $3,000 = .40

But wait — if he keeps that bond until it matures, he'll actually make more. By doing the same calculations, Casey discovers he'll get a 50 percent return, or $1,500, if he holds the bond for the full 10 years.

Sold on holding your bonds? You may miss a big payday

Let's say you bought a $2,000 bond last year when interest rates were 5 percent, so each year you'll earn $100. But now interest rates look like they'll jump to 6 percent, which means buying that same bond today would net you $120 annually. Should you hold on to your bond or sell it?

Selling your bond could get you a better profit if the conditions are right. Here are two signs you should consider cashing out.

Act early when interest rates are rising. Bonds become more valuable when interest rates drop. The opposite occurs when they rise. Experts say you should consider selling when signs point to a significant rate hike.

If the Federal Reserve raises interest rates, new bonds will pay out at higher amounts. So your best bet is to try and sell before that point, then buy newer, more profitable investments.

To help gauge the market, keep a close eye on announcements from the Federal Open Market Committee (FOMC), which decides the future of U.S. interest rates. You can find their official statements on *federalreserve.gov/default.htm*.

One exception — don't go through the trouble of selling bonds that will mature in a year or less.

High prices might mean bigger returns. Occasionally, your bonds will be worth more if you sell them now rather than holding off until they mature. It depends on factors like the current interest rate, market conditions, and how much time is left before the bond matures.

If the market price of your bond is unusually high, it may be in your best interest to sell. You'll just need to do a little math to figure out if the selling price trumps the value left on your bond.

Calculate the total return on your investment by using the holding period return yield (HPRY) formula. Subtract the price you paid for the bond from the current market value. Add that number to the interest payments you've already received to see how much you'll earn. Then compare it to the amount your bond will be worth when it matures. (See *A Closer Look* on page 248.)

These calculations will show you which bond will generate the largest profit and whether it makes sense to hold or sell.

Find the right balance for your investments

The S&P 500 has been on a bull run for nine years, rising 300 percent since 2009. Just think — a $50,000 investment back then would be worth more than $200,000 today. And with interest rates so low, it's doubly tempting to keep most of your portfolio in stocks.

But doing so could be risky if you're at a time in your life — think at or near retirement — where there's less time to recover from market losses.

History proves this true. Remember the financial meltdown of 2008? The S&P 500 index fell 37 percent while "safe" investments like Treasury bills and money market funds reported gains.

Let's say you had taken a conservative approach to investing back then, with an even mix of diversified stocks and bonds in your $500,000 portfolio. You'd have lost roughly $80,000 that year.

And if you'd been more aggressive, with a portfolio of, say, 90 percent stocks and 10 percent bonds? You'd have more than doubled your losses to $165,000.

So how do you find the right mix? Turns out, a lot depends on how much you're willing to risk. Vanguard offers a free risk tolerance test at *personal.vanguard.com/us/FundsInvQuestionnaire*.

There you'll find suggestions on asset allocations based on answers to questions about your financial situation, retirement time frame, and investment experience.

Or you could find a financial advisor to help come up with a plan. If you have a large portfolio you may qualify for free or discounted advice from an online brokerage. You could also find someone unaffiliated with a large firm at *napfa.org* or *garrettplanning network.com*. Be sure to check your advisor's record with regulators.

Time changes things for better or worse. Whatever mix of stocks and bonds you come up with, don't forget the proportions will shift over time. For example, imagine you invested 65 percent of your savings in stocks and the remaining 35 percent in bonds. You reinvest the gains.

During a bull market, your asset allocation will teeter in favor of stocks. You could end up with, say, 70 or 75 percent of your cash riding on stocks. That would make your portfolio more aggressive than you'd planned and put your nest egg at risk. On the other hand, if stocks take a beating, your holdings will shift in favor of bonds.

Adjust your risk if it strays too far from your plan. Your best bet? Rebalance your portfolio by selling some of your stocks or bonds to return to your original plan. But be aware you'll have to pay capital gains tax on profits from the sale of investments if your securities are not in a retirement savings account like an IRA or 401(k).

Another option? Stop contributing to the beefed-up portion of your portfolio, and instead invest in the securities that haven't experienced growth.

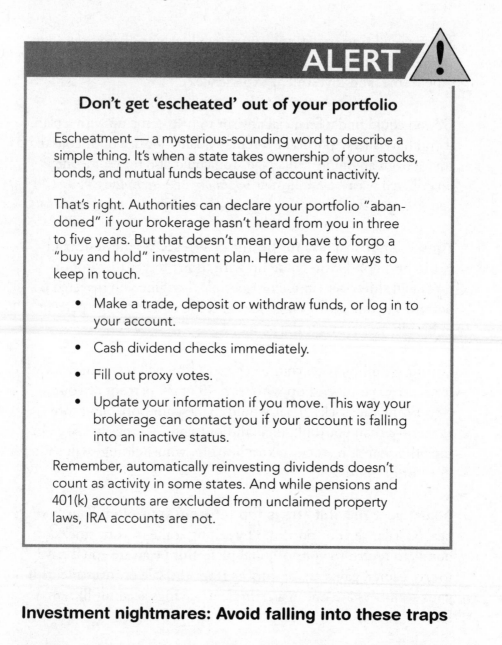

ALERT ⚠️

Don't get 'escheated' out of your portfolio

Escheatment — a mysterious-sounding word to describe a simple thing. It's when a state takes ownership of your stocks, bonds, and mutual funds because of account inactivity.

That's right. Authorities can declare your portfolio "abandoned" if your brokerage hasn't heard from you in three to five years. But that doesn't mean you have to forgo a "buy and hold" investment plan. Here are a few ways to keep in touch.

- Make a trade, deposit or withdraw funds, or log in to your account.

- Cash dividend checks immediately.

- Fill out proxy votes.

- Update your information if you move. This way your brokerage can contact you if your account is falling into an inactive status.

Remember, automatically reinvesting dividends doesn't count as activity in some states. And while pensions and 401(k) accounts are excluded from unclaimed property laws, IRA accounts are not.

Investment nightmares: Avoid falling into these traps

Ever hear of Charles Ponzi? Back in 1919 he promised Bostonians sky-high profits — 50 percent in just 45 days — if they invested in little scraps of paper called international postal reply coupons. The fact that Ponzi was tightlipped about his business plan didn't alarm investors. After all, the financial wizard had to protect his trade secrets. In all, 40,000 people eagerly handed over their savings.

Of course, Ponzi used the money from new investors to pay off — and continue to fool — older ones. When his scheme collapsed a year later, he had a 12-room mansion, servants, and a limo. His investors? They were out $20 million.

Unfortunately, modern takes on old hustles keep sprouting up. Beware the latest financial scams out there.

Don't fall for unkept promises. Are you a retiree living on a fixed income? You might be tempted by promissory notes — written promises to repay a loan — that offer high returns on your investment. That's what scammers are counting on.

Know that promissory notes are usually targeted to corporate investors. When marketed to individuals, they can be a red flag that signals "No deal!" When it comes to investing, remember the following:

▸ Don't fall for unlicensed securities or unregistered sellers. Check your investment professional's registration status at *Investor.gov*.

▸ Back away if someone offers steady positive returns despite poor market conditions.

Keep alert for impersonators. Don't fall for fraudsters who say they work for the Securities and Exchange Commission (SEC) and want to help you buy stock or "confirm" a recent transaction. They're just looking to steal your money. In some cases, they'll phone or email you after somebody else has asked you to buy securities.

If you've been contacted by someone pretending to be from the SEC, call its toll-free hotline at 833-732-6441.

Beware of aggressive sales pitches from cold callers. You may become a victim of a scam called the pump and dump.

A likely scenario? A scammer calls out of the blue and says he works for a brokerage. He'll try to con you into buying shares, perhaps giving you false "insider information" to make the stock appear attractive. He's really looking for help in pumping up the share price.

Next thing you know, the "broker" dumps his overvalued shares. He gets the profit, the stock price drops, and you're left holding the bag. Best thing you can do when you hear this type of pitch? Hang up.

4 savvy ways to outsmart scam artists

Retirees are often victims of fraud. In fact, nearly 1 in 5 Americans over the age of 65 has been taken advantage of financially.

Why do scammers target seniors? They're more likely to have built a nest egg and solid credit. And older generations were raised to be polite and willing to listen. Con artists take advantage of this, knowing the elderly find it more difficult to abruptly hang up the phone.

You can avoid becoming a victim by gaining a basic understanding of how hustlers operate. Follow these tips when making investment decisions.

Time is on your side so don't fall victim to pressure tactics.
Fraudsters will try to persuade you to invest right away, saying
your time to invest in the "opportunity of a lifetime" is limited.
Or they'll say famous movie stars or community business leaders
have already signed on. Don't believe it.

Investigate any investment pitch and talk to friends and family
before writing a check. You can research securities at
sec.gov/edgar.shtml.

Beware the lure of phantom riches that will "solve all your problems." Scammers know that lots of seniors fear outliving their savings. They'll prey on those worries, promising guaranteed returns or low-risk, high-yield offers.

> Have questions or concerns about your brokerage account or investment? The Financial Industry Regulatory Authority has a toll-free hotline for seniors at 844-574-3577. The agency also publishes investment fraud alerts on its website at *finra.org/investors/alerts.*

Walk away if a broker tells you
to "leave everything to me." If a
deal sounds too good to be true, it is. And don't believe everything
you read. The Securities and Exchange Commission says some pro-
moters write articles pushing certain stocks in exchange for cash.

Do a background check on anyone making you an offer.
Don't assume that people or organizations are legitimate. Successful con artists know how to sound professional, dress for the
part, and print out fake credentials.

So check out any person or firm making an investment offer.
Details on a broker's background and qualifications are available
for free at *brokercheck.finra.org.* For information on registered
investment advisor firms, go to *adviserinfo.sec.gov/IAPD/.*

Still unsure? Call the Securities and Exchange Commission's investor assistance line at 800-732-0330.

Stay on top of your investments. What should you do if you've already invested? Request regular statements, monitor your account, and question any trading activity you don't understand.

Be suspicious if you're told you can't cash out your profits or principal. Another red flag? Being asked to invest with a credit card. Most registered investment firms don't allow customers to fund their investments this way.

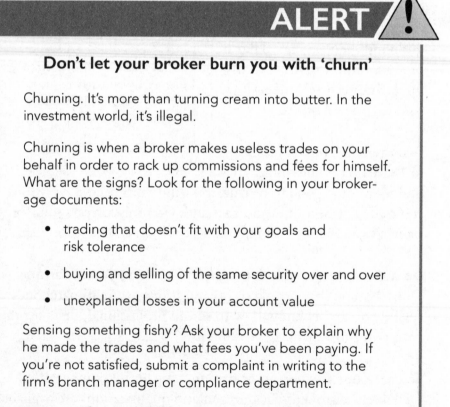

ALERT

Don't let your broker burn you with 'churn'

Churning. It's more than turning cream into butter. In the investment world, it's illegal.

Churning is when a broker makes useless trades on your behalf in order to rack up commissions and fees for himself. What are the signs? Look for the following in your brokerage documents:

- trading that doesn't fit with your goals and risk tolerance

- buying and selling of the same security over and over

- unexplained losses in your account value

Sensing something fishy? Ask your broker to explain why he made the trades and what fees you've been paying. If you're not satisfied, submit a complaint in writing to the firm's branch manager or compliance department.

You can also contact the Financial Industry Regulatory Authority at *inra.org/investors/investor-complaint-center*.

Tax secrets

Perfectly legal ways to deduct more, file faster, and pay less

Terrific tax breaks just for seniors

"April is the cruelest month..." wrote T.S. Eliott in his 1922 poem *The Waste Land*. And the most dreaded day? You guessed it. April 15, the traditional deadline to file your tax returns with the Internal Revenue Service (IRS).

But that doesn't mean you have to give Uncle Sam more than you should. In fact, you can find over a dozen little-known deductions for seniors — including six ways to slash your taxes — starting when you turn 50. Read on for some secret "senior discounts" that will help you keep more of your tax dollars.

▶ If you're 50 or older, you can make $6,000 in annual "catch-up" payments to your 401(k) in addition to the maximum contribution. That amount may change so check with your company's benefits department for the current figure.

▸ A similar rule applies to IRA accounts, but catch-up payments are limited to $1,000 a year.

▸ After you turn 55, you can put an extra $1,000 payment each year in your Health Savings Account.

▸ Want to know a secret? You can tap into your 401(k) without penalty at 55 years or older if you leave your job. But the early access benefit doesn't apply if you rolled an old 401(k) into an IRA.

▸ At the age of 59 1/2, you can start withdrawing funds from your IRA or 401(k) accounts with no penalty fees. Any younger than that, and you'll likely pay the government an extra 10 percent.

▸ The Tax Counseling for the Elderly program offers free tax advice to people age 60 and older. To find a location near you, go to *irs.treasury.gov/freetaxprep*, or call 800-906-9887.

▸ The IRS will hit you with a penalty if you take too little tax out of your paycheck and owe more than $1,000 at filing time. But if that happens during the year you retire, they may take pity on you. Taxpayers who are 62 and older can request a waiver of the penalty during their retirement year and the following year. If you fit the bill, use Form 2210 to give the IRS a reasonable cause for not having paid your estimated taxes. You may just escape the extra penalty fee.

▸ Age 65 or older? Lucky you, you get an additional tax deduction. Not only can you take the standard deduction, but you can deduct an extra $1,300 per person if you're married or $1,600 if you're single. With recent changes to the tax law, that adds up to a huge $26,600 in deductions for a married couple.

▶ At 65, the minimum income required to file taxes goes up as well. If you're below that threshold, you don't have to file at all.

▶ Some low-income seniors age 65 and up can lower their tax bill through an IRS credit. The credit also applies to some younger retirees who are disabled. To see if you qualify, go to *IRS.gov* and type in "am I eligible for elderly tax credit" in the search box.

▶ Are you insured by Medicare? You can deduct premiums paid for Medicare Part B, C, and D. But most people have to itemize to benefit.

▶ People on Medicare who run their own businesses can, under certain conditions, take those same deductions without having to itemize.

▶ Want to avoid paying taxes and do a good deed at the same time? The IRS permits IRA owners age 70 1/2 and older to directly transfer up to $100,000 to a qualified charity. The donation can solve your required minimum distribution requirement, and it doesn't count toward your income. Keep a letter from the charity acknowledging the donation. You'll need it for your tax records.

Caring for a senior parent? Don't miss these tax breaks

More than 40 million unpaid caregivers in the United States help the elderly with tasks like grocery shopping, visiting doctors, and housework. Most are sons and daughters caring for aging parents. It's a labor of love that can strain your budget, particularly if you're footing the bill for mom's medication and dental work.

Fortunately, Uncle Sam takes that into consideration when it comes time to do your taxes. If you're caring for an aging parent, take a look at these tax breaks that offset costs.

Dependent care credit. Did you hire someone to look after mom or dad while you were working? You may qualify for a credit that could lower your tax bill by more than $1,000. The catch? Your parent must have lived with you for more than half a year and been unable to care for himself. Be sure to keep receipts from the care provider.

Medical expense deduction. You could get this deduction if your parent qualifies as a dependent and you paid his out-of-pocket medical or dental expenses. To do so, the amount has to be higher than 7.5 percent of your taxable income. That figure increases to 10 percent beginning with the 2019 tax year.

So let's say your adjusted gross income is $50,000. Anything beyond the first $3,750 in medical bills would be deductible. If you paid $5,000 for prescriptions and doctor visits, you could deduct $1,250.

Employer flexible spending accounts. Your employer can put up to $5,000 of your salary into a dependent care flexible spending account. The money isn't taxed, which means it goes a lot further to help pay for things like adult daycare services. Plans differ on what they cover, so be sure to read your plan's documents before opening the account.

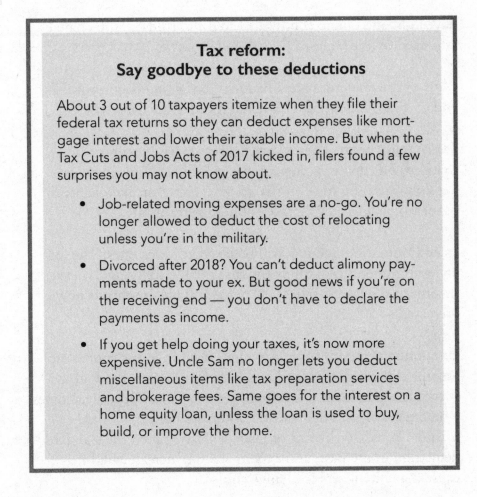

Tax reform:
Say goodbye to these deductions

About 3 out of 10 taxpayers itemize when they file their federal tax returns so they can deduct expenses like mortgage interest and lower their taxable income. But when the Tax Cuts and Jobs Acts of 2017 kicked in, filers found a few surprises you may not know about.

- Job-related moving expenses are a no-go. You're no longer allowed to deduct the cost of relocating unless you're in the military.

- Divorced after 2018? You can't deduct alimony payments made to your ex. But good news if you're on the receiving end — you don't have to declare the payments as income.

- If you get help doing your taxes, it's now more expensive. Uncle Sam no longer lets you deduct miscellaneous items like tax preparation services and brokerage fees. Same goes for the interest on a home equity loan, unless the loan is used to buy, build, or improve the home.

4 changes to tax law you won't want to miss

Joe, a single ironworker, earns $55,000 a year. This year he paid $6,890 in federal taxes. If he earns the same next year, Joe will owe the federal government just $5,400 — nearly 22 percent less. The reason? The Tax Cuts and Job Act passed in late 2017 pushed Joe into a lower tax bracket.

Of course, the tax overhaul's effect on your bottom line hinges on several factors, including how much you earn, whether you have kids, and where you live. Read on to find the top changes you need to know about the tax code rewrite.

Most of the new rules are scheduled to stay in effect until the end of 2025, unless the U.S. Congress decides otherwise.

Tax bracket redo. There are still seven federal income tax brackets, but they're at lower rates and adjusted income levels. Let's say you used to be in the 25 percent tax bracket. Most of that income will now be taxed at a 22 percent rate.

In addition, more income will be taxed at lower rates. The federal government used to tax the first $9,325 in a single filer's income at the lowest rate of 10 percent. That amount is now increased to $9,525.

Deduction revamp. One of the best ways to lower your taxable income is through deductions. Uncle Sam has nearly doubled the standard deduction for single filers to $12,000, while couples who file jointly can deduct $24,000 from their combined income. Some 70 percent of taxpayers have taken the standard deduction in the past, and experts say the increase will likely cause many itemizers to change course.

The new tax law also limits your federal deduction of state and local taxes to $10,000.

Exemption overhaul. The government has done away with personal and dependent exemptions, each of which was expected to be $4,150 in 2018. While that whittles away some of the benefits gained by the standard deduction increase, many retirees will still come out ahead.

If you're 65 or older you'll get an extra deduction of $1,300 per person if married and $1,600 if single. That brings the standard deduction for a married 65-plus couple up to $26,600.

Education expansion. Thinking about setting up a tax-advantaged savings plan for your grandkids' education? You're in luck. Tax reform has expanded 529 savings plans. Besides paying for college, you can now use up to $10,000 annually per child for private or parochial elementary and high school expenses.

In addition, you can roll over 529 funds into an ABLE account for individuals with special needs. Don't worry, doing so won't jeopardize your loved one's eligibility for government assistance.

Tax check: Are you floating the government an interest-free loan?

Chances are your tax bracket changed under the recent tax code redo. That means it's a good time to look at the amount you have withheld from your paycheck. Have too much taken out and you're giving the government an interest-free loan. Too little means you'll owe money in April.

Think you might need to adjust your take-home pay? Find out by plugging some numbers into the IRS withholding calculator at *irs.gov/individuals/irs-withholding-calculator*. Don't worry — the website won't ask for sensitive information like your Social Security or bank account numbers. Have a recent pay stub and tax return handy before beginning.

Click on the Form W-4 link if you want to download a form to make withholding changes. Just fill it out and bring it to your human resources department.

Savvy tricks to save your inheritance from the IRS

Want to prevent the IRS from touching your children's inheritance? Well, Uncle Sam has made it easy for you.

That's right. The recently revamped tax code nearly doubles the estate tax exemption. That means you can pass on almost $11.2 million to your heirs without having to pay a penny to the federal government.

Of course, the vast majority of Americans don't have estates anywhere near that size. Still, if you want to make sure your money stays in your loved ones' hands, consider lowering your assets. Here's why.

Avoid the bite of state taxes. A dozen states and Washington, D.C. currently have an estate tax, with most collecting fees at a lower threshold than the IRS. Oregon, for example, taxes any assets in your estate valued at more than $1 million. And six states charge heirs for the right to collect an inheritance.

Enjoy the gift of giving now rather than later. Are you financially comfortable enough to help your loved ones now instead of later? You can give up to $15,000 annually — free of gift tax — to as many people as you want. That amount doubles to $30,000 for married couples.

Dodge the gift tax altogether. Did you know some payments bypass the gift tax? You can pay a loved one's tuition or medical expenses without Uncle Sam batting an eye. There's a catch though. You have to make the payment directly to the school or doctor's office. If you give the money to the person it benefits, the IRS will consider it a taxable gift.

The 'taxing' truth: How much do you know?

Do you have trouble doing your taxes? You're in good company. In fact, Albert Einstein once jokingly told his accountant that income taxes were the most difficult thing to understand — trickier, even, than the theory of relativity. Why not quiz yourself to see how much you know about IRS rules?

Decide whether the following are true or false. You may be surprised at what you find out.

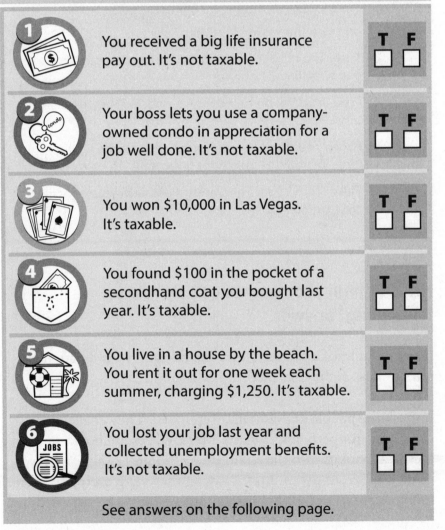

1. You received a big life insurance pay out. It's not taxable. **T** ☐ **F** ☐

2. Your boss lets you use a company-owned condo in appreciation for a job well done. It's not taxable. **T** ☐ **F** ☐

3. You won $10,000 in Las Vegas. It's taxable. **T** ☐ **F** ☐

4. You found $100 in the pocket of a secondhand coat you bought last year. It's taxable. **T** ☐ **F** ☐

5. You live in a house by the beach. You rent it out for one week each summer, charging $1,250. It's taxable. **T** ☐ **F** ☐

6. You lost your job last year and collected unemployment benefits. It's not taxable. **T** ☐ **F** ☐

See answers on the following page.

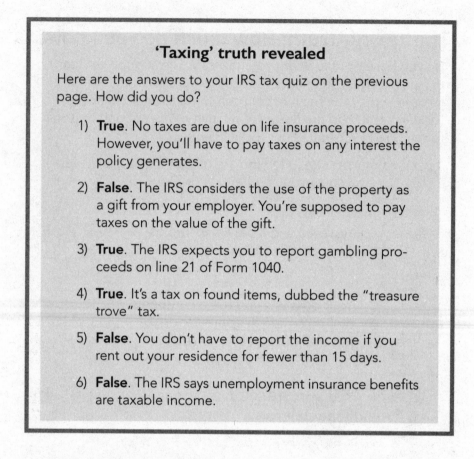

'Taxing' truth revealed

Here are the answers to your IRS tax quiz on the previous page. How did you do?

1) **True**. No taxes are due on life insurance proceeds. However, you'll have to pay taxes on any interest the policy generates.

2) **False**. The IRS considers the use of the property as a gift from your employer. You're supposed to pay taxes on the value of the gift.

3) **True**. The IRS expects you to report gambling proceeds on line 21 of Form 1040.

4) **True**. It's a tax on found items, dubbed the "treasure trove" tax.

5) **False**. You don't have to report the income if you rent out your residence for fewer than 15 days.

6) **False**. The IRS says unemployment insurance benefits are taxable income.

Hit with high property taxes? Here's an 'appealing' answer

If the thought of a property tax hike fills you with dread, never fear. You can fight City Hall.

Just ask the people of Nashville, Tennessee. They challenged their 2017 property assessments after a real estate boom sent their reappraisals into the stratosphere. Some 17,000 property owners appealed the estimates, saying they were overpriced. The result? Eight out of 10 Nashville homeowners who appealed had their assessments lowered. The same thing happened to 55 percent of commercial property owners.

Even if you're not facing a tax increase, you may think you're already paying too much. Take a look at some of these strategies to help slash your property taxes. They can save you thousands of dollars.

Take advantage of your age. Of course, you already know about senior discounts at the movies and supermarket. But did you know many states offer retirees property tax breaks?

In Mississippi, for example, homeowners 65 and older don't have to pay tax on $75,000 of their home's value. And if you add a room to your Florida residence for a parent or grandparent 62 or older, you won't be taxed on the added value of your home. Why not contact your tax department to see which discounts are available to you?

Time your improvements just right. Planning on expanding your back deck? Find out what the addition will do to your tax bill — before construction begins — by contacting your local tax authority. Is your neighborhood due for a reassessment? You might want to hold off on major renovations until after it's complete.

You don't have to allow an assessor into your home. But if you don't, he may assume you've made big improvements and tax you accordingly. If you do, walk around with him so you can point out defects like uneven floors and ceiling cracks.

Review your appraisal and set the record straight. Find out how your local government determines a property's market value. Then check for errors in your house's appraisal. The assessor's office can give you the information it used to assess your home.

Does your property record card include the correct number of rooms? Does it say you have a two-car garage when you don't even have a tool shed? Bring any mistakes to the government's attention.

You can also compare your assessment with your neighbors' appraisals. If several similar homes have a lower assessment than you do, you might be able to argue for a tax reduction.

Do your homework to build your case. If you decide to proceed, gather up photos, property records, or blueprints that back up your claims. Some property tax disputes can be settled through informal discussions with your tax office. Other times you'll have to fill out papers.

If your claim is denied, you can always request a hearing with your local or state appeals board. In the meantime, pay your tax bill to avoid penalties. If your appeal is approved, the money will be refunded.

Home sweet tax bite: See where your state stands

Thinking of buying, say, a $250,000 house? If you like palm trees, Hawaii might be a good place. That's because property taxes in the Aloha State run at just .27 percent of a home's value. You'd pay only $675 a year.

A $250,000 house in New Jersey, where the property tax rate is 2.4 percent, would cost you $6,000 in taxes annually.

For a look at where your state stands when it comes to real estate taxes, do an online search for "property taxes by state."

DOLLARS & SENSE

Paying your parents' mortgage? How to make sure you get the deduction

Bill moved into his mother's condo and assumed the mortgage payments after she fell and broke a hip. He'll inherit the property one day, but for now she has legal title to both the condo and the mortgage. When tax time rolls around, who gets to deduct the mortgage interest from their taxable income — Bill or his mother?

Turns out, maybe neither of them.

Deducting mortgage interest can be tricky. At first glance, it seems like Bill's mother is entitled to the deduction. After all, the IRS is pretty clear on its eligibility rules — you must own the property that secures the debt. Bill's mother can tick that box. But the tax code also says only the people who pay mortgage interest are allowed to deduct it. She fails that test.

Bill, meanwhile, doesn't legally co-own the condo. The IRS could simply consider his mortgage payments as a gift to his mother. Does that mean nobody can deduct the mortgage interest? This is where things get sticky.

> Taxpayers who take out mortgages may deduct the interest on a total of $750,000 of mortgage debt on a first or second home. But people who signed on for a mortgage before Dec. 15, 2017, can still deduct interest on up to $1 million.

Does the payee act like an owner? The law allows an "equitable" property owner to deduct mortgage interest. Equitable title would give Bill the right to use and enjoy the condo without having legal ownership.

Of course, the ability to "enjoy" the property comes with responsibilities. Along with taking over the mortgage, Bill would have to maintain the condo and pay taxes and insurance on it — everything a typical owner would do.

It's tax time and Matt doesn't have enough to pay the IRS. "I'll file for a six-month extension," he tells his friend. "That'll give me extra time to come up with the money, right?"

Wrong. An extension to file your taxes in October doesn't give you a pass on paying Uncle Sam the previous April. Pay late, and you'll likely face interest and penalties.

Costly mistakes like Matt's add up. That's why it's important to plan ahead — particularly if you're retired. At this stage of life, there's no employer withholding taxes from your paycheck. As a general rule, you should pay estimated taxes quarterly if you expect to owe $1,000 or more when you file your tax return.

Want to avoid the hassle? Have taxes withheld from IRA distributions and other retirement income. Consult with your financial planner to find out what percentage is right for you.

Head off problems before they occur. If you co-own a home and aren't listed on the title, have your ownership interest written into a contract.

Don't think that's necessary? You may want to look at what happened to a California man who waited to sign on the bottom line. He had an oral agreement with his family that he'd pay the mortgage to increase his equity interest in the home. The man took the mortgage interest deduction on his 2010 tax return, and his family added him to the legal title in 2013.

The IRS disallowed his deduction, saying he owed the government almost $9,000. But a federal court overturned the ruling, saying the man's oral agreement of ownership was valid. But that was only after he testified to having also made tax and insurance payments and improvements to the property.

The bottom line: make things official. Bill could have avoided a lot of problems by moving more quickly to legalize his claim to the condo. Want to avoid hassles with the IRS and possibly having to go to court? Make sure to get your ownership interest in writing as soon as you start making mortgage payments.

Small business owner? Don't 'pass through' this deduction

If you dream of launching a small business, changes to the federal tax code may just prompt you to hang out a shingle. New rules under the Tax Cut and Jobs Act of 2017 allow some small businesses to deduct 20 percent of their business income. So who's eligible?

You might be, if your business is a "pass-through" entity. Such businesses don't pay federal taxes under the corporate rate. Instead, the owners pay tax on company profits using individual rates when they file their personal tax returns.

Examples of pass-through businesses? Partnerships, limited liability companies, and sole proprietorships — the technical name for a one-person business. Considering a freelance writing gig or consulting for your old employer? Now might be the time.

While a 20 percent deduction may not seem like a lot, it can add up. Let's say you have $60,000 in qualified business income. Without the discount you'd pay $9,140 in taxes. With it, $6,500 based on a reduced income of $48,000.

Unfortunately, taking the tax break can get complicated. Generally, the deduction covers either your business income or your taxable income minus capital gains — whichever is lower.

And not all pass-through ventures can take the deduction. To qualify, your total taxable income must be below $157,500 if you're single or $315,000 if you're married and filing jointly. Once your income goes over that amount, the government limits your eligibility.

Business deductions: There's no place like home

Working from home has lots of perks — no commuting hassles, fewer interruptions, and complete control of the thermostat. And come tax time, you might get to take a big deduction. If you're self-employed, follow these rules to legally keep more in your pocket.

Use it regularly and exclusively.
You've got to use the room or area solely for work. That means guests can't sleep on the sofa bed in your home office. And don't park your car in the garage if that's where your woodcarving business is based.

> If you like to forge client relationships on the golf course, it just got more expensive. The IRS no longer allows business owners to deduct entertainment expenses. But all is not lost. Meals are still 50 percent deductible — as long as they're not lavish, and business is conducted.

That rule doesn't apply, however, if you're storing materials or running a day care.

To qualify for the deduction, the work also has to be on a regular basis, not just once or twice a year. And it can't be voluntary, like baking cookies for fundraisers.

Make it your main place of business. The IRS says your home office must be your principal place of business or where you meet with clients or customers.

It doesn't even have to be attached to your house. So if you've been itching to turn that backyard shed into a blogger's retreat, go for it.

Beware the 'nanny' tax when hiring a caregiver

Finding the right person to cook and clean for an ailing parent can be tricky. And if you decide to employ someone independently, you'll probably owe a "nanny" tax.

The IRS says you must pay half the caregiver's Social Security and Medicare taxes if you do the hiring and control how the job gets done. It doesn't matter if the worker is part-time or referred by an agency. The IRS considers you the employer, requiring you to pay taxes on wages over $2,100 a year.

But you don't have to pay the tax if you hire a self-employed worker, also called an independent contractor. These people usually run their own businesses and provide the tools to complete the job. Picture a caterer who markets meal-delivery services or a physical therapist provided by a home-health company.

For more information, download the *Handbook for Employers* at *www.uscis.gov/i-9-central*, or call 800-870-3676.

Don't fall into this vacation home tax trap

Home is where the heart is, except when taxes are involved. Just ask Brenda, a Minneapolis snowbird who winters each year at her Miami condo. Last year, when tax season came along, she decided to call retiree-friendly Florida home. That way, Brenda figured, she'd avoid paying Minnesota taxes on her Social Security benefits, IRA withdrawals, and pension payments.

Big mistake. North Star State auditors wanted proof that she had really picked up roots and moved to her Florida digs. Brenda couldn't provide it and had to pay both back taxes and a penalty.

Don't get caught in the same trap as Brenda. Follow these rules if you want to establish residency in the tax-haven state where your second home is located.

Keep a paper trail to prove your whereabouts. State laws vary, but Minnesota considers you a taxable resident if you spend at least 183 days a year there. That's why it's important to keep a log of your comings and goings if you want to establish residency somewhere else.

> Thinking of buying a house in a high-tax state like New York, Maine, or California? You'll want to look before you leap. The federal tax rewrite has limited your state and local deduction on property, sales, and income taxes to $10,000.

Don't throw away ATM and sales receipts, utility bills, or personal calendars. They can help establish the length of time you've been away.

Show your commitment to your new home. Register to vote, get a library card and driver's license, and register your car in the new state. Open and use a bank account and update your address on important papers, like insurance documents and wills.

If you're really serious about establishing residency, cut ties with the old state. Consider resigning from clubs, canceling newspaper subscriptions, and selling your home.

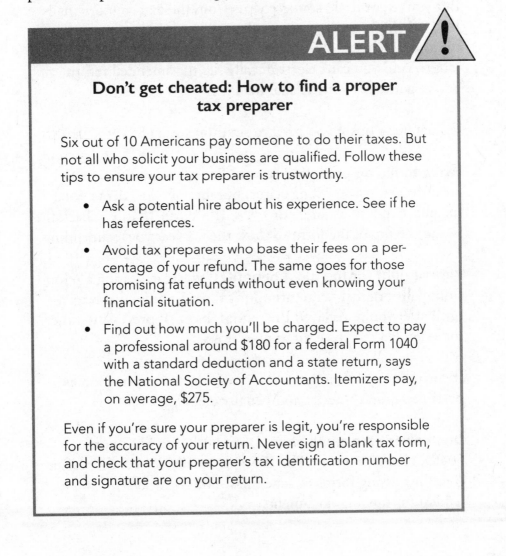

ALERT

Don't get cheated: How to find a proper tax preparer

Six out of 10 Americans pay someone to do their taxes. But not all who solicit your business are qualified. Follow these tips to ensure your tax preparer is trustworthy.

- Ask a potential hire about his experience. See if he has references.

- Avoid tax preparers who base their fees on a percentage of your refund. The same goes for those promising fat refunds without even knowing your financial situation.

- Find out how much you'll be charged. Expect to pay a professional around $180 for a federal Form 1040 with a standard deduction and a state return, says the National Society of Accountants. Itemizers pay, on average, $275.

Even if you're sure your preparer is legit, you're responsible for the accuracy of your return. Never sign a blank tax form, and check that your preparer's tax identification number and signature are on your return.

Mess up your tax return? Here's how to fix it

You missed a valuable deduction last April. Or maybe you forgot to report some of your investment income. No need to panic. The IRS will let you file an amended return.

But you've got to do so three years from the date you originally filed or within two years from the date you paid your tax. You can use whichever timeline extends your amendment deadline longer. And you can't electronically file the amended return. You've got to send it via snail mail.

Follow these tips if you need to set things straight with the IRS.

When to file an amended return. Revise your return if you need to correct your filing status, number of dependents, total income, deductions, or credits. Use IRS Form 1040X. Check the box at the top of the form to show the tax year you're amending.

Time it right for the most benefit. If you're expecting a refund from your original tax return, don't file your amended return until after you've received the refund. Normal processing time for amended returns is eight to 12 weeks.

If you're filing because you owe taxes, file and pay as soon as possible to limit interest and penalty charges.

Don't sweat the small stuff. Don't bother to file a Form 1040X for math errors. The IRS will usually correct them. Same goes for missing forms or schedules. The IRS will send you a request for missing documents.

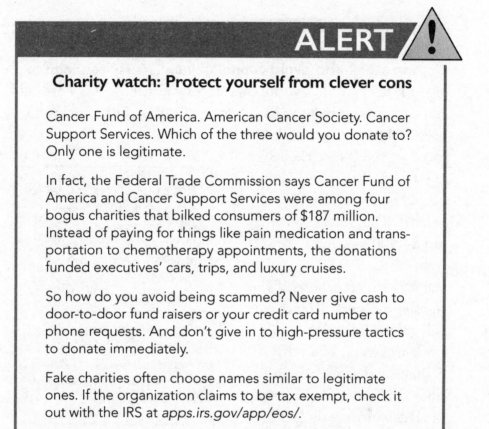

ALERT

Charity watch: Protect yourself from clever cons

Cancer Fund of America. American Cancer Society. Cancer Support Services. Which of the three would you donate to? Only one is legitimate.

In fact, the Federal Trade Commission says Cancer Fund of America and Cancer Support Services were among four bogus charities that bilked consumers of $187 million. Instead of paying for things like pain medication and transportation to chemotherapy appointments, the donations funded executives' cars, trips, and luxury cruises.

So how do you avoid being scammed? Never give cash to door-to-door fund raisers or your credit card number to phone requests. And don't give in to high-pressure tactics to donate immediately.

Fake charities often choose names similar to legitimate ones. If the organization claims to be tax exempt, check it out with the IRS at *apps.irs.gov/app/eos/*.

Get the most from giving when you donate to charity

Giving to charity makes you feel good, and deducting the contribution from your taxes makes the experience even better. But the dynamics of donating to worthy causes are bound to change.

Why? The federal government has nearly doubled the standard deduction. That makes it much less attractive to itemize — which you must do to deduct charitable gifts — on your tax return.

Want to pledge and still get the tax benefits? Here's how.

Donate stock and avoid capital gains. Let's say you want to give $5,000 to your favorite charity. So you sell $5,000 worth of stock that you bought years ago for $1,000. If you're single and have $40,000 in other taxable income, you'll owe the IRS $600 from the sale based on a capital gains rate of 15 percent. That leaves you with just $4,400 to donate.

But it's a different story if you transfer the stock. The charity will get the full value of the stock and you'll avoid the $600 capital gains tax. And since charities are tax exempt, the IRS won't tax the gift or sale of the stock later on.

Not sure how reputable a charity is? Before you write a check, look into the organization's credentials at *CharityWatch.org, CharityNavigator.org, GuideStar.org,* or the Better Business Bureau's Wise Giving Alliance at *Give.org.* You'll find information on the charity's finances, accountability, and transparency.

Consider 'bunching' to benefit from itemizing. Say you're single and eligible for the $12,000 standard deduction. At the same time, you've got $10,000 in itemized mortgage interest and state and local tax deductions. You normally give $1,500 annually to charity, which brings your itemized deductions to $11,500.

In this case, taking the standard deduction seems to make more sense. After all, it's higher. But not if you cram two or three years of donations into a single tax year. That would allow you to take the larger itemized deduction one year and the smaller standard deduction the next.

Channel your money into a donor-advised fund. What if you don't want to give away the entire pledge at once? Enter the donor-advised fund. It's like a charitable savings plan that distributes your donated cash or investments to the charity of your choice — whenever you want.

You can open a donor-advised fund at many brokerage firms, mutual fund companies, and community foundations.

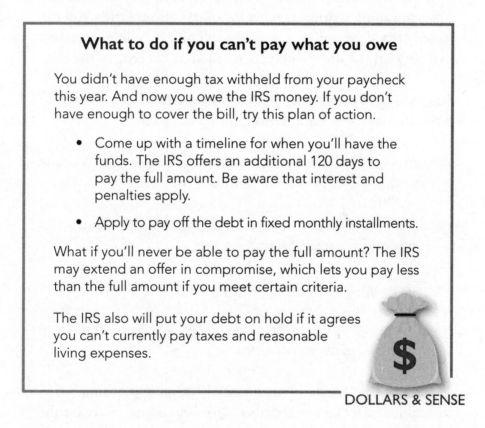

What to do if you can't pay what you owe

You didn't have enough tax withheld from your paycheck this year. And now you owe the IRS money. If you don't have enough to cover the bill, try this plan of action.

- Come up with a timeline for when you'll have the funds. The IRS offers an additional 120 days to pay the full amount. Be aware that interest and penalties apply.

- Apply to pay off the debt in fixed monthly installments.

What if you'll never be able to pay the full amount? The IRS may extend an offer in compromise, which lets you pay less than the full amount if you meet certain criteria.

The IRS also will put your debt on hold if it agrees you can't currently pay taxes and reasonable living expenses.

DOLLARS & SENSE

IRS notice: It's no reason to panic

Sweaty palms. Dry mouth. Racing heart. No, you haven't just been told you need a root canal. You've simply opened your mailbox. And there it is — a letter from the IRS. Time to head for the hills?

No need, says Joyce Mohr, EA, an enrolled agent authorized to represent taxpayers before the IRS. "Take a deep breath and don't panic," she urges. "If you're not aware that you have a serious problem with the IRS, it's more than likely you don't."

Mohr says glitches in IRS software or missing paperwork sometimes prompt a written request for clarification. Often you can remedy the situation with a phone call or by mailing in records that support the questioned claim on your tax return, she says.

Still, you need to take the situation seriously. Here's what to do if the IRS taps you for a "correspondence" audit.

▶ Check that all the information in the notice, such as your name and Social Security number, is correct.

▶ Compare their corrections or changes with the figures on your original submission.

▶ Keep copies of all your correspondence with the IRS.

▶ If you owe money, pay it right away or arrange to make payments to avoid penalties.

Mohr suggests you share the letter with a tax professional or trusted friend or family member. "You should never act on the letter if you don't understand what it's saying," she recommends. If you need extra time, Mohr advises calling the IRS and asking for a 30-day extension. Most likely you'll get it.

Of course, complicated questions about your tax return won't be handled through the mail. If that's the case, the IRS will request a face-to-face interview. But that happens very rarely, says Mohr, who owns the tax preparation and consulting business Taxes Plus in Rockport, Maine.

"I've not experienced that kind of audit in my career of over 20 years," she says.

5 audit red flags you need to know about

Funding cuts have caused the IRS to lose 14,000 enforcement agents — more than 1 in 4 — since 2010. One of the results is fewer audits. In fact, the chances of being audited last year fell to 0.6 percent, the lowest rate the agency has seen since 2002. Of course, that doesn't mean you won't get caught cheating on your taxes.

The IRS uses several methods to determine which returns it audits, including computer programs that look for mistakes and underreported income. Sometimes, it's just the luck of the draw — your return gets randomly singled out from thousands of others.

Other times, the IRS is alerted to "red flags" on your return. Here are some attention grabbers that increase your odds of getting audited.

▶ being in a high-income or no-income tax bracket

▶ mathematical errors on your return

▶ large meal and travel write-offs

▸ higher-than-average deductions

▸ not reporting all required income

Want to avoid an audit altogether? Keep things on the up and up. Don't take any deductions or write-offs if you don't have the paperwork to back them up.

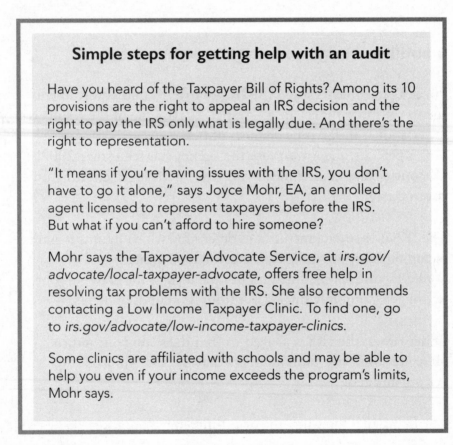

Simple steps for getting help with an audit

Have you heard of the Taxpayer Bill of Rights? Among its 10 provisions are the right to appeal an IRS decision and the right to pay the IRS only what is legally due. And there's the right to representation.

"It means if you're having issues with the IRS, you don't have to go it alone," says Joyce Mohr, EA, an enrolled agent licensed to represent taxpayers before the IRS. But what if you can't afford to hire someone?

Mohr says the Taxpayer Advocate Service, at *irs.gov/advocate/local-taxpayer-advocate*, offers free help in resolving tax problems with the IRS. She also recommends contacting a Low Income Taxpayer Clinic. To find one, go to *irs.gov/advocate/low-income-taxpayer-clinics*.

Some clinics are affiliated with schools and may be able to help you even if your income exceeds the program's limits, Mohr says.

Watch your excuses when it comes to the IRS

Accept a bribe lately? The IRS wants you to report it on your tax return. Same goes for income from illegal activities, like dealing drugs and robbing banks. Think the government is kidding? Just look at what happened to Al Capone. After being found guilty of tax evasion, the Chicago gangster was sentenced to 11 years in federal prison and ordered to pay $215,000 in back taxes, plus interest.

Nearly 90 years after Capone's conviction, people are still coming up with excuses for not paying taxes. The IRS even publishes a list of them, which it calls "frivolous arguments." So if you want to avoid a big fine — or worse, jail time — don't even think about using reasons like these.

Filing a return and paying taxes are voluntary. Not so fast, the IRS says. Use of the word "voluntary" in IRS publications refers to taxpayers' ability to run the numbers and complete their own returns, rather than having the government do it. Filing and paying is mandatory.

> IRS roots go back to 1861 when President Lincoln and Congress enacted a federal income tax to help fund the Civil War. The first tax was a flat 3 percent rate on incomes over $800. A year later, Congress lowered that amount to $600 and added a 5 percent tax on earnings over $10,000.

Wages and tips can't be taxed. The IRS disagrees with people who say only profits or gains, not wages and salaries, can be taxed. For federal tax purposes, "gross income" means all income from virtually all sources.

Citizenship relates to states, not country. Saying you're a citizen of, say, California or Alabama won't cut it at tax time. The IRS cites the 14th Amendment, saying it establishes dual state and federal citizenship.

Many happy returns: What to do if you've lost your tax files

Applying for a business loan or mortgage? You'll need a recent copy of your federal tax return. If you've misplaced it, here's what to do.

Go to the Get Transcript tool at *irs.gov/individuals/get-transcript* to view and print a free computer-generated summary of your tax information. Transcripts are available for the current and past three tax years. You can also request the document by calling 800-908-9946.

If you need an exact copy of the return you filed along with attachments, including W-2 forms, download and fill out IRS Form 4506 at *irs.gov/pub/irs-pdf/f4506.pdf*. You'll have to include a check or money order payable to the U.S. Treasury. Copies are generally available for returns filed in the current and past six tax years.

Simple and smart ways to file for free

The IRS says 7 out of 10 taxpayers qualify for free tax preparation and filing through its FreeFile partnership with private software companies. So if you're buying a pricey software package to help you do your taxes, you may want to check your eligibility for this free service.

You may qualify to file your state return for free, too. Check it out at *irs.gov/freefile*.

The IRS' latest rules say your adjusted gross income (AGI) must be less than $66,000 to qualify for FreeFile. But don't despair if your AGI is higher than that. The same website provides free electronic tax forms to fill out and file.

> File early to thwart scammers from stealing your tax refund. It won't stop the crooks from trying, but they can't claim the refund if you've already received it. Think someone has stolen your identity? Call the IRS at 800-908-4490 and file IRS Form 14039.

Looking for a human touch? If you make $54,000 or less, you can get free help preparing your tax return from the IRS' Volunteer Income Tax Assistance (VITA) program.

Another option is the Tax Counseling for the Elderly (TCE) program, which provides free assistance to taxpayers over 60 and specializes in retirement-related issues. And AARP's Tax Aide program helps people over 50 who can't afford professional help. Call 888-227-7669 for information.

To locate the nearest VITA or TCE site, go to *irs.treasury.gov/freetaxprep* or call 800-906-9887.

Protect yourself from these 4 tax scams

Over $63 million. That's the known amount swindlers posing as IRS agents stole from U.S. taxpayers over the last five years. How did the con artists do it? They phoned the unsuspecting victims and threatened them with arrest or the loss of a driver's license if they didn't send money via a wire transfer, debit card, or prepaid gift card.

Don't let similar fraudsters steal your personal information — and your shirt. Beware of the following.

The "tax refund" scam. In this scheme, hucksters steal your personal information from tax preparers and file fake tax returns. This tricks the IRS into depositing a refund into your bank account. Then the thieves, pretending to be collection agency officials working for the IRS, call your attention to the error and ask you to forward the funds to them.

What if this happens to you? Contact your bank. Have it return the refund to the IRS, and find out if you need to close your account. Call the IRS at 800-829-1040 to explain why the direct deposit is being returned.

The "verify" racket. Scam artists call during tax season, saying they have your return and need to verify your details in order to process your return. They might even have a caller ID number that makes it look like the IRS is calling. They'll ask you for personal financial information, like bank account or credit card numbers.

Don't fall for it. Hang up the phone immediately, and notify the Treasury Inspector General for Tax Administration at 800-366-4484.

The "phishing" flim-flam. Cybercriminals invented the "IRS Refunds" scam that tricks taxpayers into opening an email link that looks legit. Instead, you'll land on a fake web page asking for your Social Security number and other personal data. Such links or attachments often download malware onto your computer, giving the thieves access to even more information.

The IRS says to report unsolicited emails claiming to be from the agency to phishing@irs.gov.

The "robocall" swindle. Scammers identifying themselves as IRS employees leave an urgent message, warning that an arrest warrant will be issued if the call is not returned. Those who do respond are told they owe bogus taxes that must be paid immediately.

Remember — the IRS doesn't call and leave prerecorded messages. Call 800-366-4484 to report the call.

A CLOSER LOOK

Rita's heart dropped when the man on the other end of the line said he was from the IRS. Then it got worse. There was a major error on her 2015 tax return, he said. She had to pay $4,226 — right now — or he'd put a lien on her house.

Fortunately, Rita remembered that the IRS first contacts taxpayers through the mail. So she hung up and reported the call. Be smart like Rita, and keep these facts in mind when dealing with the IRS.

- Your first contact will never be through a phone call, email, or social media.

- The IRS won't threaten to have you arrested for not paying taxes.

- You'll never be asked to pay the IRS with a gift card or wire transfer.

- The IRS won't ask for your credit card information over the phone.

- You'll always have the opportunity to question or appeal the amount the IRS says you owe.

Forewarned is forearmed: How to outsmart fraudsters

First the good news. The IRS says the number of tax returns with confirmed identity theft has fallen 32 percent in the past year. Now the bad news. Cyberthieves are upping the ante — prowling for more detailed financial information to increase their chances of getting a fraudulent tax return past the IRS.

To lower your chances of having your identity — and your tax refund — stolen, follow these tips from the IRS.

Use security software. Use an up-to-date anti-virus program and a firewall. Encrypt sensitive files, such as tax records, on your computer. Use strong and unique passwords.

Think before you click. Be wary of emails with a link to a software update. It could be from a criminal trying to trick you into downloading a data-stealing virus. Don't download attachments from unknown or suspicious emails.

Protect your personal information. Don't carry your Social Security card with you or leave hard copies of tax records lying around.

If you must provide personal data online, make sure you do so securely. Find out how to do that in *5 smart ways to buff up your online security* in the *Credit card* chapter.

A richer retirement

Simple strategies to make your nest egg last

7 secrets to a happy, comfortable retirement

Some 80 percent of retirees say good health is the most important ingredient for a happy retirement, followed by financial security. It's really not surprising since the money you've been saving means little if you can't enjoy it.

Just as you try to eat well and exercise to take care of your health, you can also take certain steps to get the most out of your golden years. Whether you're still working or already swinging that golf club, you'll want to scope out these seven secrets for a rip-roaring retirement.

Phase into it. Instead of retiring all at once, consider cutting back to part-time work or taking on a less demanding role. The extra money might allow you to delay collecting Social Security benefits, bumping up your monthly payments in the future.

But first, find out if doing this will affect your employer benefits, such as insurance or pension.

Cut your cost of living. Controlling how much money you spend will make your retirement income go further. So before you buy anything, consider whether you really need the item. And don't forget to take advantage of senior discounts at restaurants, supermarkets, and theaters.

Envision what you want. You've been working your whole life, raising a family and paying the bills. Now is the time to think about your future in a new way. Ask yourself about the dreams you had when you were younger. See if they fit into your plans for the time ahead. Talk to your spouse about his goals, and build your future together.

Have a purpose each day. Feeling happy about being retired isn't the same as being fulfilled. After the initial retirement bliss wears off, you might be left feeling a lack of purpose. Reconnect with old friends, and make new ones. Find joy in volunteering, joining a club, or learning a new skill. Brush up on a foreign language, or take classes at your local community college.

Keep to a schedule. Set goals for your free time, and organize your activities a week ahead. It'll prevent you from getting bored and lonely. Also talk with your spouse about setting aside time to do things together, like visiting museums or going to the movies. Agree on a plan you're both happy with.

Be innovative. Let's face it. Many retirees haven't saved enough and need to monitor spending habits. If you can't afford a trip to Italy, experience the culture through books and food. Or attend lectures and films about the country. Love to go for long walks in the woods? Join a local hiking club if you can't make it to the Swiss Alps.

Stay connected with your family. Don't neglect the people closest to you. Call or visit your siblings, parents, and children. And spend time with your grandkids. Looking for a fun way to get everyone together? Organize a family vacation.

Retire these myths for a shock-free financial future

Got your heart set on retiring at a specific age, say, 65? A recent survey puts your chances at roughly 50-50. That's because many adults have misconceptions about retirement and don't factor in realities like health problems, layoffs, or having to care for a spouse.

Don't let retirement whoppers throw a monkey wrench into your plans. Here are three retirement myths you'll want to set straight.

You'll have lots of free time. Planning on getting up late and puttering around the house? You might reconsider. Many retirees find their days get filled quickly with hobbies, travel, part-time work, or visits with family. But be warned. It'll take time to adjust to your new lifestyle. The people who seem happiest in retirement are those who take care of their health and get involved in interesting activities.

Your taxes will be lower. It sounds true on the surface. After all, you won't be getting a paycheck. But don't forget that pension payments and withdrawals from traditional 401(k) plans and individual retirement accounts (IRAs) are taxable. And they may boost your income to the point where Uncle Sam taxes your Social Security benefits. Older Americans also tend to have fewer tax breaks, such as deductions for dependent children and mortgage interest.

Medicare will cover your health care costs. Need a root canal or a new pair of eyeglasses? You're on your own. Same goes for long-term care. In fact, the basic version of Medicare covers just routine doctor visits and hospitalizations. So how much will you actually need? According to Fidelity Investments, a 65-year-old couple with basic Medicare coverage will need $275,000 to pay for their health care costs in retirement. And that doesn't include the cost of long-term care, such as nursing homes.

> Figuring out when to retire can be overwhelming. If you feel you're making decisions in the dark, a certified financial planner may be the way to go. The cost? Around $100 to $300 an hour, says Susan Spraker of Spraker Wealth Management. "It's the best investment pre-retirees can make."

3 mistakes that can ruin your retirement

Marilyn was pleased as punch when New York University accepted her daughter Charlotte as an undergraduate. But she was shocked to hear the cost — $50,000 a year. Charlotte got some financial aid, but had to rely on student loans to pay the rest of her tuition. After graduation she looked for work, but wasn't able to meet her monthly repayment plan. So Marilyn raided her retirement savings to pay off some of the principal.

Bad idea, according to experts. Marilyn is risking her future financial independence and will have to work extra years to recoup the lost principal, interest, and investment returns. A better solution? Temporarily match Charlotte's half of the monthly payment until she gets back on her feet.

Mistakes like Marilyn's could ruin your retirement. Be sure to steer clear of these common blunders.

Ignoring your housing situation. Do you have more equity in your home than cash in your savings? That can happen if you spend your retirement fund paying off your house note. But then you might not have enough income to live the way you want and pay for property taxes, home insurance, and maintenance. Consider your options — from downsizing to a smaller home to moving to a less expensive area.

Wherever you decide to go, whether it's south Florida or the French countryside, you'll want to test the waters before taking the plunge. Take an extended vacation and get to know the locals. Think about renting for a while before buying. You'll be happier in case you decide endless beaches or foreign languages aren't for you.

Failing to supplement Social Security. Social Security benefits help countless seniors stay afloat each month. But the program was never intended to be a sole source of income. In fact, the Social Security Administration says retirement benefits replace less than half of the average worker's income. That's not much to live on. Try to tuck away extra savings in 401(k) plans and IRAs.

Taking on too much debt. Have a child who wants you to co-sign a mortgage? Know the risks. Although you want to help, one missed or late payment will mean a black mark on your credit. That'll make it harder to get a loan in an emergency. You'll also be responsible for the monthly premium if your child can't pay. A better option might be to contribute to the down payment — if you can — and consider it an early inheritance.

Budget your way to retirement readiness

Do you know how much income you'll need after you stop working? Many retirement planners suggest about 80 percent of your pre-retirement income. So let's say you earned $40,000 the last year you worked. You'd need $32,000 to keep the same standard of living in your first year of retirement.

The 80 percent rule makes sense at first glance. Bank drainers, like new business suits and high commuting costs, should drop. And you won't have to set aside a portion of your salary for your 401(k).

But don't be surprised if you spend more. The 80 percent rule of thumb works for some, says Jennipher Lommen, a certified financial planner at Wildflower Financial in California. But, she adds, many of her clients spend nearly the same amount as they did when working.

Lommen compares retirement spending patterns to the shape of a smile. One upper corner of the smile represents the first years of retirement. "That's when spending is at a pretty high point," Lommen says. "Possibly even higher than the pre-retirement amount because people remodel their house or travel."

Then comes the dip, or the lower part of the smile, in the middle of retirement. "When people have been in retirement for a while, they tend to reduce spending," she says, adding that at this stage retirees travel less and curb clothing and car purchases.

Not surprisingly, costs often rise in the final years, Lommen says. The second upper corner of the smile is when spending peaks again, this time on health care and nursing homes. It all adds up.

"If you even out the smile into a straight line, you're looking at more like 100 percent of your pre-retirement money," she says. "I think you'll be in for an unpleasant surprise if you assume right out of the gate that you're going to spend less."

Budgeting the right way will help you avoid this big mistake. Follow these simple steps to ensure you'll have enough money over the span of your lifetime.

Estimate your expenses. Before you retire, gather up several months' worth of credit card and bank statements. Then make a list of how much you spend monthly on essential things like food, clothing, and utilities. Also add up the amount you spend on entertainment and hobbies. Make another list of annual charges such as property taxes, insurance premiums, and home warranties. Calculate the costs on a monthly basis and include them in your budget.

Develop a plan. Ask yourself which expenses you're likely to keep in retirement and which will go away. For example, will your mortgage be paid off? Will your health insurance premiums increase if you retire early? Include money in your budget for emergency expenses, like a new roof or major car repairs.

Look at your savings. Choose the retirement accounts you'll tap first, and decide how much you can afford to withdraw from each. You might want to consult a financial expert for help determining the best strategy for reducing the income taxes on your withdrawals. Find out how much you can draw from Social Security and your pension.

Test-drive your budget. If your monthly expenses in retirement will be higher than your income, you'll have to cut costs. Once you have a budget, try living on it for a few months. If you run out of money before the end of each month, you'll need to tweak your game plan. You may even decide to work longer than you originally predicted.

A CLOSER LOOK

Not having a budget is like building a house without blueprints. It can be done, but you won't be happy with the results. Just ask Julia. She retired at 62 and used most of her savings to buy a bed-and-breakfast. Unfortunately, she failed to account for high property taxes, insurance rates, and maintenance costs. Julia couldn't afford the payments and was forced to sell at a steep loss. Her retirement looks bleak, indeed.

Don't let similar mistakes sink your dreams for retirement. Do your research and talk to an expert before making major financial decisions.

Retirement rundown: Secrets to a successful second act

Thinking of moving near the grandkids? Doing so could break the bank, says Susan Spraker, president and senior advisor at Spraker Wealth Management in Florida. What happens if one of the parents changes jobs and has to relocate the family? You could be looking at huge moving expenses every few years.

"Retirees think that when they move near the grandchildren it's going to be a permanent situation. We've never seen it work out," says Spraker, who reminds clients it may be cheaper to take extended visits instead.

Mistakes made before and during retirement can cause you to run out of funds. But follow these practical tips to remain on solid financial footing.

Expect to live a long life. If you were born in the U.S. in 1900 you could expect to live to the ripe "old" age of 47. In 2010, life expectancy was 79. And today, one in four 65-year-olds will live past age 90. All those extra years mean higher health care costs.

"There's a 50-50 chance that one member of a couple in their 80s is going to need long-term care," says Spraker. The average cost of a private room in a nursing home? Nearly $103,000 a year.

Keep your eye on the prize. Planning on retiring in a few years? Now isn't the time to splurge on a Corvette. Some folks build up nearly a third of their savings in the last five years before retiring.

And keep your feet on the ground, advises Spraker. Many people on the verge of retiring want to travel and buy a vacation home or a timeshare, she says. While you deserve to enjoy your golden years, it isn't wise to spend a big chunk of change if you really can't afford it. Take a hard look at your finances, and then make a sound decision that's right for you.

Think things through. Stop and take a few minutes before making a major decision. Spraker has seen retirees trade in their cars after the three-year warranty expired. "It's a huge mistake," she says, suggesting a simple alternative — an extended warranty.

"Cars will last, just like people, if you take care of them," she says. "All you're doing is giving lots of commissions to salespeople at car dealerships. Wouldn't you rather use that money for a trip if your car is running fine?"

The same rule applies for any major financial decision. It doesn't make sense, for example, to downsize to a town house if high property taxes and homeowners-association fees will eat up any profits you get from the sale of your current home.

The bottom line is that it's best to approach your retirement as you would any major event in life — with a lot of care and a little common sense.

Cherry-pick a spending plan to further your funds

You've saved enough in your 401(k), IRAs, and other investments to retire on. That's great. But have you figured out which accounts you'll tap into first? With a proper strategy, you're sure to pay less to Uncle Sam.

Just look at Mike and Paul, two low-earning retirees who have IRAs and stock portfolios to supplement their Social Security benefits.

Mike took out $10,000 from his traditional IRA, knowing that the government looked at the withdrawal as ordinary income. Since he's in the 12 percent tax bracket, he owed the IRS $1,200.

Paul took a different approach. He sold $10,000 worth of stock. His bill? Zero. That's right, he didn't have to pay taxes on any of the profits, also known as capital gains. That's because Paul followed a smart method for drawing down his retirement savings. It goes like this.

Turn to taxable investments first. Let's say you sell stock you've held for at least a year. The amount you pay on your earnings depends on your tax bracket. Even if you bring home half a million bucks a year, the maximum capital gains tax you would pay on investment profits is 20 percent. Middle earners shell out 15 percent. And if you're in a low tax bracket, like Paul, you'll owe nothing. Meanwhile, the funds in your IRA or 401(k) can continue to grow.

Move on to tax-deferred savings. Once you've sold your stocks, you can begin taking money from your tax-deferred IRA and 401(k) accounts. You'll pay ordinary income tax on the money you withdraw.

Consider non-taxed plans. Taking funds from your Roth IRA might be best for later in life, when you're more likely to have higher medical bills. The account has had extra years to grow, and you generally aren't taxed on withdrawals. In addition, a Roth IRA is a wonderful gift to leave to your heirs. They'll have to take minimum withdrawals, but can keep the bulk of the account growing tax-free.

This particular strategy won't necessarily work for everyone, says Jennipher Lommen, a certified financial planner in Santa Cruz. A lot depends on your current tax rate and where you expect it to be in the future.

> Heard of the 4 percent rule? It says your nest egg will last for 30 years if you withdraw 4 percent of your savings the first year and adjust that dollar amount annually for inflation. But be careful. You might want to take out less if the markets deliver below-average returns.

"Often it's the best way to do it," she says. "But I wouldn't says there's an exact order to it. It really depends on a person's tax bracket."

Your best bet? Study up or hire a professional to find the most tax-efficient way to spend down your retirement savings.

Beneficiary blunders: Heir today, gone tomorrow

Jeff, a responsible man, thought he was doing the right thing. He updated his 401(k) paperwork after his wife died, naming his adult daughter as the beneficiary. Jeff later remarried, but died of a heart attack a year later. Little did he know, his new wife would inherit the entire $300,000 in his retirement account.

Unfortunately, Jeff didn't know the rules governing 401(k) plans — your funds will go to your spouse when you die, unless your partner signs a waiver. If Jeff had been more financially savvy, he'd have rolled his 401(k) into an IRA. That's because, in most states, you can name anyone as the beneficiary of those accounts.

Don't let estate planning mistakes like Jeff's sabotage your intentions. Here are some things to think about when naming a beneficiary.

Don't forget to do it. The people you leave behind can't read your mind. That's why it's important to fill out documents naming the person or people you want to get your money.

And remember to name secondary beneficiaries. If your spouse is named the sole beneficiary and you both die at the same time, your assets will end up in probate.

Review and update the forms whenever a major event, like the death of the beneficiary or a new marriage, occurs. Think about it. Even if you get along with your ex, do you really want her using your IRA to cruise the Mediterranean while your widow is in the kitchen clipping coupons?

Naming your estate is a no-no. This has the same result as failing to name a beneficiary — probate. Plus when your heirs do finally get their hands on the account, they generally won't be able to stretch withdrawals over their lifetime. That means the account can't grow to its full potential, and your heirs might get slapped with more taxes. Not to mention the funds will be subject to creditors.

Choosing a minor could backfire. If you want to leave your retirement funds to, say, your 10-year-old grandson, you'll have to appoint a trustee to watch over the account until he reaches legal age. And who knows if he'll be mature enough at age 18 to appreciate the beauty of tax-deferred growth.

"F" is for failing to keep records. Don't assume that your bank or brokerage firm has a copy of your beneficiary form. Keep duplicates in your records, and tell your beneficiaries where they are. Check with your financial institution to make sure the information it has on file is correct.

Loosen Uncle Sam's grip with these retirement fund tax tips

Charlie, 73, is a self-described put-it-off-until-later type. So it was no surprise when he missed the year-end deadline to withdraw the required minimum from his $200,000 IRA account.

No big deal, Charlie thought. But that was before he learned what his laziness would cost — nearly $4,050. That's right. Charlie had to pay the IRS half of the $8,097 he was supposed to take out. And he needed to pay taxes on that to boot.

You know Uncle Sam is going to get a share of your tax-deferred retirement account. Why not have a say in how much he takes? The following tips could work for you.

Time your withdrawals. Thinking of tapping into your 401(k) or IRA before you're 59 1/2? You'll likely pay a 10 percent penalty on top of state and federal taxes. But once you're 70 1/2, the government will force you to make annual taxable withdrawals — called required minimum distributions (RMDs). The amount is based on your account balance and life expectancy. And with a few exceptions, you'll have to take the money out whether you want to or not.

Take advantage of the golden years. The time between ages 59 1/2 and 70 1/2 is dubbed the golden period for a good reason — you can manage your tax bill by withdrawing as little or as much as you like. Say, for example, you need $10,000 for a new roof. But that amount of money will bump you into a higher tax bracket. Why not withdraw part of it from your IRA — whatever amount will keep you in the lower tax bracket — and take the rest from your checking account?

Keep a weather eye on RMD income. Some early retirees live off the funds in their IRAs or 401(k) accounts. That means they can delay filing for Social Security and reap the benefits of higher monthly payments.

And if you start pulling money out of your retirement accounts before you have to, you might avoid large RMDs that could push you into a higher tax bracket later on. For example, how would a $10,000 RMD affect your wallet if it boosted your total income to $43,700?

▸ You'd pay a 10 percent tax on the first $9,525.

▸ The next $9,526 to $38,700 would come with a 12 percent tax.

▸ And the rest? You'd pay 22 percent on the remaining $5,000 — the tax rate on individual income between $38,701 and $82,500.

But if you had taken out money sooner, lowering your RMD to $5,000, you could have skipped the 22 percent tax bracket completely.

Help your heirs avoid a taxing situation. Forgetting to name a beneficiary on your IRA documents means, when your heirs eventually inherit the account, they will suffer the tax consequences.

▸ In some cases, they'll have to cash out the account within five years.

▸ In others, they'll have to use your age instead of their own when calculating RMDs.

And if you name more than one beneficiary and they don't split their inherited IRA into separate accounts, the age of the oldest beneficiary will be used to calculate all the RMDs.

No matter how you slice it, your IRA will lose its fantastic tax-sheltered growth potential if you don't put a beneficiary plan into place.

Retirement account Q&A — bring your questions to the table

Wading through all the rules and regulations of retirement plans can be confusing. Here's a crash course on the basics of contributing and withdrawing to help you figure out which type of account is right for you.

	Traditional IRA	Roth IRA	401(k)	Roth 401(k)
When does money go in?	before taxes	after taxes	before taxes	after taxes
If you're 50 or older, how much can you contribute each year?	up to $6,500, if you have earned income	up to $6,500, if you have earned income	up to $24,500	up to $24,500
When do you have to begin withdraw-ing funds?	age 70 1/2	never, if you are the original owner	age 70 1/2, unless still working	age 70 1/2, unless still working
When you with-draw after 59 1/2, what do you pay taxes on?	the entire amount withdrawn	nothing, provided the account is at least 5 years old	the entire amount with-drawn	nothing, provided the account is at least 5 years old

Early retirement offers: Look before you leap

What's one way companies cut costs without laying off workers? They offer senior employees, usually those collecting higher paychecks, an early retirement package. Of course, deciding whether to accept can be tricky. While the offer may look good at first — just think, getting paid for not working — you should consider several things before signing on the dotted line.

Watch how the package gets delivered. Early retirement offers are often based on your salary and how long you've worked at the organization. Suppose you've been with a company for 20 years and earn $1,000 each week before taxes. Your employer might offer you a severance of two weeks of pay for each year you've worked — that's a grand total of $40,000.

But before you grab at the chance, consider the tax consequences. If it's late in the year and you've already earned most of your income, a lump-sum payment could place you in a higher tax bracket. You might want to get the payments spread out over months or years.

Don't forget your existing perks. Health insurance can quickly eat away the benefits of your retirement package. See if your employer will continue to cover you and your family. If so, for how long?

And find out how leaving the job early will affect your pension. Some employers will boost your benefits at least until you start collecting Social Security. Others offer different bonuses to sweeten the deal.

Make a timeline. Before accepting, create a spreadsheet that lays out your future income and expenses. Make sure you'll have enough to live on. Think about what you'll do to cover any gaps. Will you need to get another job?

Remember to stress-test your plan. Let's say you decide to take the offer because your wife helps support the household. What happens if she becomes unemployed? Do you have a plan B?

Keep up with retirement age rules. Usually, withdrawals from your 401(k) carry a 10 percent penalty if they're made before age 59 1/2. But if you're 55 or older and leave your job, you can make withdrawals without being penalized. What about IRAs? You can still only withdraw penalty-free at age 59 1/2.

Know the consequences. Still can't decide whether to cash in on the offer? Know that if you do, you'll have less time to save for retirement. On the other hand, you may not want to hold out for a better offer — the first one might be the most generous. And take stock of your company's financial situation. An early retirement package is better than being fired in a downsizing.

5 factors to consider when choosing a pension payout

More than 2,000 years ago, Augustus Caesar was in trouble. The Roman Emperor feared that retired soldiers would seek to overthrow him. So he came up with a plan. Caesar bought their loyalty, promising veterans with 20 years of service a lump sum equal to 13 times their annual salaries. And there you have it — the birth of the modern pension.

What if you choose to receive your pension as a single life annuity? Payments will end when you die, leaving nothing for your spouse. Before you choose a pension plan, ask about survivor's benefits to avoid surprises later on. Some plans require spouses to sign a statement to waive benefits, but not all do.

Retirees today have more options when it comes to drawing down pensions. They can take a lump sum or spread payments over a lifetime. Picking the right option hinges on things like your tolerance for risk and how long you expect to live. Consult a professional and consider the following before deciding what's best for you.

Quick cash can come in handy. A lump sum gives you more control over how and when you spend your money. You're not limited to monthly payments, which is great if you want to splurge. It also allows you to invest the funds as you see fit. But ask yourself if you're ready to take on that job. Lean too heavily toward stocks and you could lose in a bear market, when the prices of investments fall. Invest too conservatively and you're courting a poor rate of return.

Annuities offer greater security. Monthly pension payments guarantee a specific amount — regardless of the market. That can be comforting if you're looking for a steady stream of income. But unlike Social Security benefits, pension payments aren't typically adjusted for inflation. That means, given a 3 percent inflation rate, a $1,000 payment today will be worth just $554 in 20 years.

Take your health into consideration. Choosing a lump sum often makes sense if you have a life-threatening disease. You can use some of the money to pay for health care and pass the rest on to your heirs. But generally it's best to follow this route only if your guaranteed retirement income, the money you can count on receiving every month or year, is higher than your expenses. You can use some of the lump sum for living costs and invest the rest of it.

Taxes will impact your decision. The bad news? A lump-sum distribution can push you into a higher tax bracket. The good news? Rolling it over into an IRA puts you back in the driver's seat. That's because you pay income tax only when you tap the funds. Unlike monthly payments, you can manage your withdrawals so you aren't taxed as heavily.

Some folks can have it both ways. Still unsure about which pension to choose? Maybe you can have both. The IRS recently made it easier for pension participants to take part of their benefit as a lump sum, with the remainder coming in scheduled payments. See if your company offers this option. That way, you can have both guaranteed income and investable assets in your retirement game plan.

Protect your pension from sloppy record keeping

Sometimes pension administrators get careless with records and fail to pay required benefits. Other times companies merge or go bankrupt, and information gets lost. That's why it's best to keep all your pension papers and employment records. You'll need them if you have to prove you're eligible to receive a pension.

But don't despair if you've lost track of your paperwork. Instead, check out these tips to hunt down missing pensions.

- Go to *pensionhelp.org* to connect with government agencies and free legal services.

- When you apply for Social Security benefits, the Social Security Administration will send a notice to remind you of private pension perks you may be entitled to.

- You can also search for plans that have been turned over to the Pension Benefit Guaranty Corporation at *pbgc.gov.*

When to take benefits: A question for the ages

Ready to kick back and claim Social Security at 62? Or do you plan to wait until full retirement age or beyond? It's a tricky decision. Do it early, and you're looking at smaller payments over a longer period of time. Wait, and you'll get larger payments over fewer years. Here are things you'll want to do before taking the plunge.

Take a look at your health. Your life expectancy is a major factor in deciding when to take Social Security. You'll want to look at your family's medical history and average life span as well as your health across the board. After all, there's no sense in delaying retirement if you won't be able to enjoy it. On the other hand, you don't want to box yourself into permanently reduced benefits if you live to 90.

Assuming you'd receive $1,000 each month at full retirement age, here's a comparison of your benefits if you claim early, at full retirement, or at 70.

Claiming age	Monthly benefits	Total benefits				
		Age 70	Age 75	Age 80	Age 85	Age 90
62	$750	$72,000	$117,000	$162,000	$207,000	$252,000
66	$1,000	$48,000	$108,000	$168,000	$228,000	$288,000
70	$1,320	$0	$79,200	$158,400	$237,600	$316,800

Remember, your incentive for delaying retirement — an 8 percent annual increase in benefits after you reach full retirement age — stops when you turn 70.

Know the pros and cons of working. Thinking of holding down a job while collecting early benefits? Lots of people do it, but be careful of the consequences.

▸ The Social Security Administration (SSA) will deduct $1 from your benefits for every $2 you earn over $17,040.

▸ The year you reach full retirement age, they'll knock off $1 for every $3 you make above $45,360.

The penalties stop once you hit full retirement age, when you can earn as much as you want. And the money you forfeited? The SSA will recalculate your monthly payment, permanently raising the amount to make up for the months in which they withheld benefits.

Women tend to outlive men by an average of five years, racking up higher health care costs. In addition, they're more likely to have left the workforce to care for children or aging parents, leading to lower Social Security benefits. Fortunately, many men and women can collect benefits based on the work record of their spouse or former spouse.

The upside of working those extra years is it might bump up future Social Security benefits. That's because the SSA bases your payments on your 35 highest-earning work years. And if you work while collecting benefits, the amount will be refigured every year. So say you have 33 years of earnings when you turn 62. If you work another two years, the SSA will count those years toward your earnings instead of the two "zero" years when you earned nothing. Nice, huh?

Consider partner perks. Still looking for ways to live well on a fixed income? Older men and women can get more out of Social Security by tapping into age-old options. If you were born before Jan. 2, 1954, you may be able to claim your spousal benefit at the age of 66 while your own Social Security benefits build up delayed retirement credits. This exception to the deemed filing rule doesn't apply if you were born on or after that date.

Here's another option to bring in extra money. If you're the lower-earning spouse, you might start collecting reduced benefits at 62. Your partner could wait until 70 for the largest possible benefit. If your spouse dies first, you're eligible for a 100 percent survivor benefit, as long as you've reached full retirement age.

A CLOSER LOOK

Olga, 64, hasn't been in the best of health. She fears she'll follow in her parents' foot-steps and won't live past her mid-70s. With that in mind, she claims her reduced Social Security benefits of $867 each month, or $10,404 per year. But she's still working her receptionist job. It's the only way she can afford to keep her health insurance.

Olga tells the Social Security claims specialist that she'll earn a $30,000 salary — $12,960 above the annual earnings limit of $17,040. The SSA will withhold $6,480 — $1 for every $2 over the limit — leaving Olga with just $3,924 in annual benefits.

If Olga knew how little she'd get, she might have chosen to wait. At 65, she'd be eligible for Medicare and could quit her job. Her Social Security payment, meanwhile, would have grown about 7 percent to $933 a month, or $11,196 a year. And she'd be eligible for all of it.

Size up your projected payout to sidestep surprises

Any idea how much you'll get from Social Security? For most Americans, the monthly payment is essential to making ends meet. Yet according to the Nationwide Retirement Institute, a quarter of recent retirees say their benefits are less or much less than what they were expecting. Here's what you can do to avoid falling into the same trap.

Set up an online account to estimate your payment. The Social Security Administration bases your benefit on the 35 top-earning years of your career. The average monthly retirement premium is around $1,400, but can rise as high as $2,788 for someone who begins collecting at full retirement age.

To get an idea of how much is in store for you, go to *ssa.gov* and click the "my Social Security" icon. Once you set up an account, you'll also find out how much you're eligible for if you become disabled, and what your family could get upon your death.

> You'll find free information and assistance with retirement, Social Security, taxes, prescriptions, veterans' benefits, and more at this taxpayer-funded site for seniors. Get started at *usa.gov/features/usagovs-guide-for-seniors*.

But be aware that you can't set up a Social Security account online if you have a security freeze or fraud alert on your credit report. If you don't want to remove the freeze or alert, you can set up the online account by going in person to a Social Security office.

Check to see if your earnings statement is correct. In an effort to save money, the SSA has stopped mailing statements to anyone under 60. The document contains important information on your earnings and tax history. While online, make sure your statement lists your correct name, age, and earnings for each year. It's the only way to guarantee you get all the benefits you're entitled to.

Missing earnings? Fix it lickety-split. The SSA says incorrect earnings on your statement can occur if, for example, your employer reported your salary with an incorrect name or Social Security number. Or you might have gotten married or divorced and failed to notify the administration of your name change.

If your statement contains errors, gather proof of your earnings, such as a W-2 form, pay stub, or tax return. Then contact the Social Security Administration at 800-772-1213 or visit a local office.

But don't dawdle. The SSA, with some exceptions, sets a time limit on fixing earnings records to a little over three years after the wages were paid.

Social Security and Medicare: Where to go to stay in the know

Feeling baffled and bewildered at the thought of applying for Social Security? Join the club. A report by the U.S. Government Accountability Office says many Americans don't fully understand how Social Security rules will affect their retirement benefits. To make matters worse, claims specialists often fail to provide adequate information to the public.

That's what happened to MaryAnne and Peter, a couple who applied for Social Security at age 68. An agent reviewing their applications advised them to file for retroactive payments, which they did. What she didn't tell them? They'd take a huge tax hit on the lump sum payment and see their monthly benefits reduced over their lifetimes. So how can you avoid making similar mistakes?

▸ If you're looking to unravel the secrets of Social Security, go to the official government website at *ssa.gov*. You'll find loads of key information to guide you through the ins and outs of different claiming strategies and more.

▸ Need help navigating the Medicare maze? Try *Medicare.gov* for tips on the types of federal health insurance programs and what they cover. Sister site *MyMedicare.gov* will help you manage your Medicare account.

5 Social Security windfalls you don't want to miss

The average American couple turning 65 in 2020 will have paid a whopping $574,000 in Social Security taxes over their lifetime. That's a lot of hard-earned money to hand over. Like many Americans, you've been paying into Social Security for decades. Are you sure you're getting everything you deserve? Lots of people miss out on these five provisions that can beef up their benefits.

It's well worth the wait to collect later. Some 90 percent of Americans begin collecting Social Security benefits at or before their full retirement age. Most start at the youngest age possible, 62. Collecting then might be necessary if you've lost your job or are in poor health, but your monthly check will be a lot lower.

"The best thing you can do, if you're able to, is wait until you're 70 to claim Social Security," says Charley Gillespie, a spokesperson for Nationwide, one of the largest insurance and financial services companies in the world. "If you can draw down on an IRA or have a plan to get through those years, you'll have so much more income throughout the rest of your life. It's the only guarantee that most people ever have. People leave hundreds of thousands of dollars on the table."

How much would you rake in by waiting if you expect to get $1,180 a month at full retirement? At age 62, you could collect $885 each month. But if you hold off until 70, you could bring in $1,557. That's $672 more a month, or $8,064 a year. Eureka!

Suspending benefits gives you a second chance. Regretting your decision to take Social Security before full retirement age? You can withdraw your application within the first year of claiming benefits, but you'll have to repay all the money received.

Or increase your benefits for life by suspending your payments when you reach full retirement age. You won't have to pay back any money, and you'll earn delayed retirement credits that kick in at age 70.

Marriage brings monetary perks. Social Security looks kindly on married couples, allowing one spouse to take a benefit equal to up to half of the other's. It goes like this. If your benefit is $2,000 a month and your spouse's is only $750, he can "upgrade" to 50 percent of your payment, or $1,000 a month. But be careful. You'll get less if you claim benefits before full retirement age.

Added benefits go to the one left behind. Widows and widowers can begin collecting survivor benefits as early as age 60. Then when they reach full retirement age, they may be able to switch to their own benefit if it's a higher amount. The catch? You can't get the survivor benefit if you remarry before turning 60. Surviving spouses may also receive a $255 lump-sum death payment.

You can collect on your ex's earnings. Did your ex make a bundle after you split up? Don't be envious — you can reap some of the benefits. Divorced people who were married at least 10 years may qualify for both spousal and survivor benefits.

Is your check missing money? 5 facts you need to know

Nearly 30 percent of future retirees can't identify the types of expenses Social Security withholds from monthly payments. Another 12 percent incorrectly believe the government won't take anything out, according to a survey by the National Retirement Institute.

That can be dangerous, especially if you'll rely on Social Security to cover a large part of your expenses. Here are some surprising facts to help you plan for retirement.

Benefits adjust for price hikes. Social Security payments are designed to keep up with inflation so that a dollar today is worth the same amount years from now. The most recent cost-of-living adjustment (COLA) bumped up benefits by 2 percent. That means a retiree who received $1,360 in monthly benefits got an extra $27.20 each month.

But that still isn't enough for many seniors to keep pace with rising prices, according to The Senior Citizens League. COLAs have boosted Social Security benefits 43 percent since 2000, the advocacy group says, while senior living expenses have grown 86 percent in the same period. What were the fastest growing costs? Medicare Part B premiums and prescription drug prices.

The feds withhold Medicare funds. If you receive Social Security benefits and are eligible for Medicare, the federal government will deduct a premium for Part B coverage from your monthly payments. Most people pay a standard amount of $134 per month.

Debt: There's good news and bad news. Fortunately, your bank must automatically protect two months of Social Security deposits from creditors. Uncle Sam, however, can hold on to your benefits for things like overdue taxes, federal student loans, child support, and alimony.

The IRS is at the door. You'll have to pay federal taxes on up to 85 percent of your Social Security benefits if your combined income adds up to a certain amount. To determine that figure, add your adjusted gross income and nontaxable interest to half of your annual Social Security benefits. If you file your federal return as an individual, you'll owe taxes on your benefits if your combined income is more than $25,000. For couples filing joint returns, that amount rises to $32,000.

You may uncover extra for offspring. Have children later in life? Or maybe you remarried and started a second family? If you're receiving Social Security benefits and care for dependent children or grandchildren younger than 18, they may be able to collect up to half of your full retirement benefit amount. Your own payments won't decrease.

ALERT ⚠️

Who really needs to know your private info?

Have you ever called up the cable company only to have them quiz you on your mother's maiden name, blood type, and favorite childhood pet? It's not quite that bad, but everybody from the local cashier to the mailman seems to want to know your phone number, ZIP code, and Social Security number. But the proper reply might not be what you think.

If someone is prying for private details, just say no. There's no law saying you have to give anybody your personal info. In fact, only your bank, your employer, and credit bureaus must know your Social Security number.

If companies want to know your identifying information, ask them why they need it and what happens if you don't share. The more secrets you keep, the safer you'll be.

Fraud alert: Steer clear of these 3 sneaky scams

Scammers swiped the identities of nearly 17 million Americans last year, with the amount stolen hitting a whopping $16.8 billion. But the bad news doesn't stop there, according to a recent study by Javelin Strategy & Research. For the first time ever, hackers scored more Social Security numbers than credit card numbers.

Why is your Social Security number so valuable? Armed with that nine-digit figure, identity thieves can open lines of credit, file for tax refunds, and steal medical insurance and Social

Security benefits — all in your name. Dodge these three scams to keep your Social Security number — and your identity — safe.

Don't be reeled in on "phishing" trips. In this con, criminals send you an email or text message directing you to a fake Social Security website. Once there, you're asked to fill out personal information to receive a cost-of-living increase. Or they'll call, saying you'll forfeit the increase if you don't verify your name, date of birth, and Social Security number now. Don't fall for it. Cost-of-living adjustments are made automatically. And don't assume the caller is from the SSA just because your caller ID says so — scammers can fool the phone system.

Beware fake online accounts. The SSA recommends you set up a "my Social Security" account at *ssa.gov*. That way, you can electronically change your mailing address or bank information. Establishing an account also prevents scammers from creating a bogus one and stealing your benefits. But delete emails inviting you to create an account — identity thieves put links to fake websites in their messages. Once you input your data, it's theirs for the taking.

Remember, the SSA doesn't send unsolicited emails or text messages requesting personal data that should be in your records.

Be on high alert when it comes to "high-tech" cards. In this case, hucksters pretending to work for the SSA tell you that your benefits will stop unless you upgrade to a chip-enabled Social Security card. All you have to do is verify your identity to get the modern, new card. Of course, there is no high-tech Social Security card, and if you hand over your details, you're left high and dry. So how do you protect yourself from scams like these?

▸ Don't pick up the phone unless you recognize the number.

▸ Don't respond to emails or click links in them unless you're certain they're from the SSA. Instead, go straight to the official Social Security website.

▸ Never provide personal information to anyone unless you initiated the phone call or email. If someone says he needs that information, tell him to send you a letter requesting it.

▸ To verify the legitimacy of phone calls, text messages, or emails, call the SSA at 800-772-1213. Don't use phone numbers or links provided by the person who contacted you. You can report attempted scams to the SSA's fraud hotline at 800-269-0271.

A CLOSER LOOK

Beatrice, 68, gets a phone call from a man who identifies himself as a Social Security Administration employee. He tells Beatrice that his office's IT department has detected odd changes to her account. Did she recently ask the SSA to reroute her benefits to a bank in Hawaii?

Panicked, Beatrice says she hasn't. The caller tells her he can fix the problem, but they've got to act quickly before the scammers get her money. Beatrice just has to give him her Social Security number, along with her bank account details.

Fortunately, she takes a moment before answering. Beatrice knows the SSA doesn't call people out of the blue and ask for personal information.

So she hangs up, calls the SSA directly, and finds out her account is not at risk. She's just one of thousands targeted by con artists seeking to steal identities and benefits.

3 keys to living well on a fixed income

Health care. A social life. Housing. Three major expenses that continue for decades into retirement. Worried about robbing Peter to pay Paul? Take a look at the following tips to help you live well on a fixed income.

Take control of your health to fatten your wallet. Taking care of your health won't just add years to your life. It will save you money. That's according to a report by HealthyCapital, which says a 45-year-old man who manages his high blood pressure can save $3,285 a year in pre-retirement health care spending. An added bonus? He'll live an extra three years. Not too shabby for following doctor's orders.

Keep busy and stay connected. Did you know that staying socially active — meeting a friend for coffee or being in a book club — ranks right up there with exercise when it comes to being healthy? That's because being engaged keeps your brain sharp, lowers stress, and helps ward off depression. Going out and doing things may also lower your risk of developing heart problems, cancer, and arthritis.

Don't think you can afford it? Consider visiting your local senior center. But don't expect just shuffleboard and bingo. You'll find many free activities, from yoga and computer classes to job placement programs and volunteer opportunities. Senior centers are also a great way to take low-cost day trips in your area.

Meetup.com is also a good site to find people in your area who have similar interests — whether it's knitting or Italian cooking. And remember — lots of restaurants and museums offer discounts to seniors.

Consider big ways to cut costs. Have the kids flown the coop? You might think about selling your house and moving into a smaller condo or apartment. You won't have to worry about mowing the yard or shoveling snow, and maintenance costs will be lower or nonexistent.

Want to save even more? Move to an area where you can walk to restaurants and shopping, or ask the new neighbors if they want to carpool.

You might even sell your car if you move to the city. Relying on public transportation would free up the money you're currently spending on gas, upkeep, and property taxes.

> Investing in experiences, like a trip to Disney with the grandkids or a weekend getaway with your spouse, makes you happier than buying things like TVs and sofas, research suggests. Looking to cut costs? Travel during the off-season. You'll have fewer crowds and will save on airfare and lodging.

Thinking of downsizing? Prime signs it's time to move

House rich and cash poor? Maybe it's time to sell your home. Doing so could free up a lot of cash to launch the next phase of your life. But how do you know it's the right moment? Look for these signs to see if the time is ripe.

You'll see a profit. The popular advice on stock purchases to "buy low and sell high" applies to housing as well. A tight supply of for-sale homes has created a red-hot seller's market, with median U.S. prices skyrocketing nearly 40 percent since 2012. All those gains could bankroll your future.

But remember — moving is expensive. Add up the numbers to see how closing and relocation costs will cut into your profits. Buying a smaller house or condo? Double-check the housing prices, property taxes, and cost of living in the area you're thinking of moving to.

It's hard to get around. Are you finding it difficult to climb stairs or get in and out of the tub? Staying put and making the necessary renovations to age in place costs, on average, around $9,000. But the price can be much higher, depending on the type of remodeling you need.

Then there's the issue of empty space. Are you paying to heat and cool rooms nobody uses? A smaller, more energy-efficient property that doesn't need major renovations might just be the ticket.

You're ready for a change. Selling the home in which you raised your family can tug at the heartstrings. But it can also be the start of a new adventure, particularly if you're lonely because the kids live far away or your spouse has died. You might consider moving to a retirement community where you can meet new people and enjoy an active social life.

There's a lot to consider before planting a "For Sale" sign in the front yard. Ask yourself if you're up to the task of moving. It's an emotional decision and one that might require investing in improvements before putting the house on the market.

Renting vs. buying:
Which makes more sense?

You've probably heard people say "renting is like throwing money out the window." It makes sense at first glance. After all, renters don't build equity. Buyers do.

But deciding on whether to rent or buy during retirement depends on much more. You'll need to consider, for example, how long you plan on living in a given area. If it's only for a short time, renting gives you more flexibility when it comes time to pick up and leave.

Then there's your personality. Do you take pride in owner-ship and do-it-yourself projects? Enjoy tax deductions and the price appreciation that home ownership brings? Buying might be right for you.

Renters, on the other hand, don't have to clean out the gut-ters or pay property tax and homeowners insurance. No hot water? Just call the landlord.

To see if it makes more sense financially to rent or buy, visit this online calculator at *zillow.com/rent-vs-buy-calculator*.

Leaving a legacy

Estate planning essentials for your family's future

3 reasons you must think ahead

A vacation home in the mountains. Taxes on investment dividends and interest. Your burial plot. All things you need to deal with when planning your estate. The problem is, most people don't think about them soon enough.

Don't be like Pete and Pauline whose dream of their four children happily sharing the family beach house turned into a sibling nightmare after they passed. Get ahead of the game by preparing now for these three potential problems.

Plan for the tax man, and your heirs will thank you. No one wants to think about taxes. But they're a fact of life — and death. Unless you're a multimillionaire, you won't have to worry about the estate tax. But dividends or interest from your investments can be taxed. You can soften the blow by lowering your estate's taxable income. Here are two easy ways to do it.

▶ Donate income-producing assets such as stocks, bonds, and mutual funds to charities while you're still alive. You get the added bonus of taking a tax deduction on the charitable donation.

▶ A more personal method is to gift money to your family each year. You're allowed to give up to $15,000 annually to each of your children or grandchildren, tax-free. The amount doubles to $30,000 if you're married. You lower your taxable income and can watch your loved ones enjoy the fruits of your labor.

Chiropractic assistant Joyce Tortora says her mother is following the second plan. "This year she gave each of her children $5,000. She doesn't have a large estate, but she'd rather see us use the money now, and she hopes it will help with taxes after she's gone."

> Leave copies of your funeral instructions with family members and your executor — not in your will. Several weeks, even months, may pass between death and the reading of the will. Then all your preparations will have been for naught.

A second home is not always welcome. You may not mind paying dues and fees on a Florida condo, but your kids might feel differently. Remember Pete and Pauline? Their children ended up battling for years over the beach house before settling their differences. Don't let that happen to your family. Talk with everyone about your second home or timeshare ahead of time. Knowing their wishes will make it easier to decide if you want to sell the property or keep it for future generations.

Preparing your exit saves your family grief. Would you like a farewell with all your favorite music? Rather be cremated and avoid all the fuss? Don't make your family guess what you'd like for your final arrangements. By planning ahead, you save them additional grief during this difficult time and leave the world exactly the way you want to. Here are some things you can do ahead of time.

▶ Write down your wishes for a funeral or memorial service.

▶ Draft your own obituary.

▶ Make a list of individuals and organizations that should be notified.

▶ Buy a cemetery plot, or arrange for a cremation.

▶ Find a responsible and willing caregiver for your pet. You can even set aside money for Fido's food and medical expenses and include instructions on the best way to care for him.

A can't-miss way to say good-bye

Want to share your favorite memories with your children after you're gone? Why not write them a letter while you're still healthy and alert?

In fact, write one for all your family and friends. Not only can you reminisce about good times you've shared, you can apologize for past wrongs and thank them for special things they've done for you. It's a good way to let go of grudges and express gratitude to the people in your life.

If you have trouble getting started, check out the free letter template at *med.stanford.edu/letter/friendsandfamily*. It will give you selected topics along with guidance on what to say.

Secure your finances after the death of a loved one

The loneliness of losing your husband or wife can be overwhelming. But knowing what to do in the first few months may help ease the pain and confusion. Here's a list of things you'll need to look at — and the paperwork you'll want to have on hand — if you find yourself suddenly going it alone.

Be sure your heirs don't lose out on valuable assets. Make a simple list of your bank accounts, along with PINs, usernames, and passwords. Keep it in a safe place, and make sure a trusted person, such as a spouse or executor, has easy access to the information.

File a claim for life insurance. At least $1 billion from lost or forgotten policies has been left unclaimed in the United States. Secure your share by calling the insurer and filling out the appropriate forms.

If your spouse was employed, call the company's human resources department. And don't forget to check with former employers for any workplace benefits in your spouse's name, such as a pension.

If you're entitled to an additional payout but can't find the policy, check out MIB Solutions' Policy Locator Service at *mib.com*. For a fee, the company might be able to locate policy information for you.

Look into bonus employer benefits. You could be eligible for unpaid bonuses and vacation pay. And if you got health insurance through the employer, you can apply for temporary continued coverage under the federal law known as COBRA.

Collect Social Security payouts. Call the Social Security Administration at 800-772-1213 to find out about survivor benefits, including payments for children younger than 18.

Keep up with bank duties. Be sure to pay your mortgage, utilities, and other scheduled charges. But don't rush to pay off your spouse's student loans or the balances on credit cards that aren't in your name. Also, notify the three main credit bureaus — Equifax, Experian, and TransUnion — that your loved one has passed away to protect against identity theft.

Review your own policies and plans. Check to see if you need to change your beneficiaries, power of attorney, or health care proxy. And update the names on any deeds or titles, such as your home and car.

Surprising source for savvy legal help

Knowledge is power, and you don't have to spend big bucks to get it. Expert, affordable legal advice on estate planning is at your fingertips.

The American Bar Association offers a wealth of free resources online at *americanbar.org*. Click the Public Resources link at the bottom of the page for information about the probate process, health directives, property law, wills, and more. Follow the link under Get Legal Help to find a lawyer or shed light on confusing legal terms.

Can't find what you're looking for? Type a topic into the search bar at the top of the page for a list of related articles. It's the fastest way to find legal advice, bar none.

'Til debt do us part: How to keep creditors from eating up your estate

Shakespeare famously wrote in *The Tempest* that "he that dies pays all debts." But that was in 1610, before credit cards, 30-year mortgages, and auto loans were invented. In fact, 73 percent of U.S. consumers die with unsettled accounts, according to the credit bureau Experian. And unlike in Shakespeare's time, those debts are not forgiven.

But don't panic if a loved one passes away before paying off creditors. It's not up to you to pay those debts unless you co-signed for a loan or had a joint account with the deceased. If creditors badger you for payment, direct them to the executor of the estate and tell them not to call you anymore.

> You won't get a pass on paying your spouse's debt if you live in a community property state like Arizona or Wisconsin. All income and property acquired during your marriage is free game to creditors looking to settle an account.

In most cases, creditors are paid from money — and assets — in the estate. And the law says they get paid before you inherit anything. So let's say Uncle Lou leaves you his prized Mercedes-Benz. If it's paid off and he has no debt, you're in luck. The car is yours, and you get to drive home in style. Otherwise, it's a wait-and-see game that depends on how far in the red Uncle Lou was. If the estate is short on cash, you can kiss your dream of owning a Mercedes good-bye.

Worried about leaving your own family in that situation? Here are a few tips to make sure your estate isn't eaten up by creditors.

▸ Aim to be debt-free before you retire. Stay on top of your finances and, if you have to, live below your means to reach your goal.

▸ Keep the beneficiaries on life insurance policies up to date. That money goes directly to the person you name, and creditors have no claim on it. That is, unless the beneficiary dies and you neglect to name a new one. Then the funds become part of your estate and can be used to pay off debts.

▸ Don't name your estate as the beneficiary of your retirement accounts. Instead, name an individual to keep your IRA or 401(k) from going into probate. Again, make sure beneficiaries are kept up to date.

Stay ahead of the curve with 1 important document

You know a power of attorney (POA) is important, but you just haven't gotten around to getting one. You're not alone. Nearly 60 percent of subscribers to a popular consumer magazine also admitted to putting it off.

But think about this. If you become incapacitated or disabled, a court may need to appoint someone to manage your money, perhaps that ne'er-do-well cousin you never liked. That will cost you — and your family — a bundle, not to mention a lot of stress. Then you'll really wish you had found the time.

The beauty of a durable power of attorney. A POA goes into effect as soon as you sign it and remains that way if you become sick or mentally disabled. The document gives your agent the power to act on your behalf, whether it's withdrawing money from the bank, tapping into retirement accounts, selling property, or filing your tax returns.

Pick someone who can handle the job. That's a lot of power to give another person, and deciding who to choose can be difficult. Experts agree you should have a high level of trust in your agent, whether it's a family member or a professional.

You should also consider the age of your agent, says Georgia State University Law Professor Mary F. Radford. A husband and wife in their 60s could be effective agents for each other, but that might not be such a good idea if the couple is in their 90s, she says. In that case, a child or younger sibling would probably be a better fit.

> Adding a loved one's name to your bank account won't take the place of a POA. Sure, a joint account gives the other person access to your funds. But what happens if the added person dies first? In some states, you'll be subject to an inheritance tax on your own money.

3 things you need to know. Here are some other things to consider when creating a power of attorney.

▸ Do you want to pay your agent for services? If so, make it clear in the POA.

▸ You can change or revoke your POA at any time, as long as you are mentally competent.

▸ The POA becomes invalid after your death, when the executor of your will takes over.

When is the best time to sign a durable power of attorney? "Definitely if you anticipate an onset of incapacitation," Radford says. But any time, she adds, is really a good time. "You never know if you're going to be hit by a car."

How to stop a 'no-way' on your POA

Sometimes even the best-laid plans can go awry. That was the case for Gina, who completed her estate plan — including giving her daughter, Liza, durable power of attorney (POA) — while still healthy.

Fast forward 15 years, and Alzheimer's disease has stolen Gina's independence. Liza, needing to pay for her mother's care, tries to withdraw funds from Gina's savings. No dice. The bank won't accept her legally drafted POA.

Liza learned too late that some banks require their own power of attorney forms. And Gina, in the late stages of dementia, isn't legally competent to sign one.

Here's how you can lower the odds of your agent running into similar problems.

▸ Keep your accounts in as few places as possible.

▸ Set up a durable POA, not a "springing" POA that goes into effect after you become ill. Because of privacy laws, your agent may have a hard time getting a doctor to certify that you're incapacitated. That delay can keep him from accessing your accounts.

▶ Call your financial institutions to get pre-approved for a
  POA. If your bank has its own POA form, fill it out.

4 will-writing rules that may catch you by surprise

Wills are official documents. But they can be very personal.
Comedian Jack Benny, for example, directed that his wife of 50
years receive one long-stemmed rose each day after his passing.
Hotel tycoon Leona Helmsley set aside $12 million for her
Maltese lapdog, Trouble. And rock star Janis Joplin left $2,500
in her will to pay for a party.

While some last requests may surprise you, the following rules
about wills shouldn't catch you off guard.

Beneficiaries override your will. Remember when you
assigned a beneficiary to your IRA? That person will get the
funds after you die, no matter what you say in your will. The
same goes for your life insurance policies, annuities, and company pensions.

Here's a simple tip to protect your heirs — make sure your
beneficiaries are up to date. Most brokerages allow you to
change the names online. Be sure to keep a copy of the form
naming your beneficiary, particularly for IRAs. Lost paperwork
could have major tax implications for your heirs.

**Some property can be transferred without going into
probate.** Protect any property left over after your estate is settled
by including a "residuary" clause in your will. If you don't name
a beneficiary, the state will treat those remaining assets as if you
never had a will.

Other assets not affected by probate include joint bank accounts and autos with shared titles. They go to the surviving party. The same goes for real estate held jointly as tenants in common with the right of survivorship.

Simple changes don't require a new will. You may have put off making changes to your will, thinking it will take too long or cost too much. But easy fixes, like updating a beneficiary's name, can be done by attaching an amendment to your existing will, called a codicil.

You'll probably want to write a new will if you go through a major event, such as a divorce or birth of a child. If that's the case, you'll have to revoke the old one.

Your will must meet state requirements. Waiting 'til the final hours to whisper your last wishes? That's fine if you live in Missouri, one of the few states that accepts deathbed wills. Want to hand write your will? It's only a good idea if you live in a state like Arkansas or New Jersey, where "holographic" wills are honored.

> Never put usernames and passwords in your will. It could create a security nightmare for your heirs. That's because wills become public documents, available for all to see. It's easier to update changes to your online accounts if you keep a list of them in a safe place at home.

But if you decide to retire to Florida, your will won't be valid because the sunshine state doesn't recognize handwritten wills. Whenever you move, it's best to check on whether you need to amend or write a new will, as laws vary from state to state.

Do-it-yourself will — smart savings or major mistake?

Jim thought he'd save himself a few bucks. He wrote his own will, leaving his house and car dealership to his new wife, Susan. Several weeks later, Jim died of a heart attack. His adult children from a previous marriage contested the will, saying Jim didn't clearly express his wish to disinherit them. They demanded a portion of his estate.

Unfortunately, cases like Jim's are all too common, resulting in drawn-out legal battles and family feuds. So how do you know when a do-it-yourself (DIY) will is enough?

> If money is tight, go online to *www.findlegalhelp.org* to get referrals for low-cost legal help in your area. Or call the Eldercare Locator at 800–677–1116, and ask for legal assistance. Have a law school nearby? Check to see if your will can be done for free by a law student.

When to go it alone — the simpler the better. If you're single, have an uncomplicated family situation, and very few possessions, writing your own will may work out fine for you. Websites such as *LegalZoom.com* and *Nolo.com* provide forms, starting at around $60, for writing a will. Some lawyers might look it over for a small fee.

Some experts say a DIY will is better than no will. But they warn you should be careful to follow your state's laws to make sure it's legal, particularly when it comes to witnesses. At the very least, your will should say who you want to inherit your property. You'll also need to name an executor as well as beneficiaries for any assets that are left after the estate is settled. Don't forget to name a guardian if you have underage children.

More assets require more expertise. You should hire a lawyer if you have large assets, multiple marriages, or many heirs. He can guide you through the process, making sure your will is error-free and less likely to be contested.

Be prepared to give your lawyer information on your family and how you want to hand down your property. He'll also need to know how you own each asset. For example, is the deed to your house in your name only? It's important, because the way you own something dictates how it's passed on after you die.

Longtime lawyer Amy Morris Hess strongly recommends hiring a professional. "If you do it yourself you're probably going to cause your family a problem," warns the University of Tennessee law professor. "A non-legally trained person should not try to write a legal document any more than someone without dental training would clean his own teeth."

How much will an attorney set you back? Lawyers often charge a flat fee to write a will and other estate-planning papers. Expect to pay at least $300, but prices can easily go above $1,000. Get a quote based on your wishes and estate situation. Still need to cut costs? One way is to draft your own basic will before getting a lawyer to iron out the details.

If you need help finding an affordable lawyer, the National Academy of Elder Law Attorneys (*naela.org*) and the National Association of Estate Planners and Councils (*naepc.org*) are good resources. Hess also recommends the American Bar Association Section of Real Property, Trust and Estate Law (*americanbar.org/groups/real_property_trust_estate.html*). Scroll to the bottom of the web page, and look for Public Resources.

A will gives you peace of mind that your final wishes will be respected, right? Not so fast. Take Joe and Sue, a couple who married late in life. Their wills each left their assets to children from previous marriages. After Sue died, Joe thought he'd get only a small amount of money. But then he learned about his right to "take against the will." Sue's kids, standing to lose a small fortune, were furious.

They didn't know state law allows a surviving spouse to demand a portion of the estate — in some cases up to half of it — regardless of what was left to him or her in the will. In some areas, the share is based on how long the couple was married.

You and your spouse can make sure your final wishes are respected by seeing a lawyer and legally waiving your right to a bigger slice of the pie.

5 must-do's for finding a missing will

Mary's Aunt Jean had promised to pass on a hefty sum of money when she died. After the funeral, Mary was hoping for a quick settlement of the estate. She had lost her job and was behind on her mortgage and utility bills. The inheritance would help her keep her home.

Then she got a phone call — nobody knew where Jean's will was. Her estate, and Mary's lifeline, would be decided by strangers in probate court.

If you find yourself in similar circumstances, follow these tips to track down a missing will.

▸ Comb through file cabinets and hiding places. People often store wills with other financial documents.

▸ Ask close friends and family members if they have a copy of the will.

▸ Call local banks to see if your loved one had a safe-deposit box. You might need a court order or a copy of the death certificate to open it.

▸ Contact the deceased's attorney. Some lawyers safeguard wills for their clients.

▸ Check the county probate court to see if the will was filed there for safekeeping.

Remember, an ounce of prevention is worth a pound of cure. It's a good idea to ask loved ones where they keep important papers such as wills, insurance policies, Social Security cards, car titles, and powers of attorney.

Agreed to be an executor? Avoid these 5 missteps

Attention to detail and patience. Those are the qualities you'll need if called on to administer an estate, says University of Tennessee College of Law Professor Amy Morris Hess. Oh, and an even temper — particularly if you have to deal with a beneficiary constantly calling to find out when you'll distribute the assets.

Overseeing how the estate is handled isn't necessarily difficult, Hess says, but it can be tedious. You'll have to make a list of everything the deceased owned, pay off debts, and dole out the remainder to heirs. "The process is fairly simple and could take as little as a year, maybe even less," she says.

But if you're not careful, you'll run into problems that will not only drag it out, but may even affect you personally. Here are five common financial mistakes to watch out for while serving as executor of your loved one's estate.

Paying the estate's bills too promptly. Before you start paying creditors, find out if the estate owes federal taxes, which can take priority over other financial obligations.

Doling out assets too soon. What if creditors make claims against the estate after you've given out inheritances? Trying to get those assets back could be a big problem. And in that case, you may be held responsible for the debt.

Mingling your money with the estate's. Set up a separate checking account to handle the estate's bills. If you're the surviving spouse, you may think nothing of paying bills from your joint account. But doing so can create major problems at tax time.

Leaving valuables unsecured. As executor, you're responsible for protecting the deceased's property, even if it means changing locks or getting a safe-deposit box.

Purchasing estate property. Buying anything from the estate leaves you open to accusations that you didn't pay enough for the item.

When a will is not your best choice

So, you've written your will. Think you're done with estate planning? Maybe, maybe not. Steve thought he was. His will stated that each of his three children would receive a third of his assets. But after he died, his daughter's prior drug problem reared its ugly head again. A year later, her entire inheritance had gone into her dealer's pockets.

You can't plan for every possibility, but you can try to cover the bases. If Steve had set up a revocable living trust instead of a will, he could have prevented his daughter from squandering her share of the estate.

Consider adding a revocable trust, which you can change any time, to your estate plan if you:

▸ are leaving assets to a minor child or a beneficiary you feel is incapable of managing money. In such cases, your trustee can decide when and how to distribute the assets.

▸ want to avoid the time and expense of probate. The beneficiaries named in a trust, unlike those named in a will, receive their inheritance without having to go through the courts.

▸ seek to avoid publicity. Wills are always made public while trusts rarely are.

▸ are in a second marriage and have children from a previous marriage. If you leave your estate to your spouse, certain trusts make sure your children get what remains after your partner's death.

▸ are concerned that you may become incapacitated. Your trustee can manage the assets in your trust without a power of attorney.

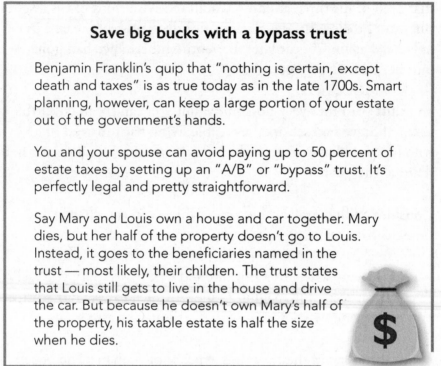

Save big bucks with a bypass trust

Benjamin Franklin's quip that "nothing is certain, except death and taxes" is as true today as in the late 1700s. Smart planning, however, can keep a large portion of your estate out of the government's hands.

You and your spouse can avoid paying up to 50 percent of estate taxes by setting up an "A/B" or "bypass" trust. It's perfectly legal and pretty straightforward.

Say Mary and Louis own a house and car together. Mary dies, but her half of the property doesn't go to Louis. Instead, it goes to the beneficiaries named in the trust — most likely, their children. The trust states that Louis still gets to live in the house and drive the car. But because he doesn't own Mary's half of the property, his taxable estate is half the size when he dies.

DOLLARS & SENSE

Put your trust in the right hands

Wondering about asking your brother Fred to manage your trust? Think again, unless he's a financial whiz who thrives on family drama.

Some things are better left to the professionals, and being a trustee is one of them. That's according to Professor Amy Morris Hess, who has taught estate planning and probate law at the University of Tennessee College of Law for over 30 years.

"A trustee needs to be a money manager who can identify the assets to invest in, the income stream to expect, and the growth potential that exists," she says. Add on to that the burden of managing the expenses and taxes on the trust, and you're looking at someone who needs extensive financial skills.

But the trustee's duties don't stop there. You'll need someone who can be "impartial and unemotional" when dealing with family members, Hess says.

Think about it. Do you really want Fred to decide whether your unemployed daughter — his favorite niece — should get a cash distribution for a snazzy new Jaguar?

Of course, hiring a lawyer or banker to manage your trust comes with a price tag. But, Hess says, you get what you pay for.

"If you think it's too expensive to have a professional trustee, think how expensive it's going to be if your heirs have to sue the family member you appointed because he mismanages funds," she says.

Don't let a catastrophic illness drain your savings

It's a fear that many face. You've saved your whole life, contributing to your 401(k), reinvesting dividends, and riding out plunging markets. You plan on leaving the bulk of your estate to your children, maybe set up a college fund for the grandkids.

But then a stroke lays you low, and out-of-control health care costs slice into your nest egg faster than a Japanese Ginsu knife.

If you're worried about your savings, ask an attorney about placing your estate in an irrevocable trust. You won't have access to the funds in the trust, which go to your heirs. But you can use the income the trust generates for living expenses. The downside is you can't make any changes to the trust after it's been created.

Some people with irrevocable trusts have whittled down their assets enough to qualify for Medicaid. There's a hitch, though. You have to create the trust five years before applying for coverage. Otherwise, you'll be subject to a "look-back" period and reduced benefits.

ALERT ⚠️

Steer clear of these 2 trust traps

You drew up a trust to provide for your family after you're gone. Here's how to make sure your assets don't wind up with creditors and former in-laws.

- Make clear in your trust that the custodian "may" distribute assets at a particular time. Using the word "shall" forces the trustee to give out money or property even when it might not be a good time. For example, when a beneficiary gets divorced or files for bankruptcy.

- On the same note, don't include a termination date in your trust. It will force the trustee to distribute all remaining assets. Instead, grant your beneficiaries, when they are old enough, the right to pick a new trustee. That will protect your assets and help your loved ones manage their inheritance responsibly.

Think twice before setting up joint ownership

Joint tenancy is a simple way to own an asset, say a house or car, with another person. But it rarely makes sense to go this route if you already own the property by yourself. In fact, it could turn into a disaster.

Take the case of June, a single woman in her 60s who wants to avoid probate after she dies. June signs a deed putting her house into joint tenancy, giving her sister, Claire, the right of survivorship.

A few years later, June's sister is sued and loses the case. The end result? Creditors go after Claire's 50 percent stake in the house, forcing the sisters to sell. June gets just half the value of her house in cash, while Claire's half goes to settle the debt.

Consider the following pitfalls before placing your home or bank account into joint tenancy with right of survivorship (JTWROS).

▸ **Relationships get rocky.** If you make your boyfriend a joint tenant on your condo, he'll own half of it. Forever. What happens if you break up? He can sell or mortgage his share. And if he goes into debt? Creditors can come after his half-interest, leaving you out on the street.

▸ **The taxman is looking.** The Internal Revenue Service looks at the transfer of property, say 50 percent of a $400,000 house, as a $200,000 taxable gift.

▸ **Last wishes mean nothing.** Funds in a JTWROS bank account go to the surviving account holder, regardless of what the deceased wrote in his will. The same goes for real estate.

> ▶ **Spouses might lose out.** By making your husband a joint tenant on real estate you previously owned, he could miss a big tax break when it is sold.

If you're looking to avoid probate, consider putting your property into a living trust. You won't be giving up ownership and can change beneficiaries whenever you want.

Living will: 3 things you must include

It's been over 40 years since 21-year-old Karen Ann Quinlan lapsed into a coma, a case that sparked a national debate over a patient's right to die. Times certainly have changed since then, and people now write living wills to make sure their end-of-life health care wishes are followed.

Each state has its own laws concerning living wills. You can find free forms online at *caringinfo.org*, or at your doctor's office or senior center.

If you're drafting a living will, be sure to include whether or not you want the following treatments.

> ▶ **Life-prolonging care.** Do you want to be put on a respirator, get blood transfusions, or have surgery to extend your life?

> ▶ **Food and water.** If unable to eat or drink, do you want to be fed through a tube or intravenous line?

> ▶ **Pain relief.** Choosing a natural death doesn't mean you have to suffer through it. You can still get "palliative care," which will include pain relievers to help you remain comfortable.

Experts recommend you talk to your family about your wishes and give them copies of your living will. Keep one in your car or wallet in case of an emergency, and make sure your primary-care physician keeps a copy with your medical records.

The end of the road: Have you mapped out a plan?

Denial and procrastination are the two major barriers to end-of-life planning, says Georgia State University College of Law Professor Mary F. Radford. Not to mention the misguided notion that planning for the Grim Reaper might hasten his appearance.

"Death is a tough thing to face, and people don't want to think about it," she says.

Just look at the statistics. Sixty percent of people say they don't want their family burdened by tough end-of-life medical decisions. Yet, according to a California Healthcare Foundation survey, almost the same amount haven't told loved ones whether or not they wish to be kept alive by extreme measures.

In fact, only a quarter of U.S. adults have an advance directive — including a living will — in place. The top reason given for not discussing end-of-life wishes? Too many other things to worry about.

Want to make sure paramedics or hospital staff can quickly reach your family or health care proxy in an emergency? Set up In Case of Emergency (ICE) entries in your cellphone, including as much information about the person as possible. For example, ICE Mary Smith, Wife, 555-111-2222.

All adults need an advance directive, Radford says, and the time to draft one is before it's needed. Along with a living will, you can outline your wishes for end-of-life treatment with the following documents.

> ▶ **Durable power of attorney for health care.** This form names a person, also called a health care proxy, to make medical decisions for you. Those can range from choosing a medical facility to refusing treatment altogether. You should pick someone you trust, perhaps a friend or relative who lives nearby. It's good to name an alternate agent in case your first choice is unable to fill the job.

> ▶ **Do-not-resuscitate order (DNR).** This orders ambulance staff not to give you CPR if your heart or breathing stops. Your doctor must sign the DNR for it to go into effect. Keep the DNR by your bedside or on your refrigerator door, where emergency medical technicians can easily see it. Be sure your health care proxy and medical providers have copies.

> ▶ **Physician Orders for Life-Sustaining Treatment (POLST).** This document, which can be used in addition to — or in place of — a DNR, is useful if you're seriously ill and nearing the end of life. It tells medical professionals what treatments you want, or don't want, in an emergency.

> POLSTs should be written with the help of a health care professional, who must sign it. Keep it with you in a visible place at home, and make sure a duplicate is in your medical records. The form varies from state to state and is often brightly colored so it can easily be found.

5 ways to dodge costly funeral flimflam

Ever hear of the Funeral Rule? It's a federal law that requires funeral providers to give you accurate price information and disclosures about their goods and services. If you're arranging a loved one's funeral, you need to know your rights. Follow these five tips to get through the difficult process without losing your shirt.

Know your budget before calling. Think about what kind of arrangements you'd like before comparing local funeral homes. Are you looking for a cremation or a burial? Will there be a viewing of the body or a religious ceremony? Share your budget with the funeral home when discussing your options.

Joshua Slocum, executive director of the Funeral Consumers Alliance, compares shopping for a funeral to buying a car. "You have to start with reality," he says. "If you only have $1,000, that means you're not going to have a funeral that costs $7,000." The worst mistake you can make is thinking you have to find the money for whatever price you're quoted, he adds. Don't be pressured into buying services you don't need and can't afford.

If you feel the funeral home has taken advantage of you, speak first to the director. Still can't resolve the issue? Contact your state's funeral board, or email the Funeral Consumers Alliance at *ombudsman@funerals.org.* You can also file a complaint with the Federal Trade Commission at *www.ftc.gov.*

Request a price list. By law, funeral directors must quote prices over the phone. Some even post their rates on the internet. When you visit a funeral home, request a casket price list before looking at models. This way, you can ask about lower-cost products that aren't on display. You can also get information on renting a casket, which is much less expensive than buying. Remember, no state law requires a casket for cremation.

Slocum recommends visiting several funeral homes in your area. "Shopping around is probably the single biggest driver of cost," he says. "Our surveys show that funeral prices within the same town usually vary by thousands of dollars for the same or comparable services."

Make sure they explain every term. The funeral industry, like any, is full of buzzwords. When you hear "coach," think hearse. Likewise, "internment space" refers to a grave. What's with all the gibberish? "Having a professional jargon makes people feel important and officious," Slocum explains. Plus, all the mumbo jumbo confuses you more. You may be willing to pay big bucks for "funeral spray" — before you realize it's just another name for a bouquet of flowers.

Choose only what you need — and want. Ask for a general price list, which itemizes charges. You can go à la carte, picking only the goods and services you desire, if it makes more sense than buying a package deal. Be sure to inquire about the basic services fee that covers common expenses like securing permits and copies of death certificates.

Ask about alternatives. Did you know embalming became popular in the United States during the Civil War? The practice made it safe for fallen soldiers to be shipped home. Today, embalming is rarely required by law. So ask the funeral director if they offer alternatives. This goes for other costly "upgrades," too, such as sealed coffins that don't offer any advantages.

The Funeral Consumers Alliance offers a gold mine of information on your rights as a consumer. Check them out at *funerals.org*.

Spare yourself a grave injustice: Write your own obit

On September 6, 1871, *The New York Times* printed German philosopher Karl Marx's obituary. The dilemma — this revolutionary was still alive and kicking. Marx would live another 12 years, giving him plenty of time to steam over reading that he was not only dead, but "obnoxious" to boot.

Journalists have long written obituaries for the rich and famous. The rest of us depend on grieving relatives to sum up our lives. Even then mistakes can happen, like misspelled names and incorrect dates. And while well-meaning, no family member can describe the special moments in your life better than you.

Enter the "autobituary." Write the notice yourself, and you get to choose if it's a short-and-sweet reflection on your life or a touching farewell. But consider these pointers before taking pen to paper.

- ▸ **It's all in the lead.** Can you tap dance? Traveled to Timbuktu? Put captivating tidbits up top to grab your readers' attention.

- ▸ **Just the facts, ma'am.** Be sure to include your full name and a list of loved ones. You may want to leave out your birth date and residence to help avoid identity theft. But leave room for information about funeral arrangements.

▶ **Make it personal.** Add funny stories, lessons learned, or historical events that influenced you.

For more writing tips, see *obituaryguide.com*. And when you're done, give copies to your immediate family.

Who knows? Composing your own obituary could spark enough creativity for a full-scale memoir.

ALERT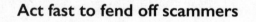

Act fast to fend off scammers

Don't wait to tell the credit bureaus that a loved one has died. It could take months for the Social Security Administration to do it — way too much time for identity thieves to dig for information and open fraudulent accounts.

When reporting the passing, be sure to include the deceased's full name, Social Security number, last address, and date of birth and death. You'll need to include a certified copy of the death certificate and papers showing you are the spouse, executor, or another person who can legally make the request.

Notify the bureaus by certified mail and ask for a return receipt. Follow up by requesting a copy of the deceased's credit report.

Say R.I.P. to grave-robbing identity thieves

Identity thieves steal $16 billion from U.S. pockets annually, and it's not just a problem for the living. In fact, scammers assume the identities of 2.5 million deceased Americans each year, running up credit card debt, setting up cellphone service, and getting tax refunds. It's called "ghosting," and it can make the grieving process for family members all the more difficult.

Fortunately, you aren't responsible for any debt resulting from a crook's abuse of your loved one's personal information. But bill collectors are likely to call, and creditors can file claims against the estate. At a minimum, you'll spend a lot of time proving the charges are fraudulent. Here are some things you can do to lower the odds of a recently deceased relative being victimized.

> Burglars troll obituaries, searching for the time relatives will be at the funeral so they can ransack the house. Don't let these bad guys add insult to injury. Try to park cars in the driveway or have friends stay at your home while you're attending the service.

- ▸ Order at least a dozen official copies of the death certificate. Send them to all the financial institutions in which the deceased had an account.

- ▸ Report the death to the Social Security Administration.

- ▸ Send a copy of the death certificate to the Internal Revenue Service.

- ▸ Pull the person's credit report to find any accounts that are still open. Contact the creditors and let them know the account holder has died.

▸ Write a certified letter, return receipt requested, to the three main credit bureaus — Equifax, Experian, and TransUnion. Have them flag the credit report as "Deceased. Do not issue credit."

▸ Gather up personal and financial documents that the person left behind. Don't leave check books or brokerage statements lying around. If you have your loved one's computer, make sure it's password protected.

▸ Cancel the deceased's driver's license to avoid duplicates being issued.

▸ Be careful when writing the obituary. Identity thieves look for personal information, such as dates of birth and death, middle and maiden names, and exact addresses, to open accounts.

Paying for a funeral the smart way

Prepaying for your funeral seems like a good idea. But it doesn't always work out that way. Look at what happened to John, who finalized his funeral plans with a $10,000 pre-need contract in Florida. Two years later, he remarried and moved to California. Guess what the funeral home told him when he requested a refund? It would keep $3,000 as a "cancellation commission."

And it's perfectly legal. Florida law requires funeral homes to place just 70 percent of prepaid funds for services into a trust. The rest they get to control.

"It's outrageous," says Joshua Slocum, executive director of the Funeral Consumers Alliance, a nonprofit agency that monitors the funeral industry. "Florida law has legalized robbery in the pre-need sales transaction. They get to keep this money simply for the privilege of having had your money ahead of time."

All 50 states have different regulations when it comes to pre-arranged funerals. That can cause problems, Slocum warns, if you want to cancel your contract in less consumer-friendly states like Florida, Hawaii, and Alabama.

But his reasons for not purchasing beforehand don't stop there. He's concerned that it creates "magical thinking" in people's minds that "everything is taken care of." But buying your funeral today doesn't guarantee you'll always live near that funeral home or you won't change your mind about your decisions later.

His advice — share your plans with your family. Let them know what type of funeral will be meaningful to you, but also ask them what would be meaningful and practical for them. Then put funds for your funeral in a "pay on death" account.

"That money stays there and nobody skims a sales commission," Slocum says. "It's available to your survivors to pay the funeral home, whichever one they choose and no matter where you are."

The only time it makes sense to buy a funeral in advance, he says, is if you have to spend down assets to qualify for Medicaid benefits. If that's the case, make sure the plan you buy is a Medicaid-exempt funeral trust.

Beware this new twist on an old scam

Con men in the 1500s would send letters to wealthy English-men, pleading for money to smuggle a countryman out of a Spanish prison. In exchange, the donor would get a handsome reward. Of course, nobody got rich but the hucksters.

Beware this 21st century take on the swindle. It's called the inheritance scam, where an "estate locator" notifies you that you're eligible to claim a large sum. Just pay a fee, and you can find out where it is.

Don't get too excited at the prospect of collecting a wind-fall. You're just one of thousands who've been targeted in a mass mailing. Remember, legitimate law firms and estate executors don't require a fee to collect an inheritance.

Going, going, gone: Cash in your estate with a profitable partnership

So you've got a house full of knickknacks and chintz-covered fur-niture to dispose of. Selling an entire estate can be overwhelming, particularly if you don't know the going rate for a Stickley hutch or Depression-era porcelain doll collection. If you're not up to the task of sorting, staging, and pricing, you might be tempted to hire an estate sales professional to do it for you.

But do your homework before picking up the phone, says Julie Hall, director of the American Society of Estate Liquidators. She has seen an explosion of fly-by-night amateurs hanging out their shingles, and you'll want to avoid them at all costs. Here are some tips to help you choose the right company.

Conduct your own research. Narrow your search by asking your friends, attorney, or local real estate agents for recommendations. Check for unresolved complaints with the Better Business Bureau or Angie's List. Hall suggests you check references and find out if the company is a member of any professional organizations. You can also drop by local estate sales to see potential candidates in action.

Pave the way for Q and A. After you've picked two or three companies, ask them how they'll market the sale and what security precautions they'll take. Also find out if they have theft and property damage insurance.

Remember, estate liquidators don't come cheap, with the average commission around 40 percent. But Hall warns against going with the cheapest bid. "You get what you pay for," she says. "If you go for the least expensive, something's going to suffer — maybe not enough advertising or not enough staff watching out for you and your possessions."

And don't forget to ask about additional fees, Hall says. For example, does the company charge extra to clean up after the sale?

Agree on a pricing plan. Think those Hummel figurines and Norman Rockwell commemorative plates will fetch a fortune? Not anymore. A combination of factors — the passing of those born during the Depression and baby boomers wanting to downsize — has caused items like heavy mahogany furniture and cut crystal cocktail shakers to flood the market. "There's too much supply and not enough demand," Hall says. And values have changed, too. Younger generations aren't as likely to buy a set of bone china for 12.

Talk with your liquidator to get a better feel for the estate's value. "Professional estate agents are savvy. They know how to advertise and how much things are worth. So even with their commission, they can bring in more," Hall says.

Get a written contract. It should say when the sale will be held, how much you'll be charged, and when you'll get paid. The contract should also describe what happens to any leftover items. But don't feel pressured into giving the green light if you're not ready. Make sure they've addressed all your concerns before you sign the bottom line.

Index

4 percent rule 299
401(k) plan
  beneficiaries 300
  catch-up payments 230, 257
  early withdrawals 258, 302
  rollover 226
  Roth 223-225, 304
  solo 226
  traditional 223
529 savings plan 263
80 percent rule, for retirement 294

A

A/B trust 342
Accident, car 150
Accounts
  changing 88
  checking 87, 93
  closing 90
  joint 332
  money market 86, 235
  online 94
  retirement. See 401(k); IRA
  savings 85
Adjustable-rate mortgage (ARM) 114-115
Adult Protective Services 9
Advance directive 347
Advisor, financial 228, 231, 251
Aging in place 199, 210
Airline rewards 60, 93
Amazon scam 10
American Bar Association 329, 337

Annual percentage rate (APR) 81, 107
Annuities 237-239, 307
Antenna 33
Anti-virus software 100
Antibiotics, free 180
Appraisal, home 201, 267
Apps
  for managing money 99
  for organizing photos 16
  for saving gas 24
  for scanning documents 14, 99
Arbitration, credit card 79
Asset allocation 250
Assisted living, paying for 184
ATMs (automatic teller machines) 88, 93, 102
Audit, IRS 279-282
Automobile. See Car
Autotrader 22

B

Bags, reusable 39
Balloon payment 121
Banking
  ATM fees 92, 93
  bundling services 94
  checking accounts 87, 93
  direct deposit 94
  for seniors 87
  online 70, 91, 94-97
  savings accounts 85
  security 96
  switching banks 88

Bargains. *See* Discounts
Beneficiaries
  for investments 241
  for life insurance 331
  for retirement accounts 300,
    331, 334
  taxes and 303
Benefits
  Medicare 163, 172
  Social Security 309-317
Bid price, bond 245
Birth certificate, replacing 15
Bitcoin 105
BJ's. *See* Warehouse club
Blood pressure medication, free
  180
Bluetooth technology 131
Bonds
  buying online 244
  laddering 246
  rebalancing 251
  selling 248-250
  terms to know 245
  treasury 244
Books, cheap 11
Budget
  apps 99
  becoming debt-free 49
  boosting 6
  retirement 294
Bundling 86, 94, 137
Burial. *See* Funeral
Business, tax deductions 271-273
Bypass trust 342

C

Cable TV 33
Calculator
  car loan 132

  debt 49
  for moving 219
  IRS withholding 263
  mortgage 112, 121
  rent-vs-buy 324
Capital gains 243, 251
Capitalized cost, car lease 130
Car
  buying 19
  insurance 54, 145-151
  leasing 129-131
  loans 20, 131-134
  maintenance 17-18, 25, 26
  modifications 162
  rental 55, 131, 154
  repair rip-offs 26
  safety 28
  scams 151, 153
  selling used 22
  shopping online 20
  technology 28, 131
  trading in 21
  warranty 27
Cards
  debit 104
  Medicare 15, 170
  prepaid debit 103
  rewards. *See* Loyalty programs
  Social Security 14
Care, life-prolonging. *See* Living
  will
Career. *See* Jobs
Caregivers, tax breaks for 259
Cellphones. *See also*
  Smartphones
  budget providers 35
  robocalls, blocking 37
  saving money on 34
Certificate of deposit (CD) 85

Charities
  donating to 277, 326
  donor-advised fund 279
  fake 277
Check fraud 73
Checking accounts 87, 93
Churning, and investments 256
Claims, Medicare 175
Clothing, buying used 12
COBRA (Consolidated
  Omnibus Budget
  Reconciliation Act) 328
Color, and homes 30, 204
Competitive bidding program,
  Medicare 174
Computers
  investment advice programs 229
  passwords 70
  security for 99-101
Condominium, buying 216
Cons. *See* Fraud; Scams
Consumer Financial Protection
  Bureau 82
Contract, cellphone 35
Costco. *See* Warehouse club
Counseling
  financial 48, 200
  for housing decisions 199
Coupon, bond 245
Coupons
  expired 42
  for groceries 41
Craigslist 22
Credit
  counseling services 48
  freezing 67
  monitoring services 83
  poor 61, 104

Credit bureaus 55, 58, 68, 352
Credit cards
  add-on services 80
  alerts 69
  arbitration clauses 79
  balance transfers 66
  billing errors 77
  cash-back 60
  chargebacks 78
  convenience checks 97
  destroying 62
  fees 63, 64, 81
  impulse buying 84
  insurance protection 156
  low-interest 60
  purchase protection 78
  reducing debt 2, 47
  regulations 81
  secured 61
  travel rewards 60
  zero-APR offers 62
Credit report
  discounts 55
  effect of inquiries 61
  errors on 56, 58
  fraud alert 69
  free 55, 84
  identity theft 57, 59
  repairing 58
Credit score
  calculating 51-52
  car loan and 131, 134
  fines and 58
  improving 52-54, 61, 119
  mortgage and 121
  retirement and 118
  shopping and 61, 110
Credit unions 90

Cryptocurrency 105
Curb appeal 203
Currency, virtual 105

D

Dark web 82
Dash cam 28
Dashlane 17
Data sharing 181
Death, reporting 353
Debit cards 104
Debt
    collectors 50, 59
    consolidation services 56
    credit card 2, 47
    estate 330
    in retirement 113, 293
    IRS, repayment 279
    medical 59, 178
    mortgage, missing payments
        126
    savings and 49
    time-barred 50
Deductions
    business 271-273
    charitable 277
    medical 260
    mortgage interest 112, 269
    standard 262, 278
    tax 258, 259
Dental care 173, 182
Department of Veterans Affairs
    (VA) 119
Dependent care credit 260
Diabetes medication, free 180
Digital wallet 105
Dining out. See Restaurants
Direct deposit 94

Discounts
    driving 147
    for seniors 44, 45, 257
    on car insurance 145, 149
    on credit reports 55
    on dental care 183
    on food 39
    on gas 24
    on groceries 41
    on home insurance 135
    on prescription drugs 46, 179
    on restaurants 42-44
Dividends, reinvesting 242
Divorce, and taxes 261
Do Not Call Registry 37, 76
Do-not-resuscitate order (DNR)
    348
Documents
    assets list 328
    for emergencies 12
    for end-of-life care 348
    for estate planning 331, 334
    organizing 13
    replacing 14
    scanning 14, 98
    shredding 74
    storing 14
Dog bites, and insurance 140
Dongle 149
Donor-advised fund 279
Downsizing 112, 218, 219, 322
DRIP (divident reinvestment
    plan) 242
Driving habits, discounts for 149
Drone operator 4
Drugs
    discounts on 46
    free 179

Medicare coverage 164
Drugstores. *See* Pharmacies
Durable power of attorney. *See*
  Power of attorney (POA)

E

Earnings statement, for Social
  Security 312
eBay 22
Education, saving plan for 263
Eldercare Locator 336
Electric bill, lowering 29
Electricity, phantom 30
Email
  cleaning out 16
  scams 10, 76
Emergency fund 50
End-of-life planning. *See*
  Advance directive
Energy bill, lowering 29-33
Equifax 55
Equity funds 235
Escheatment, and portfolios 252
Estate planning
  beneficiaries 300, 331, 334
  creditors 330
  executor duties 339
  farewell letter 327
  legal advice, affordable 329, 336
  power of attorney 331, 333
  rights of surviving spouse 338
  taxes and 264, 325
  trusts 341-344
  wills 334-339
Estate sale 356
Etsy 7
Exchange-traded fund (ETF)
  236, 244
Executor, estate 339

Expense ratio 233
Expenses
  business, deducting 272
  retirement 294
Experian 55
Eyeglasses, and Medicare 172

F

Facebook, security on 70
Fair Housing Act 213
Falling. *See* Home, safety
Federal Housing Administration
  (FHA) 119
Federal Reserve, and interest
  rates 249
Fees
  ATM 93
  banking 92
  credit card 62-64, 81
  HOA 221
  investment 227
  legal 337
  loan 106, 108
  mortgage 120, 128
  penalty 258
  prepaid debit card 104
  rewards cards 66, 93
FICA (Federal Insurance
  Contributions Act) 166
FICO score. *See* Credit score
Fiduciary 229, 232
Files, digital 74
Finances. *See also* Money
  counseling on 48, 127
  in retirement 294
  managing 1, 49
  prepaid debit cards 103
  securing, after a death 328
Fines, and credit score 58

Fixed annuity 238
Fixed income, living well on 321
Fixed-rate mortgage 115
Flexible spending account (FSA)
  160-163, 260
Floors, hardwood 206
Food
  defrosting 32
  savings on 39
Foreclosure 126
Fraud. *See also* Identity theft;
  Scams
  alert 69
  check 73
  seniors and 254
  staged car accidents 151
Freelance writer 4
Frequent flier 60
Fuel, top tier 25
Funds
  actively managed 233
  low-performing 236
  no-load 233
  target-date 236
  types of 235
Funeral 327
  arrangements 327, 349
  consumers alliance 351, 355
  costs 349
  instructions 326
  obituary, writing 351
  prepaying 354
  rule 349
Furniture, buying used 10

G

Gadgets, and hackers 101
Gambling, and taxes 266
Gas pumps, and skimmers 102

Gas, saving on 23-25
Generator 136
Gift cards, pre-owned 11
Gift tax 264, 326
Grab bars 210
Grandparent scam 8
Groceries, saving on 38-42
Grocery store
  gas savings 25
  loyalty program 41
  prescription savings 180

H

Hackers, computer 99, 101, 181
Hardwood floors, caring for 206
Health
  advance directive 347
  end-of-life wishes 346
  in retirement 289, 321
  insurance. *See* Medicare
Health savings account (HSA)
  157-160, 258
Hearing aids, over-the-counter
  171
High deductible health plan 159,
  160
Highway scams 151
Holding period return yield
  (HPRY) 248, 249
Home
  appraisal 201, 267
  business 272
  buying 194-197, 324
  cash offer 113
  downsizing 112, 218, 219, 322
  energy-efficient 31
  increasing value 206
  leasing 194
  loan. *See* Mortgage

maintenance 212
modifications 162, 182, 200, 211
outdoor updates 203
renovations 208
rent-to-own 195
renting out 212
repair scams 143
safety 208
security 136
selling 191, 195, 198, 201, 322
vacation, and taxes 274
Home Equity Conversion Mortgage (HECM) 122, 124
Home Partners of America 194
Homeowners Association (HOA) 216, 220
Homeowners insurance
comparing rates 136
coverage 138-141
discounts on 135

I

Identity theft. *See also* Fraud; Scams
credit bureaus and 67
credit report and 59
of the deceased 353
online 70
pharmacies and 180
tax returns and 288
Identity, protecting 74, 75, 82
In Case of Emergency (ICE) 347
Income
fixed 321
funds 235
retirement 4-8
Index funds 235

Inheritance
scam 356
taxes and 264
Insurance. *See also* Medicare
annuities 237
automobile 145-151
bundling 137
car 54
credit card 156
discounts 135
homeowners 135-145
liability 140, 155
life 187-190
long-term care 184-187
policy, lost 189
rental car 155
shopping for 136
title 197
umbrella policy 141
Interest
credit card 65
deductible 136
loan 107
mortgage 112, 115, 118, 193, 269
on car loans 132, 133
on checking accounts 87
on savings accounts 85
rates, and bonds 248
Internet. *See also* Online
dark web 82
hackers 99
looking for bargains 22
Investments
account inactivity 252
advice on 228
asset allocation 250
beneficiaries and 241, 300
broker fraud 256

Investments *(continued)*
  leaving to minors 242
  mistakes 230
  monitoring 256
  rebalancing 251
  scams 252-256
  transfer-on-death form 241
  withdrawals 298
IRA (Individual Retirement
  Account)
  beneficiaries, and taxes 303
  donating to charity 259
  Roth 299, 304
  self-directed 227
  SIMPLE 226
  traditional 304
  withdrawals 258, 302
Irrevocable trust 343
IRS (Internal Revenue Service)
  audit 279-282
  debt repayment 279
  inheritance and 264
  penalties 258
  problems, help with 282
  roots 283
  scams 285-288
  tax returns 276, 284
Issuer, bond 245

J

Jewelry, buying used 11
Jobs, in retirement 4-8
Joint tenancy with right of
  survivorship 345

K

Kitchen, upgrading 208, 209

L

Ladder, bond 246
Landlord 213
LastPass 17
Lawyer, affordable 336, 337
Lease, car 129-131
Legal fees 337
Life insurance
  claims 328
  lost policy, finding 189, 328
  taxes and 266
  when to keep 187
Light Reflectance Value (LRV) 30
Living trust 341
Living will 346
Loan
  car 20, 131-134
  credit card 97
  effect on credit score 53
  fees 106, 108
  for home modifications 211
  interest rates 107
  line of credit 125
  lump sum 125
  mistakes 106
  preapproval 120, 132
  prepayment penalty 107, 120
  reverse mortgage 122
  shopping for 108
  zero-interest 108
Long-term care insurance 184-187
Look-back period, Medicaid 344
Loyalty programs
  annual fees 66
  pharmacy 46
  store 41, 43
  travel 60, 93

M

Maintenance
  car 17-18, 26
  home 212
  leased car 130
Malware 100
Market, real estate 191
Marriage, and Social Security
  315
Maturity date, bond 245
Mechanic, rip-offs 26
Medicaid 165, 211, 344
Medical
  bills, lowering 178
  dependent tax deduction 260
  documents for end-of-life care
    348
  supplies, and Medicare 173
Medicare
  assistance programs 167
  benefits 163, 172
  card, replacing 15
  claim denial 175
  competitive bidding program
    174
  free screenings and tests 169
  home modifications and 211
  HSAs and 159
  medical supplies and 173-176
  penalties 168
  plans 164
  questions about 166, 314
  scams 9, 170
  Social Security and 168
  supplemental plans 177
  tax deductions 259
Medicare Advantage plan 164,
  176, 177, 182

Medicare Beneficiary Identifier
  (MBI) 170
Medicines, free 180
Medigap 164, 177
Membership club. *See*
  Warehouse club
Mold 31
Money. *See also* Finances
  apps 99
  free 3
  management 1-3
  missing 3, 189
  stress and 1
  virtual 105
  zero-spending day 5
Money factor, car lease 130
Money market accounts 86, 235
Mortgage
  adjustable rate 114-115
  balloon payment 121
  brokers 117
  budgeting for 120
  credit score and 121
  fixed-rate 115
  for rental property 213
  foreclosure 126
  in retirement 111-113
  interest 112, 193, 269
  mistakes 119
  online lenders 116
  payments, missing 126
  points 193
  preapproval 120
  prepayment penalty 120
  reverse 122-126
  scams 127
  shopping for 118
  tax benefits 112

Moving
　retirement and 216-220,
　　296, 322
　taxes and 261
Musical instruments, buying
　used 11
Mutual funds 228, 232-237
Mystery shopper 43

N

Nanny tax 273
National Foundation for Credit
　Counseling (NFCC) 48
National Park Service 5
Natural disasters, and insurance
　137, 138
Nest egg. *See* Investments;
　Pensions
Nursing home, paying for 184

O

Obituary, writing 351
Office, home 273
Online. *See also* Internet
　banking 70, 91, 94-97
　bill pay 98
　calculators 49, 112, 121, 132
　car buying 20
　coupons 43
　debt relief services 56
　financial advisors 229
　mortgage lenders 116
　security 70
　Social Security account 312,
　　319
Origination fee 106

P

Pass-through business 271
Passport, replacing 15
Password manager 17
Passwords 70
Payday lenders 103
Pensions
　annuity 307
　lump sum 307
　missing 308
Pet sitting 5
Pharmacies
　discounts at 40, 179
　privacy at 180
　warehouse club 46
Phishing 76, 286, 319
Phones. *See also* Cellphones;
　Smartphones
　landline, cutting 35
　robocalls 37
Photos, organizing 16
Physician Orders for Life-
　Sustaining Treatment (POLST)
　348
Plans, Medicare 164
Ponzi scheme 252
Portfolio, diversifying 231, 233,
　250
Power of attorney (POA) 331, 333
　for health care 348
Predatory lenders 63
Premiums
　life insurance 187
　long-term care insurance 186
　Medicare 166
Prepayment penalty 107, 120
Prescription drugs. *See* Drugs
Privacy. *See* Security

Probate
  avoiding 341
  investments and 240
Produce, savings on 39
Promissory notes, and scams 253
Property
  joint ownership 345
  rental 212-214
  taxes 266, 268
  unclaimed 3
Prospectus 234
Pump and dump scam 254

Q

Qualified Longevity Annuity
  Contract (QLAC) 239

R

Rating, bond 245
Real estate
  best time to sell 201
  buying a home 194-197
  condominiums 216
  curb appeal 203
  HOA fees 221
  increasing home value 206
  lease-to-buy homes 194
  market 191
  property taxes 266, 268
  rental property 212-214
  selling a home 192, 195, 198
  seniors specialist 199
Rebates 42
Receipts, shredding 14
Records. *See* Documents
Recycling 10
Refinancing, car loan 133
Relocating. *See* Moving

Remodeling, free 211
Renovations, home 208
  financial assistance for 210
  taxes and 267
Rental cars 55, 154
Rental property, owning 212-214
Renting, home 324
Required minimum distributions
  302
Residual value, car lease 130
Restaurants, discounts on 42-44
Retirement
  accounts. *See* 401(k); IRA
  budget 294
  credit score and 118
  debt in 293
  fixed income 321
  funding 3
  funds, withdrawing 298
  health and 289, 321
  jobs 4-8
  mistakes 292
  moving and 216-220, 296,
    322
  myths 291
  packages 304
  spending patterns 294
Reverse mortgage 122-126
Revocable living trust 341. *See*
  Living trust
Rewards cards. *See* Loyalty
  programs
Robo-advisors 229
Robocalls 37, 287
Roth IRA
  rules 304
  withdrawals 299

S

Safety. *See also* Security
  car 28
  data 100, 104
  food 39
  home 208
Sale, estate 356
Sam's Club. *See* Warehouse club
Savings accounts 85
  for health 157-160
Scams. *See also* Fraud; Identity
  theft
  car repair 26
  card skimmers 102
  charity 277
  credit report 55
  email 10, 76, 286
  ghosting 353
  health care 181
  home repair 143
  inheritance 356
  investment 252-256
  Medicare 9, 170
  mortgage 127
  phone 8, 9, 37, 72, 76, 287
  rental car 131
  Social Security 318
  tax 285-288
  towing 153
  victim resources 9
Secondhand, shopping 10
Security. *See also* Safety
  banking 70, 96
  computer 99, 101
  credit card 62
  for digital files 74
  for medical records 181
  for tax returns 288

  home 136
  mail 74
  on social media 71
  online 70
  personal 23
  Social Security number and 318
  two-factor 72
Self-employed, retirement plans
  for 225
Seniors
  aging in place 199, 210
  checking accounts for 87
  free tax advice 258
  insurance discounts 146
  jobs for 4-7
  real estate specialist 199
  restaurant discounts 44
  shopping discounts 45-46
  tax breaks for 257-260, 267
  volunteer work 8
Shopping
  discounts 41, 44-46
  for car loans 132
  for cars 19
  for funeral services 349
  for insurance 136
  for mortgages 118
  impulse buying 84
  mystery 43
  online security 72
  purchase protection 78
  secondhand 10-12
Shower, curbless 209
SIMPLE IRA 226
Skimmers, card 102
Smartphones. *See also*
  Cellphones
  freeing up space 16
  photos and 16

scanning documents 14, 98
Smoking, and insurance 137
Social media, security on 70, 71
Social Security
    card, replacing 14-15
    creditors and 317
    federal taxes and 317
    Medicare and 168
    online account 312, 319
    scams 318
    spousal benefits 311, 315
    survivor benefits 315, 329
    when to claim 309, 314
    working and 310
Software, anti-virus 100
Solo 401(k) 226
Spending, tracking 2
Springing power of attorney 333
Stair lift 209
Standard deduction 262, 278
State taxes 268, 274
Stock
    donating to charity 278
    leaving to minors 242
    rebalancing 251
    selling 243
Store brands, saving with 40
Storm chasers 143
Stress, money and 1
Supermarket. See Grocery store
Supplements, Medicare 177
Supplies, medical 173

T

Target-date funds 236
Tax return
    amending 276
    extension, filing for 270

filing, free 284
frivolous arguments 283
identity theft and 288
red flags 281
replacing 284
scam 286
Taxes
    401(k) rollover and 226
    annuities and 239
    appealing assessment 266
    business deductions 271-273
    capital gains 243
    car leases and 129
    caregivers and 273
    charitable donations and 277
    deductions 261, 262
    dependent care credit 260
    estate 264, 325
    exemptions 262
    free help for seniors 258, 285
    FSAs and 160
    gift 264, 326
    HSAs and 158, 159
    itemizing 278
    life insurance and 266
    mortgage and 111, 269
    penalty fees 258
    property 266
    qualified preparers, finding 275
    second home and 274
    Social Security and 317
    state 268, 274
    stock donation and 278
    stock sales and 243
    withholding 263, 270
Technology
    buying used 11
    in cars 28, 131, 149

Telemarketers 37, 76
Telematics 149
Telephones. *See* Cellphones;
  Phones; Smartphones
Television. *See also* Cable TV
  antenna 33
Tenant, choosing 213
Theft, identity. *See* Identity theft
Title insurance 197
Toilet, low-flow 32
Tools, buying used 11
Towing scams 153
TransUnion 55
Travel
  credit card rewards 60
  Medicare and 172
Treasure trove tax 266
Treasury bonds 244
Trust
  bypass 342
  irrevocable 343
  living 341
Trustee 342
TV. *See* Television
Two-factor security 72

U

Umbrella policy 141
Unclaimed property 3
Upsizing, in retirement 218

V

Vacation home, and taxes 274
Variable annuity 238
Venmo 99
Veterans
  free remodeling services 211
  home loans 119

Virtual banking 91
Virus, computer 100
Volunteering 8

W

W-4 form, changing 263
Walkers, and Medicare 174
Wallet, digital 105
Warehouse club
  for car buying 19
  for prescriptions 46
Warranty, car 27
Water bill, lowering 31-33
Websites, encrypted 71
Wi-Fi, security for 71, 97, 101
Will
  do-it-yourself 336
  living 346
  missing 338
  probate, avoiding 341
  residuary clause 334
  updating 335
Women, and Social Security 310
Working, during retirement 4-8
Writer, freelance 4

Y

Yield, bond 245

Z

Zero APR credit card 62, 67
Zero-interest loan 108
Zero-spending day 5